Edwardian Childhoods

Edwardian Childhoods

Thea Thompson

Routledge & Kegan Paul
London, Boston and Henley

First published in 1981
by Routledge & Kegan Paul Ltd
39 Store Street, London WC1E 7DD,
9 Park Street, Boston, Mass. 02108, USA and
Broadway House, Newtown Road,
Henley-on-Thames, Oxon RG9 1EN
Set in 11/13pt Baskerville by
Rowland Phototypesetting Ltd
Bury St Edmunds, Suffolk
and printed in Great Britain by
Unwin Brothers Ltd
The Gresham Press, Old Woking, Surrey
A member of the Staples Printing Group
© Thea Thompson 1981

British Library Cataloguing in Publication Data

Edwardian childhoods.

1. England – Social life and customs – 20th century
I. Thompson, Thea
942.082' 3' 0922   DA566.4

ISBN 0 7100 0676 4

82-266

To my mother, my son and my daughter

Contents

Plates

between pages 50 and 51

Preface

I should like first to express my gratitude to the nine men and women whose memories make up this book. Four of these, alas, Tommy Morgan, Geoffrey Brady, Annie Wilson and Cliff Hills are no longer alive but I should like to thank Mr Brady's widow and Dorothy Watsham, Cliff Hills's sister who helped me with information and photographs. Joan Altrincham, Florence Atherton, Esther Evans, Jock Yorke and Henry Vigne patiently answered my numerous enquiries, checked transcripts, searched out photographs and gave me encouragement and hospitality. Their kind co-operation is particularly valued in view of the fact that when they were originally interviewed they did not know, and nor did I, that their transcripts might be turned into a book.

I am also very appreciative of the work of Anne Burke, Jean Jacobs, Ann Jungmann, Elizabeth Key and Trevor Lummis in carrying out some of the interviews. Janet Parkin's skill and patience in transcribing the tapes and Mary Girling and Brenda Corti's help with secretarial and classification work was essential to the project. Christopher Driver of Bolton Museum, H. H. Browning of Chailey Heritage School and Jean Jacobs helped me in researching material and photographs.

In the fourteen years that I worked on the research projects and finally this book I have received encouragement and advice from more people than I could name, e.g. the twelve other interviewers, the hundred people I interviewed in addition to the ones whose lives are recorded in the following pages, the friends and colleagues who gave me support: Paul Thompson shared the work with me for ten years, his historical research contribution and enterprise were invaluable. Peter Fleetwood Hesketh and Arthur Brown took a great deal of trouble finding people for me to interview. Leonore Davidoff, George Ewart Evans, Alun Howkins, Hugh McLeod,

Raphael Samuel, Martha Vicinus, Randolph Vigne and my editor Andrew Wheatcroft have helped with bibliographical suggestions, ideas and above all, infectious enthusiasm.

Acknowledgments

The author and publishers would like to thank the following for supplying photographs for use in this book: The General London Council Photograph Library for plates 1–8; H. H. Browning and Chailey Heritage Craft School for plate 9; Christopher Driver and the Bolton Museum for plates 23–9; *Country Life* for plate 55; Joan Altrincham, Esther Evans, Joyce Hampson, Sybil King, Ralph Sewell, Henry Vigne, Dorothy Watsham and Jock Yorke for plates of Edwardian children, families and homes.

It was given to me all at once to feel that I sympathized equally with the poor and the rich in all that related to the best part of humanity – the affections.

Samuel Taylor Coleridge

Introduction

The history of childhood and family life is in its infancy. In fact, before Philippe Aries' *Centuries of Childhood* was published in 1962 it was hardly considered a subject for historical research, although social historians such as David Spring and J. F. C. Harrison had remarked on the lack of information about the interior life of families in the nineteenth century and their neglect by historians.[1] In the last decade, however, two specialized journals, dealing with the history of the family and the history of childhood respectively, have appeared and an enormous amount of new research is in progress which relates to the history of the family i.e. women's history and the study of household size; but there is still not a great deal of historical writing that illuminates the experience of family life, its struggles, pain and pleasure. Fifteen years ago when I began work on the family in the late nineteenth and early twentieth centuries there was even less. For the poor there was information about housing, earnings and budgets, but not about what men, women and children felt about their homes, work and money. There were statistics about infant deaths but not about what happened when a child died, how it was mourned and buried. For the rich there were estate papers, family papers, memoirs and autobiographies from which to learn about childhood and family life but these documents, though useful, left much for conjecture. For the middle class, a literate class, there was surprisingly little; they were too busy perhaps to record their lives, and lacking the political or romantic appeal of the working class on the one hand or the aristocracy on the other, they have failed to attract much attention from British historians. There are business histories, and histories of professions, but only an occasional autobiography such as Katharine Chorley's superb *Manchester Made Them* reveals the lives of manufacturing families.[2]

I

And yet there was, and still is, a great wealth of historical material waiting to be tapped. It was stored in the minds and memories of millions of men and women who had been born into Victorian and Edwardian families, and remembered with vivid accuracy the experiences of childhood and youth before the Great War. They were ready to give their recollections generously. It needed only time and thought on our part to record, sift and interpret what they said. So in 1967 I began to record the memories of old men and women in the villages of north-east Essex to get information on family life for a social history of the Edwardian period which was to be written by Paul Thompson.[3] I can still remember the excitement of those early meetings with people, their eagerness to tell how it was in the past, the freshness of spoken history. Paul Thompson and I pursued the recording, encouraged by George Ewart Evans whose unique studies of old agricultural methods and village life using the spoken to augment the written word, had been an inspiration to us.[4] In the end, with help from many fellow enthusiasts, five hundred interviews were collected from people born before 1906 on the first project, and sixty on the second, and it was from these interviews that I selected the nine that make up this book. Details are to be found in an appendix.

The selection of interviews was not easy. I wanted, first, to have accounts which would need as little editing as possible. They should therefore be full of matter, so that they most closely resembled the spoken word of the subject, e.g. questions anticipated or answered in such a way that points of explanation or interpolations were unnecessary. They should also make interesting reading. Everyone's childhood memories are interesting to listen to but after the spoken word has passed into the recorded word and then into the typewritten word, much is lost and in some interviews information which is useful and valuable can make dull reading, especially for those who are not in a position to recall the tone of a man's voice as he remembers his mother, or the tension in a woman's face and hands as she talks about poverty and disappointment. The tape recorder cannot do justice to those who communicate more readily with the language of gesture, eyes and body than with words.

Second, I wanted to suggest the varieties of childhood in different families, based not solely on the varieties of social class as defined by the occupation of the father, for class is not the only factor that influences the experience of childhood. Children's lives are lived on a small scale whether they are rich or poor or in between. They inhabit a home, a specific locality. It seemed important therefore to include childhoods in city, town, suburb and village, and in boarding school and day school. The character of the home is in turn influenced by innumerable factors, the parents' job and class being the most important but also their religious beliefs, personalities, education, relationships with kin, family size, housing, residential area, to name a few.

To suggest the variety therefore, I included large families, small and medium-sized families and one family with an only child. These families were in one case completely irreligious, in some cases Church of England, in two Catholic. Parents were migrants to a city, established in the country, flourishing in the suburbs, struggling in a manufacturing town. Fathers owned landed estates, earned a living at the stock exchange, represented a constituency in Parliament, practised as a barrister, sold insurance and pictures, manufactured textiles, worked a stocking frame, unloaded barges, thatched corn stacks and tended sheep. Mothers had a narrower range of occupations. Five did not earn money but ran their homes and brought up their children, with the help of servants, spending varying amounts of time on entertaining and good works. One of these became suddenly servantless and had to do her own housework and look after her own children, like the remaining four mothers, three of whom also earned money, one doing cleaning and hotel work and the other two working long hours at home in the clothing trades.

How typical are these accounts of childhood and family life? Are they representative? They were certainly not chosen to be statistically representative; with a sample of nine that would be impossible. The middle ranks of society are almost absent with the possible exception of Geoffrey Brady's family. The failure of his father's business, however, took him for part of his childhood and youth from the middle class if we accept the usual criterion of membership of that class as the keeping of at least one servant.[5] His story, however, shows within one family the contrast between wealth and poverty, a theme which I wanted to bring out in the book. The families, moreover, do not scatter with proportional accuracy over town and country, for in the 1900s less than a quarter of the population lived in rural districts, whereas one third of these nine families lived wholly in the country. Catholic families are over-represented and the families of manual workers under-represented, while single-parent families are not represented at all. One could continue the catalogue of atypicality and omissions, but it serves no purpose as these families are simply themselves and the accounts of childhood are chosen rather to illuminate the past of Edwardian families than to speak for classes or categories.

However, although the families are quite different each from the other, they do illustrate different attitudes to children, for in Edwardian England there were different modes of child-rearing as there are today. Then, as now, the nuclear family consisting of parents and their children was predominant, and ties between its members were closer than between them and their kin and neighbours. This family type is relatively new. In a pathbreaking study Lawrence Stone traces its development from 1500 to 1800.[6] A work of such breadth and scope is bound to find critics and this is not the place to enter the debate about Stone's findings and methodology. I have found his model a useful one and his accounts of the development of family types helped my understanding of Edwardian families, but I would repeat Theodore Zeldin's caveat that 'The history of domestic relations cannot be written in the same way as the history of international relations, and any description of them must be tentative and incomplete.'[7]

Our modern family originated in the mid-sixteenth century when loyalty to state or sect became substituted for loyalty to lineage or patron, weakening the ties between kin and neighbours and tending to isolate the nuclear family. In the household economy which dominated England in the sixteenth, seventeenth and eighteenth centuries Puritanism emerged as the religious ideology, and the spiritual sanctity of the family was one of its fundamental principles. The family reflected the true principles of hierarchy. The father was head and women and children were subordinated to him. This concept endured till the twentieth century and is not extinct today. It was God-given; 'Providence has ordained the different orders and gradations into which the human family is divided, and it is right and necessary that it should be maintained. . . .'[8]

It was, however, a nuclear family very different in certain respects from the one we know today. Children, for example, were less likely to grow up and less likely to live at home. More than half the children died before maturity, two-fifths died before one year and another one-fifth before twenty-one; after eight many children of the gentry lived in noble households and the children of lower classes were put out as apprentices and servants. Marriages lasted twenty years at most and the life expectancy factor meant there were few grandparents. This family type Stone calls the Restricted Patriarchal Nuclear Family; it was fused with the household as a production unit and it was therefore essential for the father to keep authority as work had to be done. But although women and children owed great respect to their household head whose duty it was to keep control, the radical sects allowed them some equality in certain spheres after religious toleration was established. They were allowed to preach and free love was advocated by some leaders.

Annie Wilson's family has many features of the restricted patriarchal nuclear family. For a part of Annie's childhood their way of life was pre-industrial, for all work was done at home, Mr Wilson being a hand frame knitter. However, although it was Mrs Wilson who supported the family with regular earnings as an outworker, Mr Wilson was head of the house, his wife seeing to it that he maintained his position despite the economic reality of the family situation.

By 1700 among upper bourgeois, professional and gentry families, a trend away from patriarchal households was apparent. The decision-making power and standing of women increased, though their economic power did not, and they became increasingly occupied with nurturing and rearing their children. They became more child-oriented and so became more permissive in bringing up their children. It is no coincidence that at this time, in the eighteenth century, the infant mortality rate began to fall and it became more worth while to invest love and care in a child. Stone notes a trend back to paternalism in the late eighteenth century, the re-emergence of the subordination of women and children, of discipline and sexual repression. This was to be followed in the last quarter of the nineteenth century by a counter-trend which by the Edwardian period had established itself as a move away from the hierarchical obedience of Victorian family life.

These were not across-the-board trends and counter-trends. Many features of the close-knit nuclear family were rarely observed among the poor until the nineteenth or early twentieth centuries;

Stone perceives them first among the urban bourgeoisie, spreading later to the landed classes. There was not so much a replacement of one type of family by another as a widening of the varieties. There was a growing pool of cultural alternatives, and shifts in family behaviour affected some classes at one time, some at another, while certain patterns persisted. As Stone puts it, 'There is reason to believe that reticence, sobriety and thrift, punctuality, self-discipline and industry, chastity, prudery and piety are qualities which had been predominant among some sections of the middle ranks since the late sixteenth century. If this is so what happened in the seventeenth century and again in the nineteenth was that these values were temporarily imposed, by a combination of repressive measures and vigorous moral and religious propaganda, upon large numbers of upper landed elite, the lower middle class and the respectable sector of the labouring class.'

The nine families in this book are more easily understood in the light of the historical development of the English family for all except the Morgans approximate to the type described by Stone as the dominant one; unstable, disorganised and rough they were unaffected to a great degree by moral propaganda. At the other end of the social scale, the Poynders were breaking free from Victorian moral repression. Like the Morgans, they are not centred on children and hearth, looking to a cosmopolitan society based on London as the Morgans looked to work-mates and pub acquaintances to satisfy social and emotional needs. The Yorkes, too, seem fairly free of Victorian repression and also have features of the child-centred eighteenth-century gentry family. The Vignes are more Victorian though fairly child-centred, the father however being the prototypical Victorian 'governor'. The Stokeses' family life takes its character from the mother who had a Protestant dislike of showing feeling or of wasting money, time or emotion keeping consequently an austere distance from her children. Geoffrey Brady's father, like Esther Stokes's mother, came from a manufacturing family and their children were instructed in the middle-class virtues of industry and self-discipline. These two families are rather enclosed. In the Stokeses this was probably due to belonging to a minority religion, Catholicism, in the Bradys to their financial reverses. Protestant virtues are emphasized by the Atherton parents and theirs is also a very child-centred family, nurtured by the father. In the Hills family we can see features of two traditions. Mrs Hills was an upholder of the respectable virtues, she accepted the social order, and work discipline, believed in punctuality and sobriety and tried to inculcate these into her husband and children. Her husband, on the other hand, was true to the tradition of the independent, rural poor of the open village, who did not need to defer to a squire, to work for him, or emulate bourgeois standards.[9]

Of the nine people who gave us these accounts, four are dead and one seriously ill. The other four read their typescripts and suggested improvements. They showed a natural desire to eliminate repetitions and phrases like 'sort of' and 'you know', to correct errors of memory, to enlarge, to streamline. After careful thought and re-reading, I made a few alterations and additions using the contributors' own words in every case, but I kept the colloquialisms, and the narrative retains its idiosyncrasies of speech. In some places I substituted a noun for a pronoun to increase intelligibility, e.g. 'My father' for 'he', and made a few minor omissions of phrases when sentences were very incoherent, which was rare. I also linked sentences together where a subject was mentioned at various stages of the interview. Parts of the interviews were not included for reasons of space, but the words you will read are the speakers' own.

NOTES

1 Philippe Aries' *Centuries of Childhood* (London, 1962) is a translation by Robert Baldick of *L'Enfant et la vie familiale sous l'ancien régime* (Paris, 1960). David Spring, 'Some Reflections on Social History in the Nineteenth Century', *Victorian Studies*, vol. 4, 1960–1, p. 60. J. F. C. Harrison, *The Early Victorians 1832–51* (London, 1971), p. xviii.

2 Katharine Chorley, *Manchester Made Them* (London, 1950).

3 Paul Thompson, *The Edwardians: The Remaking of British Society* (Bloomington and London, 1975). See also Paul Thompson, *The Voice of the Past: Oral History* (London, 1978) and Thea Vigne, 'Parents and Children, 1890–1918: Distance and Dependence', *Oral History – the Journal of the Oral History Society*, vol. 3, no. 2 for further information about research methods and findings of these oral history projects. 'The Voice of the Past' contains a useful and wide-ranging bibliography in addition to fuller details of oral history projects and methodology.

4 George Ewart Evans, *Ask the Fellows who Cut the Hay* (London, 1956), *Where Beards Wag All, The Days That We Have Seen* (1975), *The Farm and the Village* (1969).

5 Hugh McLeod, 'White Collar Values and the Role of Religion' in *The Lower Middle Class in Britain*, ed. Geoffrey Crossick (London, 1977), p. 63.
6 Lawrence Stone, *The Family, Sex and Marriage in England 1500–1800* (London, 1977), pp. 651–81. I have also used an unpublished article by Christopher Hill, 'Puritanism and the Family' due to appear in the History Workshop series on *Childhood*. For an evaluation of Stone see Keith Thomas's review in *The Times Literary Supplement*, 21 October 1977, pp. 122–6.
7 T. Zeldin, *France 1848–1945: Ambition, Love and Politics* (Oxford, 1973), p. 106, quoted in Stone, op. cit., p. 17.
8 Sir Gilbert Scott, *Secular and Domestic Architecture* (1857), pp. 140–2.
9 Raphael Samuel, 'Headington Quarry: Recording a Labouring Community', *Oral History*, vol. 1, no. 4, p. 113, on the contrast between closed and open villages.

1
Thomas Morgan

Tommy Morgan loved London and lived there all his adult life except for a period during the First World War when he worked as a carpenter in France.[1] He had learned carpentry at Chailey Heritage Craft School in Sussex, where he was sent in 1906 after he was discovered to be working under age. It was the first residential school with hospital treatment for cripples and began with seven boys in 1903 drawn from the Guild of the Brave Poor Things.[2] Tommy had a limp in his left leg but he managed to climb ladders with a kit of tools on his back and found work in the building trade until he retired. He married in 1924 but had no children. A few months after he was interviewed I wrote to him at his home in Northampton Buildings, Finsbury and received a letter back saying, 'Dear Madam, This is to let you know that Mr. T. Morgan pass away on 29th of September, 1971. From his very close friend Mrs. I. Curtis.' He was seventy-nine.

Tommy's lively narrative style brings to life a dead London of tenement buildings, courts reeking with the manure of coster-mongers' ponies, barefist fighting, street gambling, large families and teeming pubs where children played and women prepared vegetables and breastfed babies. It was a London where people had few possessions and moved house quickly because they owed rent or had had their windows broken as an inducement by the neighbours to move on. This was the only world Tommy knew. 'Course I'm talking about the Borough, Bermondsey, Southwark, so I don't know whether – well some parts of London were a bit, you know, sedate.'

It was a life lacking any pretensions to bourgeois respectability. Belief in domestic privacy and the pleasures of hearth and home could hardly flourish when a family of eight lived in one room, and even that one-room home could disappear at any time, the household goods being flung into the street. In addition to overcrowding, poverty and drunken rows caused the children to disperse, some leaving of their own initiative, some at the instigation of welfare and charitable agencies, for children like the Morgans caused grave concern to middle-class reformers from the mid-nineteenth century on. It was not just their ignorance, godlessness and poverty which cried out for treatment; their independence and shrewdness seemed unnatural and unchildlike. They were not English children but 'street Arabs', a race apart.

It was partly the desire to foster the innocence of children, making them resemble the children of the middle class, that spurred on the campaigners for industrial schools where from 1857 magistrates might send children between seven and fifteen for any period of time if they appeared to be neglected or in danger of becoming criminal.[3] Later in the century children were sent to Canada and other colonies in the belief that they would be exposed to a better life, while conveniently supplying the new settlers with cheap labour. Tommy lost one sister to an industrial school, or truant school as they were popularly called, and one brother to Canada.[4]

Today Tommy would almost certainly be in the care of the local authority. His name might well be on the register of children at risk of non-accidental injury which all Social Services Departments were instructed to keep after the death of Maria Colwell. For Tommy was clearly a victim of his mother's violence; his crippled leg was said to have resulted from an incident in which he was hurled by her at his father and hit the wall. Mrs Morgan, in turn, suffered severe beatings from her husband. But she was most solicitous when Tommy was in hospital, visiting him regularly over a long period. At home, however, he was left to look after himself.

Why was the Morgan family so poor, drunken and disorganized? There is, of course, no easy answer to this question, but two factors may be worth considering. One is the kind of work the parents did and the other their being newcomers to London, not born and bred there. Mr Morgan worked as a coal heaver, unloading barges. This work was subject to seasonal fluctuations and frequent bouts of unemployment; it was in addition paid hourly and demanded great expenditure of energy. Beer fuelled the human machine and when men were thirsty wages paid hourly were hard to save till the end of the week. Low wages also meant overcrowding. Benjamin Tillet giving evidence for the Select Committee on the Sweating System might have been talking about Mr Morgan when he said, 'The majority of the dock labourers are forced to live in either one or two rooms.' They were 'unable to pay more than 3*s*. or 3*s*. 6*d*. a week rent and that of course has to be contributed by the wife and his children.' Wives, Tillet said, often earned more than husbands and he mentioned charring as a source of income.[5] Mrs Morgan, in fact, did earn money charring, cleaning doorsteps and shelling peas and she struggled to pay a rent of 3*s*. or 3*s*. 6*d*. Her work too, was paid in dribs and drabs and she was inclined to spend it, as she earned it, in the nearby pub with her friends.

Mrs Morgan had come from Jersey as a young woman and she seems to have been without relations to help her with her hardships and big family in a day-to-day way. Recent studies of family life among the urban poor during and after industrialization have shown the importance of kin. They helped by giving support and by passing on tips about jobs, etc. The tie of the working-class woman to her mother was often a particularly strong one. Sisters too were helpful.[6] Mrs Morgan lacked that source of help. Friends were 'drinking friends' and Mr Morgan's relations lived in Greenwich, too far away to be of immediate use and inclined to drink also.

Drink, poverty, violence, bad language, open acceptance of charity were the features of a rough family shunned by the respectable working class. Tommy put it in a nutshell, 'Even in the slums where we was brought up we had our classes because some went to work regular, didn't drink and . . . "Get away from my window, get away from my door, get down further." There were another class you know, oh you were a f'ing so-and-so and all that lark, see.' Yet Mrs Morgan struggled to maintain some of the habits of a respectable woman. She kept her home clean and did not allow Tommy to wash the floor (washing was not considered a manly task). She insisted on the children bathing once a week, washed their clothes, cooked a Sunday dinner and insisted on some rudimentary table manners.

Tommy's energy, resourcefulness and friends buoyed him up. He seems never to have been lonely or at a loss for something to do, exploiting the London streets, markets and people for food, fun and money. He had the warmth and solidarity of a crowd of children all in the same position. Historians of the family, sociologists of deviance, theorists of child development may increase our understanding of 'disadvantaged', 'deprived' children but from Tommy himself we learn how one such child could enjoy life and survive on so little.

NOTES

1 The interview was done by Trevor Lummis in the spring of 1971.
2 Grace T. Kimmins, *Heritage Craft Schools and Hospitals: Chailey 1903–48* (account of the pioneer work for crippled children), pp. 25–30. See also J. H. Ewing, *The Story of a Short Life* (1885), a children's book about Brave Poor Things. Grace Kimmins was Mrs, not Lady Kimmins as Tommy Morgan calls her. Lady Dickson-Poynder, mother of Joan Poynder, was a patroness of the school when it was founded.
3 Margaret May, 'Innocence and Experience', *Victorian Studies*, September 1973, p. 19.
4 Ivy Pinchbeck and Margaret Hewitt, *Children in English Society*, vol. II (London, 1973), pp. 562–81.
5 Benjamin Tillett, SC on the Sweating System, 2nd Report, p. 135; *Parliamentary Papers* 1881, vol. 21, quoted in E. Royston Pike, *Human Documents of the Age of the Forsytes* (London, 1969), p. 230.
6 Michael Anderson, *Family Structure in Nineteenth-Century Lancashire* (Cambridge, 1971) and Michael Young and Peter Willmott, *Family and Kinship in East London* (London, 1957), are two of the studies which show the importance of kin. It must be emphasized, however, that kin were not always helpful or friendly. We do know that Mrs Morgan received help from one member of her family. A sister adopted one of Mrs Morgan's daughters. Where this sister lived or how much she and the adopted daughter saw of Mrs Morgan is not recorded.

I was born the third of August 1892 – number 5 King's Bench Street, Pocock Street, Blackfriars Road. They'd pulled a prison down to build a railway across but they left all the warders' cottages up. Now my mother happened to get one of the cottages and I happened to be born there. We nearly always had one room, she used to have a sheet on the line to separate one room – make two of it. Us children slept one side and father and mother the other side. I can only once remember my mother having two rooms – 'course they was never long in one place you see. Always got chucked out or turned out or something.

We lived down East Lane, Hard Street they called it [The official name of East Lane is East Street.]. Oh it was a terrible street! Oh we had – I forget that one – there were two rooms there we had. And we moved in there and on the same night – we was in bed about one o'clock in the morning – bang! bang! bang! bang! bang! My old man got up. He said, 'What the f-ing hells going on here?' (It's the first day they'd been in that house, there's a turning out of East Lane, Walworth.) He got up – 'What the f-ing hell's the matter here?' 'Course the costermongers only fetching their ponies through the passage, we didn't know they had a stable out in the yard. The horse dung all down the passage.

We moved from place to place I know because my mother was always thrown out. Many a time I've gone home, come home from school as a child until about seven – six, seven and eight – I've come home from school with all the other boys and girls and find the furniture outside the door in the street. There was only one decent landlord and she was a lady, well you know what I mean. She kept a little shop and she let the rooms out over the shop. I used to go down there for a farthing-worth of milk or ha'porth of bread or anything like that, and when I went down I always paid the rent. My mother always sent me down to pay the rent. I was honest there. Mother sent the rent book down. Well now and again my mother used to say, 'Go down and tell her could she let the rent go till next week – pay two.'

Well I used to go down. She used to say, 'That's all right, yes, quite all right.' See? And she was a decent one. But the majority of them used to be mostly Jews. All these slum houses. If you didn't pay the Jew he'd have you out, he'd wait on your doorstep next pay day and if you hadn't got the two weeks' rent – out! They'd put your furniture out in the street. 'Course nearly everybody only had one room. If you'd two rooms you thought you had a mansion. 'Course the rooms were only three shillings or three and six a week. One room mind you. I've seen my mother sitting down brooding – where's she going to get this and where's she going to get that. And I used to say, 'Mother – got a ha'penny?'

'Get out of it, get out – I've got enough troubles now. I've got the rent. I've got to find this – I've got to find that,' she said, 'I've nothing to pawn – get out of it.' Of course I flew out – I knew what a temper she was in. I used to get wild with her, you know, I used to call under me breath. I used to call her everything. But of course being kids you don't think, do you?

My father's father was a well-to-do man. He used to buy up land for the timber what was on 'em and he used to get men as what they called pit sawyers, see. They didn't have machinery in them days. One man was down the hole and another above. And my father worked for him some time but he finished up in Maze Hill, Greenwich as an undertaker, and my father took me and my sister Emma over to there one night, you know, early in the afternoon. And of course my father and my grandfather got on the booze and we couldn't get back so they put me in one coffin and my sister in another one and they both slept – one slept on the floor and the other one slept on the bed – a small trestle bed. I can remember that.

My father was come from Caernarvon. My mother come from Jersey, her father was one of the guards over Napoleon. When Napoleon died the Regiment got dispersed and he settled in Jersey. Well my mother was one of the children. Well when she left, and she left Jersey in the time near enough of Lily Langtry, the Jersey Lily my mother called her, they were quite proud of it not as it made any difference to her. And she come to London, straight from

Jersey to London, met my father. I don't know how they met but they met and they got married. My mother and father lived after they got married down a court the side of Greenwich church, the houses are still there. After that they come over to south-east of London – Elephant, Blackfriars, Waterloo and all round here, and that's all they seemed to – got no further, only them districts. That's why they were known as the two biggest drunkards in Waterloo and Blackfriars.

My father could get drunk three times a day. He was a coal heaver. Those days beer was tuppence a pint. So they'd go to work for a whole day – five o'clock in the morning until about four or five in the afternoon for five shillings, five men – my father was a ganger. And they earned five shillings to empty a bargeload of coal sixty to eighty ton. That was a day's wages. 'Cause they'd empty it in a day. 'Course that was all they lived for – beer – in those days. 'Cause he used to get up at four o'clock in the morning. He'd go to Lion Brewery, Waterloo – Belvedere Road, Waterloo. If there wasn't a barge in they used to go into the tap room and there was a pail of beer. They'd sit down and finish that pail of beer. Of course they got drunk. Home. Get up. Go in the pub. Get drunk again. 'Course they was open from five till twelve o'clock at night then.

And my mother was a big drinker. When I was a child she worked in Covent Garden shelling peas, peeling potatoes for the Savoy Hotel in Cherry brothers, in Covent Garden. There where there used to be the National Sporting Club. About a dozen women. And when they pick their money up, about eighteen pence, something like that, they used to go down Wellington street. Some went straight home but the others went into that pub next to the Lyceum Theatre on the corner of the Strand and Wellington Street and got drunk on what they earned. She also did charring and that, cleaning. Used to go doorstep cleaning down Kennington Park Road, you know, 'cause they were all actors down there. Well you know Charlie Chaplin's mother and father were down there. In fact she worked for Charlie Chaplin's father and mother down in Kennington Park Road, only cleaning doorsteps you know.

We mostly had our dinners in school, 'cause you know the old milk churns, well they used to be delivered at all the School Board for London. After it was the LCC. But they were big milk churns delivered at the school full of soup see. Very rare we had a gas stove. 'Course gas was very cheap then, five hours a penny – put a penny in the slot it lasted five hours. But it was very rare we had a gas stove. Always had a coal fire. Everything on the one fireplace. Always had a regular meal on Sunday, and of course why we had it on a Sunday – Saturday I was the only one – and the youngest brother of the two, Jerry they used to call him, we used to all have a place to go to buy food. I used to go to Jermyn Street for twopennorth of giblets. We lived in Waterloo or Blackfriars – as I say we were never in one place long – my regular jobs was Jermyn Street, two-pennorth of giblets, you know, that was the insides of the chickens, the liver and all that. Another one had to go to the Strand for stale bread. Another one used to have to go to Hart's Corner, it's there, still there now.

'What do you want?'

'Two pennorth of block ornaments.'

'Right-o.' About five or six pounds of good meat. 'Course they didn't have no fridges in them days. So it was better meat than what you get today. What you get today is twelve months old they reckon. But having no fridges it was either sell it or give it away or throw it away you see.

The shops was open – it was common for them to be open at ten o'clock at night, see. And I used to go with my mother, 'Here you are, take this bag – put the 'tatoes in.' Peas was sold in pods then, but they didn't used to weigh 'em. They used to measure the peas then, be sold by the pottle and that was the biggest cheating way agoing, 'cause my brother, the one who used to be the coster-monger, he used to say to me, he had a stall down the Cut, near the Victoria, 'Look after the barrow, anybody come up "pottle of peas". Put 'em in and push 'em down.' And my brother come along, 'What the bleeding hell you doing', he said, 'Cor blimey, I'm losing money!' He said, 'When you measure 'em out,' he said, 'Get 'em like that and go like that, don't press 'em.' Used to get half a pottle for a pottle that way, see.

If we got a bit of a joint we used to have a roast, done in front of the fire on what they called a Dutch oven. Pot on one side and Dutch oven in the front. And 'course it was coal – it was good coal although it was only about a shilling or one and two or one and four a hundredweight then. But it was good coal. English coal. But the last coal they got here, cheap coal, was Belgian coal, no good. Newspaper on the table, pot used to come off the hob on to the paper, dished out like that see. Frying pan was used for meat, fish and anything else. I always used to say, 'I don't want that fat, I don't like fat.'

'You've got to eat some fat.' Pot of 'tatoes – the potatoes come out and smacked on your plate. The biggest you know used to get theirs first, 'What do you want? How much do you want?' See. And we the littlest ones, we were served last. Whatever she got we had to have. You couldn't pick and choose. But we were never allowed to put our arms on the table, like that. 'Get them arms off!' Wallop – you know. Put a knife in your mouth – you got a hiding for that. Oh she taught us good manners as far as she could go.

Christmas Day we used to go in the pub with 'em, us children, see. 'Cause children were allowed in the pubs then and we used to play down on the floor in the sawdust and men who used to spit down there. And all the women used to sit on the seat peeling the 'tatoes and shelling their peas and of course they was mopping it up all the time and us kids used to be playing in the sawdust, spit and all that. But after a while – I think it was about 1904 – they stopped it. I don't suppose we was ever home at Christmas time. We all went to a Christmas party at some mission, see. That was the usual thing for all the poor kids then.

We used to sing a few hymns and they used to have a magic lantern service, 'Twinkle, twinkle little star' or something. Then they'd show us a few pictures of different lands you know, and after that they used to say, 'Well come and have the cocoa' and buns or biscuits, whatever it was, and that was the meal there. When we was at Shaftesbury Hall, in Trinity Street, Borough, we used to get a proper Christmas dinner there you see. We used to have turkey – 'cause you could buy turkeys five shillings each then. When they used to buy it wholesale it used to be about half a crown. So they could feed a lot on one turkey.

Clothes – always secondhand. Off the barrow down the market place. Penny left and ha'penny right we used to call them. Oh you could buy boots in them days, I can remember when they were in the money you could buy a brand spanking new pair of boots for half a crown, hobnail. 'Cause I mean to say, you could buy a suit for about ten bob. A man could buy a good suit for eighteen shillings. And when I used to go to an outing or anything my turnout was a halfpenny collar. All us kids – halfpenny paper collars. 'Course when we got home they were torn up. We lit the fire with them then.

But in regard to bedclothes, sheeting, my mother never bought sheets out of a draper's shop. She used to buy scenery out the Victoria – Vic we called it, you know – the Opera House in Waterloo Road. Used to buy the old scenery – fetch it home, put it in a bath in the yard and let it soak for about a week. And when that was done two or three times we had a bedsheet. You could never tear 'em. My mother never used to buy new sheets because the old man, in his drink, he used to flop on the bed in his coal clothes and everything see. So what was the good of sheets? So that's what she used to do.

My mother was strict on us having a bath once a week – the old tin bath. She used to bath one, dry us, put our clothes on – 'Go on – hoppit!' Then one of the sisters used to have her bath. Bath her, clothe her again, 'Go on – hoppit! Go down the court – play down the court'. She used to do her regular washing once a week. Sometimes she used to go to the public baths – very rare. Always done it at home in a bath on two chairs, same bath we bathed in she used to wash the clothes in. And of course they were coal fires and a pot of water on the hob that side, pot of water on the hob this side, and it was all done in a bath. I used to go for all the errands and that – 'course there was none of the others there. Go and get the coals and sometimes if I took a fit in me head I used to sweep up and all that. But my mother would never let me try and scrub the floor. 'Cause we never had no lino, it was all bare floors in there.

'Course my mother and father used to get, you know, for drunkenness, they used to go and do like seven days or fourteen days and me, or whoever was at home at the time, used to go round to a sister or a brother who was old enough to take us in till they came out. And then they got another room and then they took us back. Not for long. They soon got drunk and got inside. My father went and chopped up wood many a time to get relief. He used to go down – well my mother used to go down mostly, 'Look he ain't been home for three days – we've got nothing to eat – I've got – you know – two or three children. They're hungry!' Right. Used to get a loaf, butter or something like that – not much. 'When your husband comes home you'll tell him he's got to come straight down here'. Well when he did come home my mother'd say. 'You've got to go to the Guardian – Relieving Officer.' Well he used to go down. Right. He didn't used to come home. My mother used to go down to him, 'He ain't home – he ain't come back again'. He said, 'No. He's in the casual ward. He's in for three days chopping up wood for the food you've had.' That was the system then.

Well I can remember, only just remember – what was the name of that – you know, where Oliver Twist supposed to ask for more? Well it's still there now. What was the name? Anyhow, I can just remember my mother carrying me 'cause I was only very small – carrying me and knocking at this pair of doors, big doors. The door was opened and my mother carried me in and that was the last I see of my mother. He got hold of me and they put me on a spring bed and away my mother went and where she went I don't know. That was in where Oliver Twist was supposed to ask for more. It's still there now but tumbling down. And on the other side of the street they had a women's lodging house. Three hundred women lived in that lodging house. All the filth of the earth, dregs of the earth.

It ain't so long ago – in between the wars – if you had a piano – you went to see the Relieving Officer – you was told to get rid of it. If you had anything decent they'd tell you to pawn it or sell it. Not give it away but sell it, to make up money to keep yourself. They were very abrupt, very abrupt. They bullied you. Oh sometimes when I see them bullying my mother I used almost to cry and I used to creep out of it.

Oh what a life! But it's true though, I'm not making it up. If I could find some of the old 'uns you know like myself, they'd tell you the same thing. And yet we was happy. That's funny. Never wanted a meal because we knew all the shops where we could go and get a soup ticket. Oh we had a dozen shops. And we used to go to a mission hall nearly every night. Bread and jam night, bread and fish night, all like that. And we used to go away once a year or twice a year for a fortnight's holiday, Princess Christian's Home, Windsor. Two of them turn outs a year we used to get. Shaftesbury Hall, we used go to them a lot, used to try to teach us. Now I think they got broke up or something 'cause they gathered so much money on charity. What they got stopped for was they only used to share out two shillings and eighteen shillings theirself. They got stopped at it. That was Shaftesbury Hall people. But they weren't the only people, mind you. All these here big people you know, looking after the poor, they were looking after theirself.

And another place we used to go was Southend side of the gasworks. The house is still there but not as a convalescent home now, or holiday home. And last time I remember going there, the matron says to me, 'Look Tommy Morgan', she said, 'I'm going to give you sixpence if you take the boy in a wheelchair,' she said, 'and give him a good wheel round.' Of course sixpence is a lot of money for us kids then. So I said, 'Oh yes matron.'

She said, 'Whatever you do', she said, 'don't take him near the water.' Well at the side of the pier that belongs to the gasworks there, there's a big open gate. I said to the other boys, 'Come on, let's put him down on the sand and we can go up and spend our tanner.' So he says, 'Yes.' So we pushed him down a bit too far. Well when we come back about two hours after the water's right up to his knees. 'Course we got a ticking off for that.

'Cause as I say, I lived in St Margaret's Court and I used to earn many a penny because – the boy used to come in – come round to me and say, 'Mother said she wants you'.

I say, 'What does she want?'

'I don't know.'

'All right, I'll go.'

She'd say, 'Would you go over to Thomas's hospital or Guy's hospital and tell them "you'll be needed in a couple of hours"', something like that. Well I used to dash over to Guy's hospital – I knew where to go, 'Mrs So-and-so says would you go over there in a couple of hours.'

'What another one! She only had one last week,' you know. Oh I had that job many many times. But as for medicine – used to pay threepence. Well nine out of ten used to write a note, 'Father's out of work, we've got no rent' and all that. Well they used to get the bottle of medicine free in Guy's, well I suppose all the hospitals. But I know for a fact that Guy's did do that.

We used to get a barrow and we used to go down Bronti Close, Walworth, and we used to get a barrow, 'course it's only about fourpence or sixpence a day to get a barrow and you had the weight on the barrow – two or three hundredweight on that. Well we used to go down Bronti Close, Walworth – that's a small turning out of East Lane, Walworth, you know – big market place there, and we used to buy salt, hearthstone [a soft stone used for whitening hearths and steps], vinegar – what's that stuff that poison stuff? Anyway, we used to buy this stuff – I forget the name – and we used to go round Kennington shouting out 'Salt! Hearthstone! Vinegar!' About ten or eleven years old.

I used to run papers. I used to buy three copies for a penny and of course the paper used to come out with a horse and van then – a two wheeled cart like. And of course, they were very quick horses or ponies, very fast. And we used to wait at this spot where they used to pull up – three copies – penny. Well you used to dash round. Sell the three – you earned a penny. Well you'd dash back again when he come up again. You might be able to have six copies, see. Well that six copies earned you another penny. All them tricks – oh yes. I can't remember any youth associations. We used to go to the Gospel Lighthouse and we'd do fretwork and there was a gentleman there he sent my brother to Canada. He used to look after us as best he could and he used to get us to do fretwork and string knitting and all that sort of thing. But we only used to go there for the bread and jam. Mother used to go to a Mothers' Meeting. She'd go to a Mothers' Meeting in Tower Bridge Road, Hadden Hall. It's still there the Hadden Hall. They used to go all the year round and they used to get a turkey on the Christmas. That's all they used to go there for – but you know all the old cronies. 'Course it was a big market place there at that time.

Having the run of the streets like that in those days, there was always a clique of us – about twenty – none of their mothers and fathers looked after 'em, like me, see. And we had the run of the streets, fetched ourself up in the best way we could. Well, as I said, we used to all get together, play up at the court or the street, or the roadway where we lived, and we'd be playing up there twelve o'clock, half past twelve, one o'clock in the morning, see. And I can remember an occasion when we had all stopped out, slept in some buildings underneath – some in the lavatory, some under the sink – Westminster Bridge Road, opposite Oakleys where they made the glass paper. And we got a hiding for that. She was going to put us away and all that but she didn't.

I did keep some mice once. I made a cage. And I had no glass so I took a picture down, took the glass out of the picture for the front of the mouse cage. My mother come home and she sat down and about half an hour she was looking at this picture, 'Where's that bloody glass gorn out that picture?' Of course, she see the cage. Wallop! I get the wallop. She didn't hit us hard you know with the flat of her hand, but always had a cane up on the line – ha'penny cane. Every oil shop had a bundle of canes you know. 'Course what we used to do we used to break the cane up or chuck it out. 'Where's the cane? Here y'are – go down the oil shop and get a ha'penny cane.' Never without a cane. In their drink you got a hiding. What they called a hiding. But when she was sober we got a slapping. Two different moods you see. But she knew where to hit us properly. Never in the head or shoulders. Always on the backside. No I didn't used to sulk – used to scream and shout and holler you know, sounded like I was being murdered. But anyhow, after she'd given us a good hiding we used to get out and go down and – 'What's the matter Tom?' 'Oh the old woman ain't half hit me.'

I can never remember my father hitting me or any of my brothers or sisters. He was very cruel to her. He used to hit her like he'd hit a man, although my mother's a big strong woman. He'd hit her like he'd hit a man. He was a strong man and all. The only time he was in he'd come home and get sober – then go out again and get drunk. I've seen 'em stand up – I can remember several times – stand in the middle of the room. He get hold of her, punch her. She'd punch him back and they'd finish up on the floor both of them, punching at one another. Oh they were very crude that way.

He was a big gambler, very big gambler he was. He named me after a racehorse. My name is Thomas Morgan. He told me when I, you know, was a big grown up. He said, 'Do you know what,' he said, 'I think it was 1896,' he said, 'I backed a horse called Tommy Tittlemouse.' He says, 'A couple of days after' (cause you know it was big money they won – about three or four pound, see – that was big money then) 'I named you after that racehorse, Tommy Tittlemouse – that's how your name become Thomas.'

Well it didn't make no difference to us whether he lost or whether he won. The only trouble was that when he used to go out four o'clock in the morning, very likely wasn't a barge in. He'd come home, he'd say, 'What's those on here?'

'Three and sixpence.'

'What's that?'

'Mother told me to pay the rent with that.'

'Oh all right – pay two next week.' He'd take the three and sixpence and go out and gamble with that three and sixpence, see. 'Cause he used to go down a place called East Lane there. He'd have sixpence each way. Davey Cope – one of the biggest book- makers had a threepence each way – kept the barber's shop.

'Cause I mean to say my father used to come home and say, 'Well I don't know – no money! Go round ask Lily whether she's got any money.' I went round to Lily see – that was a daughter, 'My father says – have you got any money you can let him have?'

So she said, 'What? Not me,' she said, 'If I had a mint of money,' she said, 'I wouldn't let him have it to get in the pub.' See. I remember when my father did come into money, that was when his father died, that was my grandfather. He left them four hundred pound apiece and sixty pound for me, being the only cripple in the family – 'cause I was the last one. Dad was on the beer and Mother come home. Father was lying on the bed blind drunk. And the money on him. She pinched his trousers, corduroy trousers. It was in the front page of the *News of the World* that was, yes. She nicked his trousers with all the money in and he had to wake up and see her dashing out the door with the trousers. He dashed after her, nothing on, and caught her at the Elephant. I can't remember where we lived at the time, but it was on the front page of the *News of the World*.

Nearly all day Sunday was gambling or getting up to some mischief, since I was eight years old. Wherever we lived we used to go playing cards you know, banker and ha'penny pack of cards. That was the only enjoyment we had. Otherwise we was always in trouble for what we called knocking down ginger, you know. Big line of us, knocking at doors and running away, we called it knocking down ginger, all that sort. We didn't play football or anything like that. It wasn't like it is today. Back horses, yes – go down to Cope's in East Lane – threepence each way.

The police treated us in a decent way but if we was obstreperous well they treated us in an obstreperous way, in regards, you know, we'd been playing banker you know with a packet of cards down the street. Copper used to come along and he used to stand there and say, 'All right, Tommy Morgan, I know your name and I know where you live.' And he'd start rolling down – we'd snatch our ha'pennies and pennies. Well you didn't used to trouble about the cards because they were only a ha'penny a pack and away we used to go. But he used to stop, pick the cards up, tear them up. And it was, 'All right Tommy' – always Tommy Morgan.

If anybody died in the family everybody had new mourning. Men had new suits, the women had new dresses, all black. But you don't see 'em now. I mean to say, do with a black band now, don't they. And you know how they mostly got their money to buy? Off the money lender, penny in the shilling. Plenty of money lenders round. They used to sit in the pubs – rows or rings. Someone used to walk in, 'Morning Mrs So and so' (whatever her name was) nearly all women, 'Would you let me have a pound?'

'Pound enough?' 'Cause they only got twenty shillings – one and eightpence for that pound. If you had five pound – well they got five times as much. They knew they'd get it back, otherwise it's spoiled for good – the word went round, no other money lenders would lend them money. Nine out of ten were women. They lived local, they were neighbours really. I knew one woman, she started ha'penny in the shilling. Well she didn't last long 'cause she had all the other 'penny in the shilling' after her.

The only funeral I can remember – well it wasn't a funeral it was a wake. I can remember it just before I went in hospital with this leg. Only about five minutes' walk away was the hospital in Southwark Bridge Road, facing the fire station – the hospital's still there. Us kids was playing on the floor. And my mother and father, one or two of the oldest ones and neighbours, they was all drinking. And we was playing on the floor and I can remember looking over to the man, Old Roache, and he was laid in the coffin. And I happened to look and somebody threw a fag end in the coffin. So I got up and I said to my mother, 'Mother, Mother!'

'What?' properly drunk like.

'That man in the coffin is alight – look!'

'What!' She looked over and she shouted, 'Old Roache is alight, he's alight, he's alight!' They all got their cans of beer and jugs of beer and slung it all in the coffin – I can remember that distinctly. Oh he was a funny old man old Roache. He was a pioneer of lino and rank Catholic.

I had two brothers – five sisters. But there was several died in between you see. 'Course they had no control over me 'cause I was the only one left. I was the last one of thirteen. I don't know nothing about those that died. I don't know nothing about one sister, Ada, she died about twenty-five. One sister was sent to a truant school. She got sent to a truant school for stealing a haddock underneath a stall at the Elephant and Castle, in London Road, more for, you know, like larking about than anything. They sent her to a truant school. After she came out at fourteen they sent her to Wales as a servant on a farm. That's the last one that died. I had one decent sister, she was a nurse at Romford hospital, but my mother's sister adopted her and her husband was a big sea captain. Of course he had plenty of money. He could afford to have her sent to college. But all the others they all left home before they were twelve year old, somebody took 'em in. I left home about thirteen when they sent me to charity school. So they all found a place – lived with different people, neighbours mostly. Well most of them started work for about twelve years old. Now and again one used to come back for about a week, but they soon went again, 'cause of the rows and fights with him and her you see. I had nowhere else to go. Nobody didn't want me being a cripple, see. That was the trouble. All the others was strong and healthy, wiry and everything.

My sister Mary they say was the cause of me being a cripple – so they say. It's only a rumour mind you. Because my mother says to her, 'Take him round the jail' (that was where they used to hang 'em – wasn't so far back before I was born that they used to hang 'em there) and she put me in a swing and left me. She'd gone with the other girls. 'Course I fell out this swing and the park keeper picked me up, took me over the hut, says, 'Where's your brother and sister?' I said, 'I don't know, my sister's gone over there – gone over there with the other girls.' Well he found 'em and came back and she took me home. But some time after that my mother said that I was crying night and day so she reckons that was the cause of it. But somebody else says that my mother threw me at my father, missed him and hit the wall.

I was about four and a half then. I was crying day and night. I don't know who it was advised my mother to take me to the hospital to see what was the matter. She did. She took me to Evelina Hospital, Southwark Bridge Road, opposite the fire station. And they transferred me from there to Westminster Hospital, the old one – not the one what they got now. And that's where I went when I was about five years old near enough, when they operated on me. And I was out about twelve months when I got an abscess. I had to go back into hospital again – the old Westminster Hospital. But since then I seem to have got hardened, you know, mixed with the other boys and roughs and that. And yet I was quite strong, wiry and quick. I was as good as any of the others although I'd got this leg. I'd had a fight with another fellow in Burman Street, London Road. I was on crutches. As he come in so I hit him with the crutch. He come in again. Another fellow come up and set about him. 'Course I was all right, I sat back and let 'em get on with it. I got all them. I suppose, you know, me being a cripple and the yellow boys they used to say, 'Oh he's easy, we'll have him.' That was always me you see. And I always got mixed up with a gang down the street. 'Cause that was the only amusement we got mostly in the South East was street fights.

I had a St Thomas's splint, you know. It was buckled round here right down the leg. But my mother used to take the patience of washing me and dressing me and putting this 'ere Thomas's splint on. But after a few weeks she got fed up with it and so did I. But I never wore – they tried to get me to wear a high boot – an iron on me boot. I wouldn't. I came out the hospital. I was six near enough. I lived down Deacon Street, Walworth. After a few months I went to this school in Sayer Street – School Board for London. 'Course they didn't put me in the ordinary school on account of the leg. They put me in the part where most of them – you know – mental cases in there. Star School they called it. I don't think I was there twelve months. When I left there I went to the Old Kent Road cripple school. It's a deaf and dumb school now. It's still there. They had all sorts of cases there. Some had heart trouble, some had hunchbacks. Some like me.

Yes I did like it. I don't know why I used to keep on hopping the wag, I'm sure I don't. 'Cause I was a rare one for hopping the wag. What I used to do to get away from school, I used to get a button, you know, a bone button, and I used to press it in me throat just before I went into class see. And I used to go up to the headmistress and say, 'Mother said, could you tell me what this was?'

'Oh ringworms – oh'! I was away from school three or four months at a time. Over Covent Garden with a sack – sackful of broken up wood, you know – flower boxes. Back over Waterloo bridge, down Tenison Street where Waterloo station is now . . . knock at a door. 'Firewood, ma'am?'

'How much?'

'Tuppence the bagful.'

'No – give you a penny or three ha'pence.'

'No.'

'All right!' Shoot it down the area and back over the garden – four or five times – and earn about eightpence or something like.

Used to go over Berts', Farringdon Street, next to Earl's Corner. A packet of envelopes and paper in a pub – 'cause you was allowed in, we used to play on the sawdust in pubs then – envelopes and paper, penny a packet. I'd sell a packet. I'd earned fourpence out of that. Back again for another. That's how we used to get hold of money. No, we never used to get anything out of our parents, not pocket money anyway. They never had enough for their beer.

The headmistress there she used to invite us down to her place at Brixton – Tulse Hill I think it was. I forget the address properly, but it was at Tulse Hill. And even going down there – four of us altogether – I started a fight in the Brixton Road. A college boy came along and one of the others said something to him and I said, 'Mind your own business', something like. I interfered – it was me had the fight not him. And when we got to the headmistress's place she said, 'You've been up to it again,' she said, 'You've got a black eye.'

I said, 'Well,' I said, 'He hit me first,' I said, 'I hit him after.'

'Oh,' she said, 'I know you.'

They used to try and teach – but what I didn't like about it, we had to do girls' work – knitting, crochet work, paper flowers. I didn't like that part. But in regards to geography and stuff like that – I didn't mind. But you couldn't learn nothing 'cause everyone was interfering somebody else you see. And the only part I really did like was Friday afternoons when we used to have to put all work away, all lessons away, and we sat back and listened to a story she read. Used to like that part. Used to teach us table manners a lot. We had the dining room in the hall. 'Cause we used to pay tuppence a day for our dinners. We used to all get there and we used to have to go and wash our hands first, see. And she used to stand there and she used to say, 'Look your nails are not quite clean, go and wash them again.' And, 'Look just comb your hair, there's a comb up there.' And when you got in the hall you had to sit there, they said grace there, and if you was talking to another one over the other side of the table, 'Tommy Morgan, do you mind taking your arm off the table please. And don't fiddle about with the knife and fork.' All that. You know what kids are. Poking their tongues out at one another and that.

'Course there was mostly trouble with the girls. I don't reckon they ought to mix us with the girls. They used to torment us and one nearly got me into serious trouble but somehow or other I escaped it. She put up her hand and said I called her a c---. Mind you it's not a word that should be used but it's used today more than what it was then. She put her hand up see, so the teacher said, 'Yes, what's the matter?'

'Tommy Morgan called me a c---.' But she didn't say c---. She said, 'He called me a nasty name.'

'What name did he call you?'

She said, 'Well it begins with c.'

So the teacher said, 'Well come out here.' Goes up to the desk, 'write down what he called you.' Of course she wrote the full word down. So after a little bit, 'Come out here Tommy Morgan. Can you read that?'

I said, 'Yes. . . . Oh,' I said, 'That's terrible isn't it? Ooh ah!' you know – I used me wits.

So she said, 'Did you used that word?'

I said, 'No, I didn't'.

'Did you call her that?'

I said, 'Oh yes, I called her something 'cause she kept on pulling me back and pushing me over,' I said.

'What did you call her?'

I said, 'I called her a big cat.'

So she didn't know whether to believe the girl or believe me. So anyhow I got the benefit of the doubt. Mrs Mare. I remember her name now. She was a good old girl. 'Course the majority of children in London, round the Borough and Bermondsey, they were nearly all the same type. You had to drag yourself up.

While I was at the Old Kent Road Cripple School, they sent us to see the opening of the Kingsway. They took so many from each school and they put us into a Salvation place, or Church Army – and the beds was in between two windows. Well they put two of us each side so that all of us could see. And they gave us a medal – opening of Kingsway. I don't know whether it's silver or gold but it must have been of value because when I got home my Mum said, 'What did they give you?' as usual.

I said, 'Look they give us a lovely medal.'

I remember her saying, 'Oh that's nice isn't it. That's very nice.' So she said, 'Put it on the mantelpiece.'

I put it on the mantelpiece, went out as usual, you know, with the other boys, come home at twelve o'clock, and I was telling the other boys about this medal and they all wanted to see it. When I got home that medal had gone. I never see it any more. I'll bet it's worth some money today.

Thirteen I left school and I went and got a job as a van boy. But I left school when I was about twelve really 'cause I don't suppose I done three months' schooling in the year. Always out after money you know, pocket money really. 'Cause as I say I always worked the trick – either I was bad with me leg or else I got ringworms or something, always worked it like that. That's why the school board was so hot on me. If I hadn't been crippled you know where I'd have gone – truant school. Most of the boys they used to work at the railways, van boys. Well one of them said to me ''Ere – over the railways yard', he said, 'The yard shed,' he said (Compton their name was – well they had a name like Compton) 'Compton wants a van boy, why don't you go after it?'

I'd say, 'No, I'm not fourteen yet.'

'Don't matter, tell him you're fourteen.'

'Course they didn't ask for birth certificates, we had no insurance cards or anything like that then. I went over, I said, 'You want a van boy sir?'

'How old are you?'

'Fourteen sir.'

'Oh, when can you start?'

'Now sir' (four o'clock in the afternoon). 'Now sir', you know, so eager to get the job.

'All right – start in the morning.'

'Right.' Well we used to work Borough Market, Billingsgate Market and all round. 'Course it was hours and hours – eighteen hours a day sometimes. All for five shillings a week. But my mother was fair. She used to give me half a crown out of five shilling. 'Course the other half crown went in beer.

He had a horse and van and a traction engine from London to Cobham. He used to work Billingsgate, Borough market and all that. He used to come home back to the yard and we used to have to shift all the lot onto the traction engine. Then he used to say, 'Come on jump up – and we used to have to go to Cobham'. That's about eight o'clock at night. Time we got to Cobham it's about one or two o'clock in the morning. Unload and come back again. Go out and have some breakfast, if there was any, and start work again. There weren't no one very soft there I'll tell you. It was quite exciting going round calling in shops, 'Have you anything at Cobham's?'

'Yes, here you are.' (Sack of stone, weighed about two hundred-weight.)

I said, 'I can't lift that.'

'No I know you can't but your carman will.' And he did lift it and all. And he got a trolley and got it up a little higher and he got it on his back – like a sack of soda or a sack of flour. Bag of flour weighed two hundred and forty pounds you know. We had cement, fish, bacon, eggs, everything all mixed up in our van.

The carman was quite all right. He used to say, 'Had your breakfast?'

'Yes sir.'

'What did you have? . . . that's all right, come on, go in and get a cup of tea and a slice.' Cup of tea ha'penny, slice ha'penny. When we got in Billingsgate, they used to sleep in there a lot and all – open at four o'clock in the morning. They used to go in there – have a cup of tea, sleep there right up till twelve o'clock you know, to get out the cold. We used to go in there. He'd say, 'Go on, go and have a cup of tea and a bit of cake.' He was very good that carman was. He was a countryman. And I'd been there about a few months and they come up to me one morning, he said, 'Hoy Tommy, how old are you?'

I said, 'Fourteen, sir.' 'Cause I used to be quite proud carrying a whip being a bad boy. He said, 'How old are you?'

I said, 'Fourteen sir.'

'All right, run over and get your birth certificate.'

I went home. My mother happened to be in that morning. She said, 'What do you want? Aren't you going to work?'

I says, 'He wants my birth certificate.'

So she said, 'Oh that's had it,' she said, 'You're not fourteen yet.' ('Cause everybody left school at fourteen then, not sixteen, fourteen then.) Oh she did swear and all. Oh she was a proper ruffian!

And after I got the sack I remember I was laying in bed one morning about half-past-nine. This 'ere constable in plain clothes walked in. He didn't knock or anything. I was in bed and so he come over to the bed. 'Cause we only had one room in St Margaret's Court. 'Come on what are you doing in bed this time, come on,' he said, 'I've come to take you over Spring Gardens.'

I said, 'What for?' I said, 'I'm not going to no school.'

He said, 'This is no school', he said, 'So', he says, 'come on.'

And I was in pain with this leg at the time. Anyway I hobbled over Blackfriars – on to the Embankment. The other end was, you know, Spring Gardens, County Hall. When I got there I had to go in front of a great big table. They was all round it and one says to me, 'Oh, good morning Tommy, well we're going to ask you whether you'd like to go in for a trade.'

So I said, 'Yes.'

'What would you like to be?'

I said, 'A bootmaker.' I distinctly remember – a bootmaker.

So they all 'yap, yap, yap, yap' all around the table – 'I see, all right, all right.' You know, they give me a book to read, a paragraph or a simple sum. I done it. 'All right – right. Well – we'll see what we can do for you to be a bootmaker.' I said, 'Thank you.' And this 'ere fellow, big ex-copper he was 'Come on, come on.' So one spoke to him about it, 'Don't be too rough with him, see.' Oh he was a brutal fellow. So after that he was all right.

Well we walked down the embankment again see, over Black-friars Bridge. When we got over there he said, 'Any breakfast?'

I said, 'You know I ain't.'

So he says, 'Well come on.' He took me in this 'ere coffee shop – oh rough old coffee shop because it was full of cockroaches all in the window. So he took me in so he said, 'What do you want?'

So I says, 'Oh, I don't care.'

So he says, 'You going to have some eggs and bacon?' quite nice to what he was, so I suppose they'd ticked him off, see.

'All right,' I said, 'I'll have two eggs – and a rasher.' I can remember the two eggs and a rasher. 'Course you know the lot only come to sixpence. Cup of coffee ('cause it was tea, coffee and cocoa then – they had three urns, tea, coffee and cocoa). Well I preferred coffee at the time. When he paid, I don't know what it come to exactly but anyhow you could get the lot for sixpence at the time. He went out, left me. Well about three weeks after we got a letter from Chailey to say I'd been accepted. This lady had sponsored me and paid for me. The LCC didn't. It was an elderly lady kept a grocer shop like. When she retired being old I suppose she thought she'd do some good with the money she'd earned. Well she sponsored me. I think it was sixty pound a year she paid at Chailey for me. And the only time and the last time I see her she took me up to Camberwell – big park at Camberwell Green and she said, 'All right you have a run round.' She sat down on a seat and I run round or hobbled round somehow. And she said, 'Oh,' she said, 'You're quite strong on that leg.'

I said, 'Yes, that's all right.' Well when she came home she spoke to my mother. That was the last I see of that woman.

At the Chailey School we used to do lessons in the morning from nine till about ten – reading, writing or drawing or ideas – if we got any ideas in our heads for a bit of furniture or something like that, we used to put it on paper. And then after ten o'clock, we used to go from ten o'clock till twelve on the bench, planing and whatever job we were on. They started us on toys and simple things. The first question they sked you when you went there I remember, Mr Sykes, he was the headmaster, 'Well Thomas,' he says, 'You want to be a carpenter?'

'Yes.'

He said, 'But you're not going to be a carpenter, you're going to be a cabinet maker.'

I said, 'I want to be a carpenter,' I said, 'I wanted to be a bootmaker,' I said, 'They sent me down here to be a carpenter,' I said, 'Now you want me to be a cabinet maker.'

'All right,' he says, 'all right, that's enough.'

So he says, 'Have you ever done any woodwork?'

I said, 'Yes sir.'

'What did you do?'

I said, 'Oh we made our own motors.'

'Motors?'

I said, 'Yes, four wheels on a box you know.'

'Oh,' he says, 'I see.'

'How did you bore the holes?'

I said, 'With a red hot poker.'

'Yes,' he said, 'A good idea,' he said, 'Did you ever set the house alight?'

I said, 'No.'

'What else did you used to make?'

I said, 'Well I used to make hutches for my white mice.'

'Oh did you? How did you make the box?' Told him how I made a box you know, got an old wooden box and turned it upside down. I took the glass out the picture to make the front.

'Good ideas', he said, 'Now look,' he said, 'see that chisel.'

I said, 'Yes.'

He said, 'Look', and he hit the chisel. The wood split. So he said, 'What did that do? Did that cut it or split it?'

I said, 'Split it sir.'

'Good idea,' he said, 'We're going to make something of you.'

See I asked to be a bootmaker, but when I got there they trained us to be cabinet makers, not bootmakers. Well I was too rough for the cabinet makers so they made a carpenter of me. We had our own bench, we had our own machinery there – had all our own timber yard there. It was run by Lady Kimmins and her friend Miss Rennie. They started off on simple things such as toys you see, and they worked us up to a gate-legged table and all that sort of thing. All what we used to make was all sent away to be sold and they used to make a lot of money out of it. And while I was there – we were the first boys to have a ride in a Rolls-Royce car – because a lot of people used to come down, well-to-do people you know, rich people – Lord Llangattock, Lord Harcourt Rose, all them people come down. Of course it was more pity's sake than anything and some big pot come down with this Rolls-Royce and give four at a time a ride from the Chailey School down to Newick and Chailey station.

I think there was about twenty of us there at that time. Now there's about four hundred. I'm going there. I go every year. They send me a lot of tickets you know, sweepstake tickets, seven-and-sixpence or half a quid's worth. When we first went there we had a dormitory, the new boys had a dormitory. When we got there we used a bigger hall – farmhouse it was. They say it was a truant school at one time. But anyhow, they got this place. And when you started you settled the last one on the row down here, a table in the middle and a row down the other side – table, table and a big table in the centre. Well, as you got on you worked your way down, till you got to the other end on the other side. When you got to the other end on the other side you went to the middle table and what marvellous food you had there! We had an old sailor there, you know, on the sailing ships, and he used to be our physical instructor. He used to learn us all the drill, you know, sword drill but not boxing. But when he went the other fellow who come he learned us boxing. Or taught us boxing. Cutlass? Oh no, we only had a stick. We'd have cut one another to pieces. No, it was only an ordinary copper stick like. Guard – cut one, point parry. You know, we used to face one another, a line here and a line facing see.

33

And of course when he left, he got so old – had another chap come, he come out here – some Lancers, I don't know what number Lancers, anyhow, he learned us boxing and that. Mr Sykes and an assistant. That was two, four, six – about eight altogether.

We got on all right. I only had one quarrel there. When I refused to wear this college cap. I refused to wear it because she said, 'Look you can't go around in the rain without a cap on. I'll get one of Anthony's – Anthony's'll do you'. She had two sons, Anthony and Brian. Both went in the Navy and Anthony was at college and so was Brian. And I wouldn't wear this cap. Only had a cloak, a short pair of knickers, a coat you know, ordinary coat like. And if it rained we got a cloak. Yes, that was the uniform. And shoes – thick soles as thick as that. Proper clogs they were. My mother come once while I was there, only my mother, not my father – he wouldn't be bothered with it. My mother come down with about another twenty mothers. Oh what a lot they were! They nearly got half drunk before they come in, we heard singing and that.

After three years they sent six of us to Brighton in a mineral water factory, name of R. Fry's mineral water people. Not R. Fry's the chocolate people, mineral water people, Middle Street, Brighton. Been taught as a cabinet maker, started work as a carpenter repairing mineral water cases. Well that's a waste of time and money it is, 'cause I was very disappointed over that. We used to be in at six. I lived in Hove when we first started and I had to walk from Hove to Brighton. Middle Street was one place, the Level was the other place. The Level was along further than what was Middle Street. And you had to be there – I used to get up about half past four, 'cause the landlady was a very clean respectable woman. I had to be very smart. Washed myself – couldn't go upstairs with me boots on and all that. And we used to start at six. If you wasn't there by five past six you were shut out – quarter of an hour. No lunch in the morning. Dinner time – one to two. And from two up till six you was finished. Worked Saturday mornings and all.

I was there about two and half – three years. And I got home-sick. I left the job, come back to London. And I let myself go. Went out selling – all that sort of lark. Took any sort of job on then, you know, the docks or the warehouses, down Bankside you know. [Where did you live then?] Well mostly furnished rooms and I stopped in Rowton House a lot. 'Cause it was very clean and different to what they are today. There were no Irish about then. Well we used to get with the boys, come back to the Elephant and get mixed up with the boys round the Elephant and that. Drinking mostly, drinking, dart playing and all that. Used to go to a lot of boxing – very little football, very little. 'Cause I mean to say you always like to get back to where you come from. And many and many a time I'll go round the Elephant, Blackfriars and all round there – you can't keep away from it somehow.

2
Clifford Hills

I first met Cliff Hills in 1968 and began recording his memories that summer. We both lived in Great Bentley, Essex, but whereas I had been there only four years it was Cliff's native village and he had deep roots there. Cliff had been a widower since the age of thirty-two and was childless. He lived alone and was usually in when I called for a drink and a chat, sometimes with the tape recorder, sometimes not. Our acquaintance deepened into a friendship which extended to our families, and when he died on 23 July 1975 we mourned him deeply.

Clifford Frank Hills was born on 21 May 1904, the fourth son of William and Lily Hills. The eldest boy, William, born in 1886 was the son of Mr Hills's first marriage. Jack was born in 1900 and Lance in 1902. The youngest was a girl, Dorothy, born in 1909. Cliff's father, born in 1864, was from a Great Bentley family and his mother, born in 1874, came from Thorrington, a village a mile away. Cliff loved the village and never lived anywhere else except during the Second World War when he served in the Royal Armoured Corps. He had given up farm work in the early 1930s to be gardener/chauffeur for Dr Athill whose house looked out over the 42-acre green. Cliff enjoyed this work and up to the onset of his last illness when he was seventy was always to be seen clipping hedges and pruning roses at the edge of Great Bentley Green.

Although Cliff as a boy knew only farms and fields, Edwardian Britain was the most urbanised country in the world; only 8.3 per cent of the employed population earned their living in agriculture.[1] It was 'a land of overcrowded towns and cities with a countryside of dying villages round them'.[2] Nearly nine-tenths of the farming land was owned by the gentry, the farmers rented it and the labourers worked it. But although Essex was seriously affected by the agricultural depression Great Bentley was full of life and interest for Cliff. There was a tradition of dissent and independence, non-conformity was strong and although the village people had lost two pieces of common land under the eighteenth-century Enclosure Acts they had succeeded in keeping their large green as common land.[3]

Steam power had made some impact on Great Bentley farming, but despite the use of threshing machines, reapers and reaper-binders, work was carried on by men and animals much as it had always been. Everyone lived by farming and there were very few opportunities for work or recreation outside the village. The motor car changed all that but when Cliff was young he belonged to a community so close-knit that sixty years later he could remember over one hundred nicknames of village people.

But although his membership of this community gave Cliff great satisfaction and security it also caused him pain as he began to feel aware of the humble position accorded his family in the Great Bentley social hierarchy. It was at church that the facts of class first hurt him just as they had Joseph Arch, the Warwickshire-born farmworkers' leader, eighty years before. One Sunday when he was seven Arch had peeped through the keyhole to see his father take communion, 'First, up walked the squire to the communion rails; the farmers went up next, then up went the tradesmen, the shop-keepers, the wheelwright and the blacksmith; and then, the very last of all, went the poor agricultural labourers in their smock frocks. They walked up by themselves; nobody else knelt with them; it was as if they were unclean – and at that sight the iron entered straight into my poor little heart and remained fast embedded there. I said to myself, "If that's what goes on – never for me!"' Arch, like Cliff, resented the pressure on farmworkers from better-off people not to dress above their station. His daughter was sent home from school for wearing a hairnet with beads, while feathers, flowers and buckles adorned the tradesmen's children's clothes and shoes. But Cliff got a different response from the young Arch when he deplored class distinction to his mother. Mrs Arch was a dissenter and 'gloried' in her son's spirit, while Mrs Hills tried to convince Cliff that it didn't matter and 'we can't all be rich'.[4]

Mrs Hills had a deferential respect and liking for the doctor's family who lived next door. She chose to give Cliff the doctor's Christian name Frank as his second name and she could not bring herself to refuse the doctor's requests for Cliff's services as a beater in the shooting season although the boy found the work utterly exhausting. Cliff shared some of her attachment to the family. He enjoyed playing tennis and having strawberry teas with the doctor's nieces when they came to stay. Yet he also shared his father's scorn for the dinners the doctor's brother brought over on a plate on Sundays. It was however a scorn that was concealed behind a polite acceptance, for Mr Hills, although he preferred the economic uncertainty of being self-employed to serving one master, was not one to express discontent openly.

Mr Hills went out to work only when there was a job he could do which would command a price he thought fair. He was therefore far more in his children's company in the home than other farmworkers, indeed more than most fathers in general, for he stayed at home when he was unemployed and made his thatching equipment. His brother-in-law envied him as he called in at five o'clock for a cup of tea, 'You're all right. You can set in your backyard in your old shed, riving your brauches for a house or a barn, I've got to go down to the old farm, Sturricks Farm and that old cold barn all day, mending a few old sacks', but his wife found the financial uncertainty very burdensome. The boys saw more of their father at work too than other boys did because they helped him. Lance and Cliff enjoyed this though they were reluctant to pull beets, a wearisome job; Cliff worked long hours on his own from an early age for after the school leaving age was raised to fourteen in 1889 some children were exempted from full-time schooling before fourteen. From the age of eleven in agriculture, and from twelve under the Factory Acts, children might work part-time. But Cliff was missing the first hour of school well before his eleventh birthday; it was a common practice for village children to miss school when farmers needed their labour, and during the First World War many local authorities allowed children total exemption at twelve.[5]

The hard work had its lighter side; Mr Brooks's eccentricities and Miss Newman's squeamishness were a source of pleasure and the monotony was broken by funerals, fairs, ferreting, fights, bareback riding, bathing, football and cricket. Animals too were a source of interest as well as labour. Today horses are not used on the village farms and the animals are less visible; a Great Bentley child now would be unlikely to learn the facts of life by watching animals, or earn money by tending them.

NOTES

1 Paul Thompson, *The Edwardians* (London, 1975), p. 38.
2 Dorothy Thompson, *The British People* (London, 1969), p. 22.
3 A. F. J. Brown, *Essex at Work* (Chelmsford, 1969), pp. 44, 144.
4 Joseph Arch, *The Story of His Life told by Himself* (London, 1898), pp. 19–20; pp. 50–2.
5 Pamela Horn, *The Victorian Country Child* (London, 1974), p. 72.
  For children's work in a rural community see also Raphael Samuel, 'Quarry Roughs: Life and Labour in Headington Quarry 1880–1920' in R. Samuel (ed.) *Village Life and Labour* (London, 1975), pp. 203–7.

We lived near the post office. It was a very old house. It's been pulled down. There was a very low back door I remember. They were short people in those days I think, and two upstairs rooms and two down, plus two small rooms at the very back, more or less attics I should think. They were quite warm, plastered walls. The house was wood. Wooden house with slates on the roof, very low ceilings. [Downstairs?] Front room and a kitchen. The stairs was just a ladder, wooden ladder. No stairs that we know these days. The kitchen was just a very low room with a brick floor, always damp, with a bowl to wash in you know, and a shelf with pots and pans, usually all smokey because it was an open fire we had to cook on. No, there was no oven. In the fireplace itself, yes, there was an oven, by the side of it. But the top was wide open, you see, so the saucepans had to stand right over the flames, which gave us smokey tea, smokey food quite often. We used to stand a bar of iron across the top so it would take four saucepans, three and four saucepans, plus the kettle, sometimes.

It burned coal and wood which we collected sometimes from the woods. We didn't have much coal, or rather we didn't have much money in those days to get much coal, about half a hundredweight a week, that's all. Most people were very poor in those days. We just went in the woods or the fields and collected big pieces, anything we could get hold of and Father would saw it up you see, in the back yard. The old fashioned saw.

We all washed in the same bowl. There was no sink. We had to go about 50 yards to a well and draw water up with a bucket, crop and a bucket. Mother just said, 'Cliff (or Lance or Jack) would you fetch a bucket of water?' and sometimes two buckets at a time. But we weren't very big in those days, so we couldn't bring them full, even across that distance. Sometimes in my very younger days – I suppose we were about four or five or six years old – we used to wait at the well head for some old man to come and draw us a bucket. We weren't strong enough to draw it up.

We in those days lived from hand to mouth. There was never enough money to store anything, no fridge or anything. There was never any stores, only as she made jams and fruits, bottled fruit and so on. We had a cupboard, near the fireplace, actually just an opening in the wall with a few old shelves made with orange boxes and so on. Everything was dilapidated in those days. We never had any cooked meals for breakfast, usually bread and jam or lard and brown sugar. When I speak to people about it now they are horrified, but it was nice. We liked it anyway. Or bread and margarine. Tea with sugar and milk. Never a glass of milk, yet milk was cheap, but as I say nothing was cheap if you hadn't got the money. A pint of milk was a halfpenny then, you could get a pint of skimmed milk for a halfpenny, but if you hadn't got the halfpenny it was dear, wasn't it? The three brothers we used to sit at the table. My mother was very particular. She wouldn't let one start without the other. We all had to start at once.

We had visitors quite often, neighbours for a cup of tea. Almost any day of the week. Any time. Mother used to have friends each side of the cottage, you see, and they used to come in for a cup of tea and a chat. I remember very well, the tea was usually very weak. I can almost see it now. Of course, let me say again, there wasn't much money to spare then, hardly any. We had to buy things in ha'porths and penn'orths, you see. Nothing is cheap if you haven't got the money to buy it with.

She made nearly all our clothes, the children's clothes. But my clothes were always made out of some kind of material that Mother would have given her, or perhaps get it from a rummage sale, or something like that. Yes, I well remember that, her making my clothes. Usually velvet. I don't know where she got the velvet from, but to make things pretty she used to put some little pearl buttons down here. I remember them, little white buttons down here. You see them in the picture, didn't you? She was a good mother.

Saturday nights were bath night. We were called in from the Green at seven o'clock every Saturday night, and we wanted to play, but we knew we had to go. And in front of the fire was the rather big galvanized bath and on the fireplace were three or four saucepans of water, kettle and all. And we bathed in the same water, of course, although it was topped up each time with a saucepan of water which we had to stand clear of because of lifting it over the high guard which prevented us falling into the fire. And we used to have this bath, the three of us, on Saturday nights. I don't remember wearing knickers, shorts, in those days, just our little shirts. I don't really remember having those underclothes. I don't think so. But anyway, she used to seem to be delighted to bath us, you know. This was in our school days of course when we were seven, eight or nine. And this was the Saturday night high tea. Father would come from the pub – this was the only time he went out, Saturday nights, and start frying this supper, which I said before I got with threepence – three penn'orth of pieces.

So after the bath we'd sit round the table waiting for Dad to come in and he didn't drink much, but what he did have made him happy, you know, a little merry. Then he'd get a pan and fry this food, bits of sausage and bits of meat, and we had a good tuck-in on Saturday nights, and so to bed, early. And usually there was enough meat for Sunday morning breakfast. But what I thought about a good many times since – with my brothers we've spoken about it – nearly every bit of meat we got was suspect. Dad always smelled it first, but we never seen him put a bit to one side, he always put it in the pan but we've since said, you know, sometimes, but we used to eat it. And talk about the flies, I've wondered since why we didn't get some kind of disease because the meat had gone off, the flies were crawling all over the place.

It was a great day weekends, you know, with this fry-up on Saturday night and Father cooking the dinner on Sunday, because Mother always went to church on Sunday morning, as we did, in the choir. When we came home there was Father – lovely smell – roast beef, Yorkshire pudding, potatoes – [what else?] Probably peas or cabbage, something like that. And for tea we would have bread and jam of course, that's usual; bread and butter, lettuce, celery. Celery – we had a lot of celery in those days. Oh and mother would make some cakes for the week-end. When we were getting more money Mother would make more cakes. She called them harvest cakes, but we used to call them rock cakes. They were hard. She wasn't a very good pastry maker, Mother wasn't, and you could drop them on the floor, which we did sometimes and say they wouldn't break, but anyway we used to like them. And Sunday, it was really a lovely day, with this extra food and Father being happy and we enjoyed the Sunday School and going in the woods. Did ever you see a nicer shade of blue than bluebells in the shaded woods? Have you seen them?

Nearly everybody kept a pig in those days for one reason, to pay their rent. My father kept a pig from about eight weeks old and he used to fat it up and sell it about September time for about £10 or £12 which paid his rent, which was £10 per year. The other couple of pound perhaps went on clothes for the winter for himself and us kids. I remember him killing a pig once; I think he had two. Yes, I remember that, he had two pigs, one for us to sell to pay for the rent and one to eat. I remember that we used to hang it up in a spare cavity room. It used to turn black. They used to pickle it, you see, pickle it so it was black pickled right through, and it lasted for some months. It had swill, with swill from neighbours to help sometimes, who didn't keep a pig. Also my brothers and I had to collect acorns in the autumn from the trees, used to go miles with a little cart for acorns for the pig, to help out, feed it, you see.

Yes, my brothers and I always had to dig the garden and dig the allotment which was about a quarter of a mile away before we were allowed to play on the Green. Three brothers had to do all that. In the spring is allotment time, you see, when the nights began to lengthen in March and if dry enough we used to go and get it dug first, that was important. Father used to come along and plant most things. I think I'm talking now of when I was about the age of eight or nine, because I got a kitchen boy's job when I was about nine years old, so I wasn't able to do much on the allotment.

We used to do a lot of cross-country running and jumping bars. We used to do a lot of jumping. We used to go into the local builder for a couple of stakes with a few nails in and a cross bit, which we either cut out of the hedgerow or perhaps he gave it to us and the two posts and the bar was raised on the nail 2 inches at a time. You see we done a lot of that. But we didn't have any gym shoes in those days, or white shoes or slippers, we just kicked off our boots and just jumped in our socks. And for a football we used to just go to the butchers and ask him for an animal's bladder blown up. And a cricket bat we just used to make out of bits of wood, the stumps were sticks. The goal posts were somebody's caps or coats chucked down. Everything was made up by ourselves or found. Catapults, of course, we always had a catapult we made ourselves. We made kites, not run into Woolworth's and buy yourself a kite. We used to make them with a bit of willow and a straight stick and a bit of mother's wallpaper left over from the previous year's wallpapering. The catapult was made with a piece of wood – twig with a fork and elastic.

My grandfather was a shepherd for many years. He was a shepherd at the Lodge Farm. My father was a shepherd eventually. Before then, before he went to work on the farm he was a bricklayer, and he helped build Clacton and parts of Walton. He was a man who liked variety. He didn't like to be tied down in the middle of a field for about twelve hours a day then, I think. He'd work hard for a few weeks when he'd got the work to do, from daylight till dark, and enjoyed it, but he didn't like to be tied down to a farm on regular work from six till six, that wasn't in his line. He was a man who wouldn't work on a regular job. He wanted to take the job, so much per job, you see, so I think he had to start on a farm.

He did general farm work at eleven shillings per week when he got married, and he learned to thatch stacks, corn stacks, he learned to clip sheep and dip sheep to clean them. He learned other farm work and he became good at it so that in the summer time when the corn was gathered and all the stacks were made he would thatch that lot of stacks for so much money which was probably four or five times more than he would earn per week on a regular job, you see. And then he would do this sheep shearing, which was good money in those days, there wasn't many sheep shearers about and he was very good at it and he earned lots of money then. But you see, by doing those kind of jobs there was many weeks when he was out of work, so perhaps he wasn't any better off in the long run.

He was very good at poaching rabbits. My brother and I used to go with him. He'd put the snares out at about four o'clock on a winter's afternoon and collect them in the mornings about four or five. My brother and I would go with him quite often. I don't remember anyone being summonsed for it. They were threatened by farmers, by the police, but I don't remember Father ever being summonsed for it and he wasn't the only one who went poaching. Sometimes they had permission, mind you, to catch rabbits on certain farms. But there wasn't always rabbits on a farm where you had permission and sometimes there was plenty of rabbits where you couldn't get permission. He never had permission to get

45

pheasants but there was ways and means of getting them late at night – catapults. And in those days if you had money you would invest in a torch. They just began to manufacture torches, I think in those days, or a paraffin lamp. And late at night you would go up to a little woodland place where the pheasants used to roost and shine the torch on them in their eyes. Dazzle them. And with a long stick you just hit them on the head and drag them down. But for those too high up or too far away you had a catapult, you see.

Father was very good with the catapult. He could even kill a rabbit with a catapult. Most boys had a catapult in their pockets in those days, which I believe was illegal. I think so. I think that if the policeman saw you with a catapult he'd run you in, because we quickly hid them when the policeman – who was always on our track in those days for playing games on somebody's property. Or as boys we've many a time gone in with our catapults even with sparrows roosting in the tree, we just killed sparrows for the fun of it. Mother's father had a gun, double-barrelled gun, and working on the farm he used to shoot sparrows and pigeons, wood pigeons. I remember Mother often made a sparrow pie. Us kids used to pluck them, you know, very tiny things too, when you get their feathers off. But they were tasty. And pigeons. Father had permission to shoot wood pigeons, which are pests, eat a lot of corn.

He was very good at catching a hare. He could pick a hare up in a field. Pick it up with his hands. Now you might wonder how he knew it was a hare that was there wouldn't you? But he could see a hare all round nearly a mile away. He had a wonderful sight. And going through Sturricks Farm early one morning, my brother and I and Father, my father was looking ahead, oh it seemed miles ahead and he suddenly stopped. He said, 'One of you boys go over that way, and the other one go that way and we'll walk together.' We were about twenty yards, thirty yards apart you see. 'When I put my hands up like this, you walk towards each other.' So we did, and as we walked towards each other, my Father kept on his line of walk and suddenly stooped down and picked up a hare. He knew that it was sitting there, he knew that it would be watching one of us, because he made that hare watch one of us before he moved. And often he did that with a rabbit too. Now, how he spotted that rabbit or hare all that distance away I don't know, because it was a long distance that we had to walk before Father would pick this rabbit up, or hit it with a stick. It seemed that he could smell a rabbit.

And most days we had fried rabbit, baked rabbit, boiled rabbit. But we were never short of a turnip or swedes to go with it. Mother made dumplings you see, with a bit of flour in those days. We had a good dinner when the rabbits were around. And he sold some of the rabbits of course. We had enough for ourselves, but I think they were about sixpence or ninepence then and you could sell the skins for about a penny or tuppence. In those days the rag and bone man used to come round, a man usually with a sack, and he'd examine the skins to see if they were in good shape and give you a penny for them.

That farmer Brooks was a terrible man. They were always quarrelling. My father worked for him for many years and there was always trouble between them. I believe Father manhandled him two or three times for different reasons. And in those days when Father was thatching, we had to draw the water from the pond you see. We used to have a plank going into the pond, about eight or ten feet to rest it on a big box or boulder, then you walked the plank and then you could heave a good bucket of water out where you couldn't from the water's edge you see, because it was too shallow at the edge you see.

And they'd be arguing quite a bit, and the master, the lunatic you see, the old man down that farm, Brooks, and Father went in to get this bucket of water, arguing on the pond's edge, and this stupid farmer walks the plank after my father on the end of the plank and they both struggled on the end of the plank and fought until they both fell in the water. Wasn't very deep – well it was about two feet deep, you see. Father was up to his knees, you see, and the old man Brooks was on his knees in the water. Father had to go home and change and Mr Brooks went running back to his house, just running, never said a word. Next day they started again friendly, nice and friendly. But Mother said, many times, 'I wonder you work for that lunatic,' but Father said, 'Well as long as I get me money it doesn't matter about a few arguments.'

And we were delighted because that old man had some false teeth, I should think about the only one in the village who ever had false teeth. They made them in those days. He used to stick his tongue underneath them and sometimes they'd fall on the floor or the ground. He'd pick 'em up, wipe them on his trousers and put them back in his mouth again. My brother and I were delighted to see this. You see, it was an interlude. Work stopped and we had fun. Another morning we went to this farm, I haven't been to the farm for years, often think about it and the fun we had at that farm, Sturricks Farm. Overnight we left the ladders in position, one ladder on the big corn stack my father was thatching and the other up on the straw stack, where we had to climb up and turn the straw down and shake it up properly, you know. And this ladder was missing one morning. Mind you this was about half past four or five when we used to go in the summer holidays near dark. And we couldn't understand where this ladder was because we knew we left it laying the night before, in the dark nearly, and it was nearly dark when we got there the next morning and the ladder had gone.

So my uncle came, the head horseman he was then (not this one with the leg but another one). My father asked him about it and he said, no, he hadn't had it, so my father said, 'Well you boys go and have a look round and see if you can find it.' And we found it up at a window of the house where you're living now. I think the window was facing Sturricks Lane way, to the best of my recollection. And that ladder was up at the window. My brother and I just wondered how it got there, but we were after the ladder and took it down when a voice suddenly said, 'Half a mo', mate. You can put it back again so I can get out.' So we put it back again, and that was the local porter. [Their eldest brother, then in his mid-twenties.] He'd been spending the night with the housemaid down there. And he said, 'Here you are, there's a bob,' he said, 'Don't tell Father, will you?' And we didn't. He gave us a shilling, and evidently he'd been going there a good many times but you see, we was too early for him this particular morning, or he was too late getting out, putting the ladder back. And my brother and I have often spoken about it since. We told Father in later years. We always had fun at that farm. Just before we went into school one morning at nine o'clock we see Mr Brooks taken to the asylum in this Mr Gosling's trap. And Mr Brooks was potty.

On Sundays we had to dress up all day. We had to go to Sunday School in the morning, about nine o'clock till ten, three brothers, as well as the other boys in the village, and we had to march to the church from the village hall that is now. Then we came home and had a quiet hour before dinner. Then we had to get washed and Mother would take us to Sunday School again, or rather come with us to see we went in. We weren't always willing to go to Sunday School, of course. And this was at the village hall, what was the

Sunday School in those days. Mother would be waiting outside for us when we come out of Sunday School and we had to go for a walk with Mother, the three brothers again, through the woods, being very quiet all the time. Then we came back to tea, washed again, done our hair, off to church again, in the choir again, back home again, and so to bed. No playing on Sundays anywhere at any time.

Later on my sister came along and when she was four or five years old, perhaps younger, my father bought an organ, like a church organ. It had pipes and no end of stops, he bought it cheap, he'd been earning some money, I think for £5 for my sister. Of course, being the only sister they thought the world of her and she used to get on this organ and she could play! But first of all my mother used to play every Sunday after tea, hymns, and my father and the three brothers all had to stand round and we all used to sing hymns before we went to church again. But Father used to go to chapel. Every Sunday night Father went to chapel. And he used to sing these what they call Sankey hymns. Lovely hymns. I used to like them. There was more go in them than the Church of England hymns I thought.

Mother didn't like us to go to chapel. I think it was probably when we got old maybe fifteen or sixteen, perhaps we had an occasional Sunday off from church. My mother was proud of us in the church choir. Sometimes the surplices didn't look clean enough. I don't know who used to do them, when we walked up the aisle and she used to sit near the aisle you see, so she asked the vicar's wife if she could do her boys' surplices and she made a good job of them too. They were spotless. White not grey. Whiter than white! Mother was very fond of me too; I don't know why but she seemed fonder of me than the others, but the usual surplice had a collar, rather straight collar all round. But she made mine sort of frilled, so it looked frilled. She thought I looked fabulous in this surplice compared to the other boys and I could feel Mother's eyes on me, and only me, as we marched up the aisle.

And at Easter time we used to sing that lovely hymn 'Forever with the Lord, Amen, so let it be' and we used to stop in the aisle and sing one verse, there was about twenty or more boys in the choir then, men and boys, and we used to stop in the aisle and sing one verse, why I don't know, but we did. And nearly always when we stopped Mother would be sitting in our seat here. I was so shy and I used to dry up when Mother was just there, you know. I expect I didn't feel like singing. And she said, 'You can sing if you like, you know you've got a lovely voice and you can sing it at home, why don't you sing when you're close to me. I like to hear you sing.' But that was a certain shyness I had just at that one spot. It wasn't 'Forever with the Lord', it was, 'Now Thank we all our God', a Good Friday hymn, an Easter hymn.

In those days as kids, grandfathers and grandmothers were dying, you know, and of course when relatives came to the funeral they had to find them food or something special, so when they did there was cakes and wine, mostly wine, homemade. Ginger cakes, I remember, nearly always ginger cakes and jam sandwiches and what not. And as kids we used to go up to the funeral and have a good tuck-in. It was something like the Irish have, the Wakes, you know. I had an uncle who played the accordion and after the funeral, with this homemade wine which was getting the better of them, Uncle would play the accordion and those who could dance would dance and those who could sing would sing and it ended up with quite a nice gay evening. We enjoyed people dying in those days. They used to know lots of songs in those days, and I've heard my father sing perhaps a dozen or fifteen verses. These days some of them only know about one line and start humming all this, but in those days they used to learn lots of verses. They used to tell lots of funny stories at these receptions, some drawing-room and some not. One thing about it, however drunk people were then, I don't remember them ever using bad language in front of women and children. I don't remember my uncles or anyone using bad language. I won't say they got blind drunk or anything of that kind. They got lively and sung songs altogether or by themselves.

There was no particular celebration for birthdays. There wasn't too much money to celebrate, only Christmas. We always had a Christmas tree for Christmas, Father always had a Christmas tree. I think Mother used to remark about our birthdays but I don't remember Mother or Father making any fuss about birthdays to each other. Just like an ordinary day. But we were reminded it was our birthdays when we were kids. I had a grandmother alive in those early days and she used to save my pennies and we were always earning pennies, we'd go around trying to earn pennies somehow, even searching the local pond for a beer bottle and get a penny on it, or a monster bottle, and my grandmother used to save

1 King's Bench Street, Southwark, London in 1907. No. 5 where Tommy Morgan was born is the cottage behind the lamp post. The cottages had been lived in by warders of the Marshalsea prison where Dickens' father had been imprisoned.

2 The public house on the corner of Pocock Street and Wellington Street known as the Duke's Head. This was a stone's throw from Tommy's home and was probably a home from home to his parents. Men appear to be erecting scaffolding planks for demolition. The date is 1907.

3 Southall Place in the Borough, London in 1913. The women are hatless and so not dressed to be photographed outside their doorways. Their clothing has the dark colour universally worn by working class women of the time and, although their faces and hair indicate that they are probably still comparatively young, their slumped posture, with arms folded for support, show them prematurely aged with work, child bearing and poverty.

4 The Saturday market at the Cut in 1894–5. The Cut is off Waterloo Road. Here Tommy helped his costermonger brother sell from his vegetable barrow and was taught how to stretch the profits. Nearby stood the Old Vic where Mrs Morgan bought scenery for sheets.

5 Nos 146–52, Borough High Street in 1904. Before the deep freeze, meat was hung up outside, to prevent it decaying in the close air of the shop, and auctioned off cheaply on Saturday night.

6 Nos 309–17, Borough High Street, London in 1904. J. Shuttleworth's was the sort of coffee shop Tommy patronized when he had the money. It was in just such a shop that the policeman bringing him home after his interview at County Hall bought him two eggs, a rasher and a cup of coffee. The boy in front of the shop appears crippled, possibly with tuberculosis of the spine.

7 Borough High Street in 1895–66. The vehicles on the left are brewers' drays transporting barrels of beer. At right angles to this street runs Trinity Street where Tommy had Christmas dinner in the Shaftesbury Hall. Shops and shopkeepers were important to Tommy. The majority gave soup tickets for a meal. 'If you was one of the naughty boys which I was many a time I was, but I always' knew I'd get one at one shop, a big linen draper's shop name of Brooke's in the Borough High Street.'

8 Westminster Hospital, London in 1913. Tommy was transferred here from Evelina Hospital. 'My mother never missed a visiting day. I think it was a Thursday afternoon and a Sunday afternoon for eighteen months. My mother never missed a visit and my father never came up once.'

9 Boys doing lessons at the Chailey Heritage Craft School, Sussex. This photo was probably taken about the time of the First World War after Tommy had left the school.

10 The village school which Cliff Hills attended.

11 'I remember going to school. Grandfather was a roadsweeper then. . . .'
Cliff's Grandfather is holding the wheelbarrow.

12 Great Bentley Green. The house second from the right is Pond House where the Athill family lived when Cliff was a boy. In the background can be seen the tower of the parish church, St Mary's. The building on the extreme right is the Red Lion pub.

13 This is the home of the Barker family of the Hall Farm at the edge of the village green, Great Bentley. Cliff's father would sometimes pull beet for Mr Barker and Cliff worked here from the age of nine until after his marriage.

14 Jonathan Hills and his wife Phoebe, Cliff's paternal grandparents.

15 Cliff's childhood home next to the Post Office, Great Bentley. In the doorway wearing a white apron is his mother. The child is Dorothy Hills, Cliff's sister.

16 Cliff with his father, William Hills. Although Cliff is wearing his Little Lord Fauntleroy suit his father is wearing his usual working clothes and is with his dog, Bob. The boy is modelling himself on the father—hand on hip and the other clasping a stick.

17 William Hills thatching. With him is his daughter Dorothy.

18 Dr Frank Athill, Great Bentley village doctor and neighbour of the Hills family in 1903. He is mounted on his first motor cycle outside his home, Pond House.

19 A car belonging to a friend of Dr Athill's, Sir William Avery, which was brought down from London with special permission to a fete at St Mary's Farm, Great Bentley. It was the first car to come to the village.

20 Soldiers outside the lodge of Brook Farm during the First World War.

21 The wedding of Jane Hills, Cliff's aunt, to Jimmy Lodge in about 1910 in
Great Bentley. On the bride's right is Jonathan Hills, Cliff's grandfather and on
the groom's left is Cliff's brother Lance seated next to his grandmother,
Jonathan Hill's wife. Out of the thirty-eight men, women and children in the
group only four are not blood relations of Cliff's including the groom. Cliff's
sister, Dorothy, was often told by her parents that she was the result of that
wedding. She was born exactly nine months later. 'I expect Dad had a few
drinks!'

22 The wedding of Cliff Hills to Annie Cooper in January 1927 at Ainger's
Green on the borders of Great Bentley village. Annie came from a gipsy family.
Her mother has bare arms and is not wearing a hat in contrast to the 'home-
dwellers'. Her husband is wearing a handkerchief round his neck. Cliff's
mother was not happy about him marrying into a gipsy family and did not
attend the wedding. She died a year later on his first wedding anniversary. His
father attended the wedding but is not in the photograph.

23 Two young girls in a Farnworth spinning mill in the early 1900s. The name of the mill is not known. Girls this age would usually wear their hair loose down their back, but it was dangerous in a mill to have loose hair and so it is worn up.

24 Vicar's Row, Farnworth, near Florence Atherton's home. The street is celebrating the return of the troops from the First World War. This is the Plodder Lane area close to many of the mills such as Barnes's, Phethean's, Almond's, Century Ring Spinning Co., etc.

25 Howarth's shop stands at the junction of Market Street and Rawson Street, Farnworth, a few hundred yards from the streets where Florrie Atherton lived as a child. Queen Street, where she was born, is almost a continuation of Rawson Street. The Farnworth bus, marked F is approaching.

26 A group of children on the corner of Barncroft Road and King Street. The children are wearing duck-toed clogs which are only found within a twenty mile radius of Manchester. There was a great home production of stockings. Note the sign 'Stockings knitted and refooted'. The girl in the front row minding her little sister or brother is typical of the period. So is the boy second from the left. His coat is bulging with an item redeemed from the pawn-shop. These were usually concealed under a jacket so as not to alert the neighbours.

27 St Gregory's school walking day on Whit Friday, 1896—possibly at Moses Gate. The band probably belonged to Barnes's Mill.

28 Farnworth Market in the early 1900s. Customers are listening to a portable phonograph through stethoscope type ear pieces. A girl wearing the usual hat, black stockings and pinafore stands at another stall.

29 Brabin's outfitters and hosiers decked out for the coronation of Edward VII. Brabin's was in Market Street, Farnworth. Next door to the left was Devonport's butchers.

30 Geoffrey Brady at an early age.

31 Geoffrey and his sister paddling at the seaside. The sweater and shorts were typical seaside clothing for boys in the middle class. The children's heads are protected from the sun.

all the pennies, put them in a handkerchief, put them in her pocket in her old dress underneath her pinny, and she didn't tell me how much I'd got till I went to the Sunday School treat. And I remember once I had four shillings and I thought I was a millionaire.

One thing as a boy I didn't like and it sticks in my mind today. I came to the conclusion that church-goers were something like the railway carriages were at one time – first, second and third class. You see my mother was a person of the lower class, she was a poor woman, and she and her friends were all poor, but they were great church goers, regular church goers, kindly gentle people. But they had to sit in the middle of the church, or rather at the back, I say 'middle' because there wasn't so many going at that time. They had to sit in the back pews. In the middle of the church were the local shopkeepers and people who were considered to be a little bit superior to the others, better educated perhaps. And right at the top of the church, behind where the choir used to sit, were the local farmers, the local bigwigs, you see, posh people. And when people left the church, although as I said he was a nice kindly vicar, he didn't seem to have any time for the lower classes. Mother and her friends would pass out of the church door, the vicar would stand near the church door, and he would just nod and smile, perhaps not that even.

But when the higher class people came out he would shake hands and beam to everyone of them as if they were somebody far superior to my mother and her friends, the poor, the very poor. And I didn't like that. I thought my mother was worth a handshake as well as the rich. There was the Captain Peele and other local farmers who were considered to be rich in those days, they were select. They had chosen seats, reserved seats. My mother's seat wasn't reserved. If there was something important on and the church was full of people, it wouldn't matter to anyone whether she got in the church or not, although she went so regular. They did most of the work. They did all the cleaning. They did all the decorating I remember. I must have been perhaps twelve when it used to strike me. Yes, it did because I used to discuss this, and only me used to discuss this sort of thing with my mother, the other brothers never talked about it. I said it wasn't right, it wasn't proper. I said she shouldn't go to church. She said, 'Nothing will ever stop me from going to my church.'

I should think I was fifteen before I ever had a new suit, brand new suit, which Mother bought on the never-never for a shilling a week. I should think it was somewhere about 1914 or 1915 during the war, 1914–18 war, because I remember the soldiers saying to me, 'Hello, Mother bought you a new suit,' and that's the first new suit I ever had. And one more thing about that, living next door to the post office we used to take telegrams for the post mistress, I've gone over to Little Bentley or Bromley for sixpence, you see and one Sunday morning I had to take a telegram to the local baker, lived round there on one of the new estates, man named Smith. And this was the first Sunday I had this new suit on, and when I took this telegram he said, 'Let me see, your name is Hills, I think, isn't it?' I said, 'Yes, sir.' We always called them sir. We were brought up to call men like that 'sir', the doctor and the vicar whom we thought were rich, even the local baker we thought was important. 'Ee' he said, 'I see you've got a new suit on. It looks like a new suit to me. Good gracious me,' he said, 'some of you people are going to be as well dressed as we are.' I've never forgotten that. That's what we had to put up with from the so-called rich and intellectuals. I told my father and he said, 'It's no good taking notice of that old man,' he said, 'Let him go to chapel with his Bible under his arm.' He used to go to chapel every Sunday morning with his Bible under his arm as if he was the most important man in the village, but he was a very mean-minded type of man. Mother just said, 'Don't take any notice,' I think she said once or twice, she said, 'We can't all be rich. It wouldn't be right that we should, no one would do the work if we were all rich.' But she had a nice nature. You couldn't make her turn against anybody or tell anybody off or anything. I never knew her, or my father, get bad tempered over anything.

I think mother used to have a book occasionally, to read to herself mostly, not to us. But she used to like, I think to have a read in the afternoons for a little while. She said, to the best of my recollection, that it relaxed her. It prevented her going to sleep, because she hadn't time to go to sleep, she said, having three boys coming out of school, rushing out of school. Mother used to see us off to bed with a candle, no paraffin lamp in the bedroom, only a candle. And what's more she used to take it away with her. She was always fearful of fire, us getting a match from somewhere and lighting it. But over this candle and the little dressing table there was the Bible. And mother held it underneath this candle and we all had to read a little passage out of the Bible before we got into bed, and then our prayers. Every night. We always had to read a little verse, perhaps twenty or thirty words wherever it stopped you see, the three of us, and then the candle was snuffed out and Mother would go down, not stairs, it was only a ladder in that cottage. And off we went to sleep, the three boys. Things have changed now, I don't think that's done now. As I said, my mother was a great church goer.

Father wasn't interested, I don't think, in newspapers or books. He used to do a good day's work and think of what he'd done, how good it was or if he was puzzled by anything, and when he came home at night he used to sit in front of the fire and just smoke his pipe, as if he was a lord, very happy thinking he'd done a good day's work. Only smoked a pipe. He never smoked a cigarette but he seemed that he was happy with everybody in general. One of the happiest men I ever knew. And as I said, when he brought bread home sometimes it was pretty dry, in summertime especially. He would put it in the basin, put some hot water on it and pepper and salt and enjoy it. It's amazing the things those people enjoyed in those days.

In my case and my brothers I think, we did speak a little better, if you call it better, differently to the other local children because, as I said before, my mother was a nurse in London with a lady, Mrs Morgan Brown, and she was more refined than some village people. And children do copy their parents. We all know that don't we? Mrs Morgan Brown used to come at least once a year, that was before Christmas, with the gifts, sweets, and little trains and things like that as kids had in those days, little engines and little motors. Nearly always, either in the summer or Christmas, there was a little box of soldiers which we were delighted to have, which we used to play with on the table, mostly in the old British uniforms, Hussars and Dragoons and Guards, mostly horse soldiers. And we used to arrange 'em between us as battles. That time I used to wish I could be a soldier. Even when I was ten when the soldiers come about here I wished I could be a soldier. My wish came true eventually.

She always had tea, used to sit at the table with Mother, just as if she was my Auntie, or something like that. She was refined but not pompous or nothing at all. Quite humble. No airs and graces. Not like with some people today even, who have no title or not much money. Yes she was a lovely lady, so friendly, and I'm sure she loved my mother. My mother was so excited when she came. We were excited too, believe me, because we knew we would get something. Mother didn't need to tell us to be on our best behaviour, we were already aware of that.

There was nothing said about sex at all when we were young, not in front of children, I don't remember anything being said about sex. I don't remember the birth of my sister at all. I don't remember even mother being pregnant or nothing at all. I hadn't the faintest idea, I didn't know how babies were born then, no. The old story that we were taught, under some gooseberry bushes. I don't think other boys knew either. I didn't remember noticing whether another woman was pregnant or not. I don't think other boys did. I think one reason was because they wore such heavy thick clothes then you see, so they weren't noticeable like they are today. They had heavy floral dresses and overalls and pinnies and coats and they weren't noticeable even if we knew. We were very innocent. Well everyone are innocent until they're told or taught or they read about it. Well we didn't have books to read about that sort of thing. The only thing we knew was the goings on of animals. That's how we learned those days, on the farms.

I remember mother's mother coming from Thorrington when her husband died, my grandfather died. I should think I was only three or four years old. I remember her being there when I started school, because my brother took me to school for my first day at school and I promptly ran home again, the very first day. He was porter on the railway and he took me on his shoulder to school, I remember it very well, and took me right into the school and left me with a teacher. And as the teacher entered the door, thinking I was going to follow her in, I didn't. I scooted down the corridor and went back home in a twink. The school-teacher went and told my brother. My brother came after me again but my granny tried to hold me. She tried to console me but my brother took me and the teacher looked out I didn't run away only that once.

No, I can't say that I did enjoy school. We were glad to get away from school. We got the cane and we played truant, you know, for no good reason. We played truant when the fox hounds would come on the green and we used to follow the hounds sometimes, all round the fields, be gone all day. We knew what we'd get in the morning. We always got the cane, one on each hand. And another time there was an aeroplane, one of my first sights of an aeroplane, came down in Little Bentley in a big field there. We saw it come down. 'Course we all left school and went to see it. We all got the cane for it though the next morning. See, once we started on anything we didn't try to go back to avoid getting the cane, we just kept away. There's no going back once we started to play truant.

And then the soldiers came about here. The schoolmaster was fairly lenient then. And in front of my mother's house they used to cut up the rations. A big supply waggon used to bring the food for the different regiments, and that little bit of grass in front of where I lived, we had chickens on that green too mixed up with soldiers and some meat and cheese and butter they were issuing out to different units. Us kids, we were round them as well, hoping to get a bit of this and that, which we did. And we used to get in these waggons and go round with the soldiers to different farms when they issued rations and playing truant again. But it paid off because we got something to eat, you know, cheese and a bit of butter, a bit of fat, bit of meat. But I don't think the schoolmaster came down hard on us, because I think he knew what we were on for, a bit of extra food with the soldiers. We had to admit where we'd been. I think he turned a blind eye more often than not. Sometimes we got one strike but never two for that. My parents always said if the schoolmaster, knowing he was a just man, and I think they knew the teachers pretty well, if we got the cane or a tap on the backside with the cane, they said we deserved it, we didn't get it for nothing, we'd been doing something. Never once did I know them to go up to the school to complain about the teachers. In fact they were full of praise for our schoolmaster, Mr Richardson. I liked history and geography better than anything simply because it carried me away over Asia and Europe and the Far East, different countries I was interested in. And at that time, going with the soldiers, I used to think to myself, 'I wish I was a soldier. I wish I could be a soldier.' But when the time came I didn't relish it at all.

And before we left school we used to look forward to our five-week summer holiday, and for why? It was only to work hard. And we used to go to work at daybreak, half past four or five, not my elder brother who was the studious one, the middle brother, with Father day after day for this solid five weeks, unless it rained. Fror daybreak till dark nearly. Some bread and cheese and then we had a few extras then. Mother used to buy a little jar of potted meat, shrimp paste, ham and tongue and so on. We thought that was wonderful to have that put on our margarine. We used to go off with our own little pack of food for the day. Father had a bottle of cold tea, no sugar or milk, 'cause if it had milk it would have gone sour, you see, in the summer months, and my brother and I had a bottle of lemonade each. We used to go to the shop and get a penn'orth of lemonade crystals, a penn'orth mind you, and you got an ounce for a penny, which made two pints, and that was our drink for the day. Usually it was gone long before dinner and we had to drink water for the rest of the day. We had threepence each per week pocket money. We were a great help. You must remember that boys from nine to fourteen were men nearly in those days, you know.

After laying on the Green mostly in the mornings we used to go down to this brook they called it, a brook at the meadows, and we built a dam across the stream and we dug out an area as big as this room first you see, and about three foot deep, and then we built a dam across to make the water hang fire and we made a lovely bathing pool. We used to go down every Saturday and Sunday and most afternoons if we weren't at work and at that age, I should say we were about nine to thirteen something like that. We hadn't left school anyway, and we had a lovely time down there, boys and girls together. And the oak trees were on a huge bank, grassy bank, and to dry ourselves we used to roll down the bank. We never had any towels or bathing costumes in those days, we never even had any money. If someone had a ha'penny they'd get a bottle of lemonade crystals which we all drank out of the same bottle, all laid on our belly to drink the water out of the stream where the ws had been paddling through, but we didn't take any hurt. And ° was cows and horses in the meadows – sometimes a bull 1 we had to beware of. And he wasn't always allowed to come he meadow but he used to break out from a farm sometimes e and get with his ladies and we had to post a lookout. mes he was allowed to come with the cows, they used to take om the meadow about two in the afternoon and milk them, ing them back to the meadows about four and sometimes d to give the bull a break, come with them and the first t wretched bull would do was bounding up towards us you see. There's nothing more frightening than a bull coming towards you, but we always prepared for that sort of thing.

We had lookouts and escape routes, which I've made a sketch for you to see presently. We had great fun. This particular summer he was coming round quite a bit with about twenty cows and we got used to him bounding ahead of the cows towards us but he never got within twenty or thirty yards of us and he'd just stop dead, then run back to the cows you see. So we got a little bit careless. One of these times we thought he might have continued and come after us but mostly the lookout saw it in time, in fact we could hear them sometimes coming down the road at the bottom of the hill and lookout would shout, 'Look out!' you see and off we went down the escape routes towards the stiles and the gates we knew and we always left our clothes on one side so that we weren't stranded over one side of the hedge and our clothes were safe. There again we had posted a guard. We weren't fools in the way of getting organized in those days, you know, we had to be thankful about these things because every field had animals in in those days. First of all they come through the churchyard. There was a meadow there, there was a huge boar there and sows and the very dangerous boar, we had to beware of him.

In those days there was a lot of tramps about you know, walking through the footpaths and the roads, most of them harmless. But we didn't risk losing our clothes, because as I said many times we had no money to replace things and no girls or boys had clothes on. Nobody took any notice of it, neither did we, until well, say suddenly it came to a stop – quite suddenly we became shy of each other and thought it was rude to be seen without clothes, so we kept the girls away, not that all the girls came in the pool with us but there was a couple of girls who did.

I went to work at the age of nine for two shillings per week. I went at seven in the morning till ten and then went to school. I come out of school at four o'clock and went as kitchen boy till half past five, mostly it was nearer six. And on Saturday morning I went from seven till one, for two shillings a week. I had to go to this Hall Farm. Well this farmer sometimes didn't leave the two shillings on the dresser, or on the table for me, he'd forgotten it or gone out, and there was a Miss Barker, his daughter lived with him. And I used to go home without this two shillings. I was almost crying in tears. I knew Mother was waiting for it, and she used to send me back for this two shillings. Eventually I got it from waiting about a long time, perhaps a couple of hours, and I probably had to go to the butchers with this two shillings to get the Sunday joint, which lasted us for Sunday dinner time and perhaps Monday dinner time, a small joint for perhaps one and ninepence, threepence change sometimes. It was beef, nearly always beef. It seemed to go further, or make more gravy or something like that. But she had to be economical you see.

This threepence-worth of meat was every Saturday night with the threepence I earned as a paper boy. The two shillings for the joint was what I earned as a kitchen boy. So one can say I nearly always bought the meat with my two and three. My one brother was a kitchen boy too. He earned I think two and six. He got half-a-crown for his job, working over the green there, working the same hours. I think that half-crown went on bread for the week. The other brother he was more studious. That's the one who didn't ever work. Only mugs worked, he said, in later years. He never did work either, not with his hands. He was a good scholar, always writing, doing figures. But he always took part in any feast that was going. He'd be at any party or feast. So with my two and three and my brother's half-crown, that bought quite a bit of food, bread and meat. When Father was in work, of course, we lived better, much better, but there were some weeks when there wasn't much more than this four or five bob going into the house.

The farmer had a son and he often asked me what boots Father had got on any particular morning because if his father had a certain pair of shoes on he knew he'd gone to London, you see, on business which enabled him to have the day off going on the spree with the pony and cart. And he used to give me sixpence to go and get some cigarettes with, because he knew I smoked, really that's how I started smoking, him buying me cigarettes, you see. I used to go and get his tobacco at the little shop near that farm, just over the road and he give me sixpence to get some cigarettes. And that's when I was smoking in the woodshed, chopping sticks, when the farmer caught me, and picked up a twig and give me – not a thrashing because I didn't stay long enough. I just bolted but he caught me two or three times. No, that was before I had a regular job. That was when I was still going to school. And when I got to my house, this was near ten o'clock, my father was at home and I was crying and I told him what had happened. He said, 'Well, I'll go along and see him. I'll beat him.' He said, as an afterthought, 'what did he hit you for?' I said, 'because I was smoking.' I don't know why but I did. So he give me a clip with his hand. He couldn't find a stick otherwise I'd have got the stick, but anyway, he managed to get a backhander in right across my cheek, and off I went to school crying. By that time, you see, it had gone ten. So there was another boy allowed out till ten and I went down to the other slaughter house, to where he used to work. We both went in late. And that's where the headmaster was strict. If you were allowed out till ten it had got to be ten, irrespective of what the farmers or who you worked for kept you at work. And so we got one on each hand then, the cane on each hand, both of us.

Mother used a stick sometimes, a little cane, but not violently, we had to be corrected. We wouldn't have been human if they'd always been nice to the boys. Usually a smack on the backside with the hairbrush with a handle on. She did once hit me, accidentally I'm sure. She was cleaning my shoes before we went to school. Something I'd been naughty about and she threw the brush at me, not a great distance, and that hit me in the eye and I had a black eye. Mother cried about it. She didn't mean to do it, of course, and I didn't blame her for it of course in later years, and not then. But you know that black eye got me the nickname of 'Shiner' for the rest of my life. There's one or two people in the village who I went to school with call me Shiner, just because of that. But my parents weren't cruel at all, they only used to correct us properly. They were kind and good to us and they used no bad language. Of course, we grew up as they did, really, as far as I remember. I don't think they had much reason to make any rules themselves, because I believe we were more or less sociable and polite people with our teaching from the school and the vicarage. We had particularly to respect the schoolmaster and the clergyman and the doctor. We had then to raise our forefinger to him and say, 'Good morning, Sir.' Always 'Sir'. And we were taught, of course, never to be rude to people, or answer back.

I wasn't unhappy, I accepted – it was a way of life. But I had so much to do, so many jobs to do before I went to school, so I couldn't help being late sometimes. Clean the knives, clean shoes, sift cinders, clean the dogs' kennels, scrub the bath house, no end of jobs to get in. Pluck birds, pheasants, partridges, skin rabbits, hares. That was when I was kitchen boy and then of course I had the same work to do when I left school, plus going with the farmer in his pony and cart round the farms. There was only one servant and I was only allowed in the kitchen to get the knives and the shoes. I had to take them out to what they call the old wash house. And there was a paper up there, a list of things I had to do before I went to school. I remember a brass coal scuttle which I could hardly lift when it was full of coals. And I ran out of Brasso once and I knew they kept Brasso in the shed, the stable for the horses' harness, so I thought 'Well I'll go and borrow their Brasso.' And I went in to get it and this farmer's son was in there with a girl. He picked up a stick and he chased me and threatened me never to go there again. I couldn't win, and it was a terrible job to clean these knives on an old board with some brown powder, sprinkle the powder on the board and rub the knife up and down, backwards and forwards, and I just couldn't get them clean just round where the handle was on the steel. I was sent back no end of times because they weren't clean just there properly. Even when I got a rag and put it in the powder and rubbed just there. They just wouldn't come bright like the other part. Only steel knives, blades you know. But you see, they expect so much from a boy of that age.

Miss Barker the farmer's daughter was over me. She was a very stern person. When I was cleaning windows and I was looking round at German aircraft she threw up the window and nearly frightened me to death. I nearly fell off the ladder. She was always stern. She stopped me from having this cup of tea. I hadn't been there long when the servant there gave me a cup of tea, soon after I got there one morning. And unexpectedly Miss Kate Barker came in, the farmer's daughter and saw me drinking this tea. She really frightened me the way she went on at this maid, cursed her right and left and she said, 'Never, never give him tea!' They were very mean people. So if the servant said to me sometimes did I want a drink, it was this wretched skimmed milk, had all the cream taken off, from a big pan in the pantry.

I must have been only about nine years old when I was doing this kitchen work, because when the 1914–18 war broke out I was delighted when the troops came into the village and into that farm and that was in 1914. Well I was still only ten years old then and I worked as a kitchen boy till twelve and a half and the farmer came to the school one morning and said he wanted me to work regular every day, all day, could I leave school because his gardeners had gone to the war. And I left school and I went to work for him every day from six in the morning until half past five at night and then till five o'clock on Saturdays for five shillings a week, all those hours for five bob, and I was still doing the paper round every night, because when the war broke out there was a big camp at the bottom of the hill, hundreds of soldiers there and I had to take newspapers to this camp, and I sold many more papers, of course, and I got one and three a week then because I was selling so many papers, but I had to work about three hours for it, plus a black eye sometimes, the troops used to put us in boxing gloves to fight the band boys down there.

As kitchen boy and also when I worked there all day your duties always seemed to be to enter the house and pick up your master's shoes and clean them, or do some other indoor job so that they knew you were there you see. You see they wouldn't allow you to go to work at six in the morning and your job was a couple of miles away. It seemed that you had to enter the house for some reason or other. I had to enter the house and first job was to pump water from an old-fashioned pump. I did all the kitchen boy's duties, and then went in the garden you see and helped the gardener. And then each gardener, this was in 1914 and onwards, joined the Army and more and more I was responsible for the garden at an early age. And then the farmer used to take me with him in a pony and trap to open the gates and close the gates behind him.

After my kitchen duties I was on the farm with the men, driving the horses away with the waggon loads of corn, when the huge horses would take no notice of my tiny voice, my quiet voice. If I said, 'Whoa' they didn't know what I was talking about, I don't think they ever even heard me and they'd never 'whoa' or even go sometimes unless I whacked 'em with a stick. They'd been used to gruff shouts from the men, you see. I had to work very hard at that stage, thirteen and fourteen. I worked with four or five men, helping the men in the farmer's field pull down the traves they call them of corn when they'd been damp, wet and then help them stand up again. I was the only boy there at that time.

Almost one of my first jobs was rook scaring, in a big field on the way to Thorrington adjoining the railway. And of course you musn't leave your job between one and two to go home half a mile home to dinner because as soon as your back's turned the rooks are after what you're supposed to protect, the corn. So mother used to pack up sandwiches, the usual bread and jam sandwiches, and it was a terrible long day from half past six in the morning and on one occasion it was foggy, very foggy, and I was half afraid of being in the field, really I was. And the only thing that overcome my fear was men working on the railway. I could hear their picks and the shovels on the gravel underneath the metal you see. So I kept as near the railway as I could just to hear them and then I'd go and listen, go within about a hundred yards of the railway and listen to see they were still there and off I'd run back into the middle of the big field again, see the rooks weren't there. One day I thought it must be breakfast time. I seemed to be there a long time, so I ate my breakfast, probably wasn't about seven o'clock, and looked at me sandwiches, had a good mind to eat the lot but I had to keep them for my dinner. So off I went into the field again after listening for the men on the railway and presently I came back again and couldn't hear the men. So I thought well it must be dinner time. So I ate my dinner. And I went back into the field again. And after what seemed a couple of hours which wasn't perhaps only about half an hour, I went back to see if I could hear the men and I could hear them this time. So I thought to myself well I'll ask them the time, see if it just be getting knocking-off time which was round about five to half past you see, when it's getting dark. So an old man named Almond, big stout man, had a belt to keep his big belly up, so I asked him the time. I said, was it time to leave off yet. He said, 'What time do you leave off?' I said, 'Half past five.' 'Half past five!' He looked at his watch. He said, 'It's quarter to twelve in the morning.' It was terrible. And they hadn't had their dinner. They had their dinner at twelve.

The reason that I thought it was dinner time was I heard no movement. They were having a little break I suppose, you see, even five minutes. Just a break from the work, probably lunch perhaps at eleven o'clock. How I got through that day I don't know. And I told mother about it. By the time I got home at half past five, well it was nearly six time I got home. And I didn't half have a dinner that night! I was ravenous. The usual rabbits, baked rabbit, dumplings, swedes, like turnips and roast potatoes. But you see the railwaymen then left off at five. And I had to stay till nearly dark, till nearly six you see. So that hour after the men knocked off at five that was dreadful for me to be there, all alone in the middle of that big field with a thick fog. I should think I was thirteen then.

That was, as I said, one of my first jobs after leaving school. I used to get an old jacket and some straw and a stake and put it in the field hoping it would frighten them but it never did you know. Scarecrows they call them.

Another job I remember I had after then was in the early spring. An old man named Robinson was spreading manure out of the stockyard which was hard lumpy stuff, straw stamped down hard you see, and this old man had to spread it about. And I had to do what you call knock it, break it up into smaller pieces to spread evenly over an area. It was heaped up, the carts used to bring it, the manure in the fields and make a heap, about a barrow load in each heap about every ten or twelve yards, see. And it had to be spread about. And it was from six in the morning until six at night. Dreadful long day. And I wasn't big enough to wield a big fork and knock this stuff about at the age of thirteen and this old man used to just fling it about and leave me to do all the hardest work you see, so he used to go half a mile before, I couldn't keep up with him you see. Then the old master, old Barker was the man, brutal old man, he used to come along and swear at me awful for not keeping up with the man. Oh I had tears in my eyes many a time from that old man.

My mother and father were sympathetic but of course they couldn't do nothing about it. But I'd got a job and the money was useful, that was five shillings, five shillings a week that's all. And we thought it was wonderful being off at five o'clock on Saturdays. And the other days it was six till six, for five shillings a week. And the men were only getting twenty-five then, twenty-five shillings a week. When I was about fourteen or fifteen that old farmer sold the farm and the market gardener took the farm over. Mother told me to ask the foreman if he could give me a job, the new farmer, and I asked him, I was still the only boy on that farm, and he said, 'Yes, I think I'll see the boss. I think we can give you a job. How much do you want?' Well my mother said, 'Ask for eight shillings,' I'd been getting five you see. She thought I deserved a rise, I was getting older, and I asked for eight and I got it.

3

Annie Wilson

Annie Wilson was born in 1898 in Nottingham, the ninth child of
Enoch and Elizabeth Wilson.[1] Three children were born after her,
two of whom died in infancy, and as an older sister also died in
infancy only nine grew to maturity. There were seven girls and two
boys. Nottingham rents were high by national standards, in 1906
most families paid six shillings a week, and it was probably failure
to find this sum weekly that resulted in the family moving so often.
Annie remembered five homes in the first thirteen years of her life.

The family were not solely dependent on Mr Wilson's earnings.
This was fortunate as after the death of his father the family workshop, where he had earned a meagre living as a hand-frame knitter
was closed down by his mother and his efforts to go it alone at
home with a hired frame resulted in earnings of about ten shillings a
week. Mrs Wilson was the regular bread winner also working for
the hosiery trade at home; its labour force was traditionally
composed of women, and had been largely domestic until relatively
late in the nineteenth century. For, despite the early inventions of
power looms for the trade, fine work and intricate patterns
continued to be done by hand frames or by hand work in the home.
It was cheaper too for the manufacturers to use outworkers in a
trade subject to severe economic fluctuations.[2]

Despite his failure to provide adequately for his family, Mr
Wilson was head of the household and his wife took care to bolster
up his position even to the extent of giving him money to give to the
children as pocket money. Males and females were assigned
separate tasks and roles in the Nottingham home to a greater
degree than in some other areas and it was considered emasculat-
ing for a boy to wash up, hang washing on the line, etc. Mrs Wilson
therefore got very little help from her husband and did not seem to
expect it, expressing gratitude at his making the fire and bringing

her tea and seeing that he had more to eat than herself and the girls. Her life was truly one of unending toil; visits to relations, church, entertainments were too time-consuming or too expensive or both.

Annie's relationship with her parents was typical of many girls in large poor families in the Edwardian period. She had a great deal of domestic work, was expected to contribute to the family income at the earliest possible opportunity and received little affection or praise. Mrs Wilson's burden was particularly heavy because her family was so large, being twice the average size of families of women married in the 1870s.[3] This big family, however, was a source of great companionship, affection and help to Annie. With her sisters and brothers she enjoyed the amusements of town life, the street games, the odd behaviour of adults.

Two other features of Annie's childhood and youth are typical of her class: the strict Sabbatarianism and the surveillance of her sexual morals. In the Edwardian period middle and upper class parents began to allow their children a more cheerful Sunday than they had experienced, tennis and other games were played in many families and there was a relaxation of rules about what might be read. This was not normally the case in the respectable working class, where church and chapel activities still provided the only permitted activities apart from a sedate walk. Concern about the chastity of girls before marriage was prevalent in all classes though methods of enforcing it took different forms appropriate to the family's style of life. In the working class firm rules about what time girls should be in were laid down, and the Wilsons were no exception to this. These rulings usually governed boys too. Mrs Wilson's dislike of the cinema is another indicator of her concern over her daughter's sexual behaviour. Bodies such as the National Council of Public Morals deplored unsupervised groups of young people associating together in the dark of a cinema, and Annie was only able to go once.[4] The sharpest conflicts of all would often arise over the choice of a partner and timing of marriage. Mrs Wilson had been married at seventeen, already carrying her first child. It is not surprising that she looked with disfavour on Annie's friendship with a young man when she was seventeen. A little later when Annie wanted to get engaged she tried again to use her veto. This time Annie openly refused to obey her. She pleaded the unusual circumstances of war, as many young people did, to try to get free.

George and Annie married in 1917 during his leave and moved into two rooms at the Wilson house. A month later George lost an eye and was prematurely discharged from the army in 1922 with no pension and only a disability allowance. Four years' unemployment followed and after that a succession of casual jobs which he never managed to hold for very long: labouring, canvassing, window cleaning and finally nightwatchman's work. The couple had four children and Annie supported the family as best she could doing home work as her mother had, until her sister Grace found her a job as a lace mender on the machine next to hers. Annie kept on at this lace factory until she was sixty-three except for a period as a telephonist during the Second World War. She was the first woman on the switchboard at the Nottingham fire service and would have liked to continue with the work. She would also have liked more education, 'If I'd have had a chance to have gone to university I might not even have done anything, but I felt as if I wanted the change.' She died in the mid 1970s having been a widow for several years.

NOTES

1 Annie Wilson was interviewed by Jean Jacobs in 1971.
2 Sandra Taylor 'The Effect of Marriage on Job Possibilities for Women, and the Ideology of the Home: Nottingham 1890–1930', *Oral History*, vol. 5, no. 2, pp. 48–9. Raphael Samuel 'The Workshop of the World: Steam Power and Hand Technology in mid-Victorian Britain', *History Workshop Journal*, 3, p. 52.
3 E. A. Wrigley, *Population in History* (London, 1969), p. 197.
4 Paul Thompson, *The Edwardians* (London, 1975), p. 69.

It'd be number seven Union Terrace where I can remember most. The living room that was the kitchen and the scullery that had the sink in and the copper. You know, one that you used to light the coal underneath with. The kitchen was quite a big room but came under the garden at the front, I think that's why they called it a cellar. The coal place was in one half of it, where you stored the coal, and in the other there was stone slabs round to put your food. And then there was the front room on the first flight of stairs and the back bedroom went off together like that and there were two more bedrooms above there, quite big bedrooms. And then there was a big attic that went across the whole of the house.

The big room at the top they would have had for the shops. For the hand frames. I should think it was an abbreviation of workshop you see from what I could gather. But Dad always called it the shop. And when I've gone to take a message to me grandma's I can remember quite well going down Coltham Street and I used to look up at the houses and used to say, 'That's the living room – oh and all those windows all up at the top. . . .' And I asked me Dad once, 'What's all those?'

He said, 'Oh that's the shop love, where all the frames are.' And he once took us to Keyworth, there was a lot of these little villages. I believe some of it's still done. And Dad showed me. He says, 'They don't have to go up three flights to their shop.'

I've heard my eldest sister saying, from time to time, Mother was only seventeen when she got married, and Dad was eighteen. They lived near each other. Dad lived at the back of Batlock on Coltham Street, one of the streets that ran off here. In those days the hand frames were doing the hosiery, the power frames hadn't been invented in those days and in these little tiny back-to-back houses there were two bedrooms one above the other – then what they called the shop with windows all the way along. They're all pulled down now but there's quite a lot left out in the countryside, Keyworth and all around there where they did a lot of this work, and they used to hire the frames from I. & R. Morleys and several more hosiery places and all the boys would walk up – the father sort of was the foreman and he taught them all to do this, but it was shockingly paid. They made this hosiery by hand on these – it was a sort of knitting machine really, made ever such a funny noise and Grandad lived to be quite old but his other brothers struck against it. Grandad was a martinet, you know what I mean, and Dad was the only one who'd put up with it. So he used to say, 'You'll have to take over the shop when I go.' But unfortunately when he died Grandma said she'd had quite enough of the shop and she sent frames back so me Dad had nothing.

He mostly worked as a lad you see in his father's shop, from nine or ten, I believe I've heard him say, but I couldn't be sure of that exactly. But they never went to school. So as soon as they could use their hands they'd got to do running errands and this winding and anything they could do. And mother was telling me once that after they'd got married she felt Grandma wasn't quite fair to dad. She says, 'I should look round for some kind of a job and not be dependent on the old people.' And he did go for a while as a steel rod maker. He trained for a steel rod maker, somewhere on Ashforth Street, off Hartford Street. I remember that quite well. And he was there for quite a while. And then there was a slump in the trade as there often is, and Dad was one of the last to go and the one that would be most inexperienced so of course he went. He had to go. There was no more for him. And then he had a brother who'd gone to Yorkshire in a mine and he wrote and said, 'Well, I think you can get a job down here if you can come.' And we all scratched up the train fare for him to go. But he went down below but he was not well, so he wasn't long away. He came back again.

When Grandad died I could read and write and I'd gone to school so I should be approximately perhaps ten or twelve – more like twelve I think. Anyways we were talking it over and I said 'It was unkind of Gran to do that, wasn't it Dad? You haven't nothing have you?'

He said 'No.'

I said, 'Well, you used to take the work into I. & R. Morleys, for grandfather, should I draft you a letter out and you copy it and ask them?' ('Cause he couldn't write. That's when I began to teach him to write you see.)

So he said, 'Won't be any good.'

'Oh,' I said, 'Don't be downhearted, it may be.' I said, 'If they only gave you just one frame for yourself you'd be something.'

So he took a lot of persuading, he wasn't a man who could – you know, force himself.

So Mother says, 'Well, it's no harm in giving a try.'

I was thinking for Dad because he was so unhappy and we used to talk it over with me eldest sister, the one next to me, Grace. She used to say, 'Go on, I dare you to do it.'

I said, 'Well, I'm not going to do anything wrong, Grace, just ask this man if he could give Dad a frame just for himself.'

So she says, 'Does he know his name?'

I said, 'Yes, he does.' Can't remember it now but anyway – and I wrote this letter for him and I guided his hand to sign his name at the bottom. I said, 'Now you take it Dad, and don't give it to anybody' (this was the man who gave the work out sort of). And he came back and I was oh, you know, so excited.

'Well, what did they say to you?'

And mother says, 'You be quiet.'

I said, 'Well, I want to know.'

'He's going to give it his . . .' (he tried to think how to say it) I think it was 'careful consideration'. 'What does it mean?' he says. 'Cause he's had no education whatsoever, except these few hours at the Ragged School on a Sunday afternoon. So, of course, wasn't many days and this letter came and it was printed, and I taught him how to read print first. And it says 'Will you please call here and we will arrange a frame. Have you room at your home for it?' And all this. And it was fixed in no time. The front room was empty so we scrubbed it out. We worked so hard and we got it really nice. Bare boards with nothing on. And of course we were all fascinated when it came but we didn't like it when we heard the noise it made. It went sssssh. That was when he was running the thread along and then it was worked with his feet underneath to move the thing. It went pop-pop-pop-pop and we used to be playing around. They gave him so much yarn and they knew exactly what it would do and they perhaps would say 'You must make four vests out of this.' Or 'you must make two vests and two pairs' – those long pants men wore those days. Or even only one pair. And it all depended on the yarn they could give him, for the more he turned out he got a few shillings more, you see. Well, Dad hadn't been having the frame at home ever so long when he came home very disheartened. He said, 'They can't find me any more work.' It was such expensive stuff to do by hand. It was like hand knitting you see. I mean, now they'd got these things that went by steam and they could do hundreds of dozens. And they'd got this big factory on Newark Street, still there to-day, and they said that they'd have to fetch the machines back. They couldn't give him any more work. So I said, 'Well, did you not ask if they could find you a little job in the factory?' Because I knew how worried Mum'd be you see.

So he said 'Well, if it comes to that I could.' He said, 'Well, I've got to go on Friday to fetch what bit is due to me.'

I said, 'Don't go and ask for nothing other than you ask that man who let you have the machine, Dad.'

He came back beaming. I said, 'Well, what happened?'

He said, 'Yes.'

Oh, we had quite a jubilation. They said all they could find him was a sweeping up job at the factory. It was more money than he'd ever earned in his life. Hours were from six in the morning till six at night and it was thirty shillings a week. I thought he would never get over it. He's been getting about ten shillings on this for years.

Mother'd never been to school, she was like Dad. And I've heard her say that from a tiny little girl she started at chevening. Her mother taught her and she was only allowed to play for a little while in the evenings, she'd got to go back home. Her mother did it. Her sister did it before her. Well in those days round there if they didn't do lace work from the factories, the drawing and scalloping, they did chevening. Or hairnet spreading. But more women than men did because the men couldn't get the work. [Could you explain what chevening means?] Yes, well, you yourself I suppose have bought your husband's socks with embroidery on like that on here and up there on the point. Well you'd never dream it's all done by hand – but it is. And they can do it on the machine up to where the top is. I've put spots on by the hour by hand because they can't do them on the machines. But when mother was little and the ladies had beautiful little forget-me-nots, little sprays of lilies on the tops of stockings. Fine cashmere stockings, right up to the knee. About five or six rows.

Oh I was fascinated by them. Most of it was done in silk and you had to do five or six threads. It was so very fine. Thread it up and make it lay nice and flat. And they had middle women – well, they used to send them hampers full of it and then the people like mother have to go to her and pick up what she could. She'd spread it out amongst as many as she could, this lady. A dozen or two dozen, you see. And you'd got to get it done by a certain time. That died out too you see. They did it by machinery what they could. And what they couldn't do – they used to train little girls in the factories to do. They didn't want to send it out if they could possibly help it. Mind you I've done it. I've done a dozen men's socks with these on – two on each sock, that's twenty-four in a dozen, for one and six a dozen. Imagine. I was fascinated. I was always watching her. 'Let me look – let me see.'

Me eldest sister she says, 'You're not going to do it.' She says 'You're pale faced enough as it is, you want to run and play the same as the other children.'

I says, 'I should just love to do it' – because I used to think it was wonderful. I watched her. And in the evenings she'd get the hose on her hand and would keep it like that and she could go like this all the way, like lightning. And in the evenings we always used to say, 'We've got to be quiet, the lamp's coming out.' You see, if she was counting. You often had to count the stitches. And sometimes she'd sing to us. 'Course there was no television or anything like that.

And this lady, this dear old lady who used to give the work out, she came to Mother's with this parcel. She said, 'I want you to be sure to put a clean white apron on when you do these.'

So Mother said, 'I don't work anything if it's light without my clean white apron.' She'd got an apron for every job mother had, oh yes. And she said 'These are for Princess Mary, you know, the one that's going to be married.' And she had to put HRH – Her Royal Highness Princess Mary in cross stitching. And they were fine silk. When she showed her the pattern I said, 'Can I look Mum?'

'Oh,' she said 'you are nosey.' So when Mrs Hallam had gone she says, 'Well now you can look.' And it was cross stitching. Oh but you couldn't tell a hand had touched them when·she'd done them. And I really think she got a thrill out of it. Each stocking as she was doing it was rolled up in this white cloth so that there was nothing but just the part that she was doing. And she paid – forget how much she paid – I think double what was paid for an ordinary job. Oh, but no one would have thought it was worth the deed. We were all just as excited as she was. Keep your dirty fingers off – don't you dare touch them – if we went anywhere near it. Can't remember the date of that.

She had to work. She's told me she's sat up at night, all night long, doing. She never stopped working until she couldn't see. She was quite old. The out-of-work phases were when the younger family were coming along. I wasn't born then. Mother didn't like to talk about it very much – odd things she'd tell us. And he'd tell you little bits. I only knew that all her life she had this resentment against his mother because they took his livelihood away. That was the only thing. I believe I can remember her once saying, she could go without food herself but she couldn't see the children. I can't remember it happening but it did. And she did go to the Board of Guardians and they gave her a big loaf of bread. And that's all she ever had, 'cause as soon as she got some chevening again she could get us some food.

We felt cheated in some way or other. Well, particularly when you got the idea other children were having this and when you played together, why don't you have one? – when other girls and boys were going to have such and such a thing. It may be something trivial – and I used to see it at a theatre – I said to our Grace, 'She was ever so upset 'cause she couldn't give us these coppers.' I said 'Don't ask her any more.' We were all very loyal to her – we wouldn't give her away at all – but it hurt us. And once when I said 'Can't have anything, we're poor.'

'Don't say that word here.'

She'd got immense pride. And I don't know where she got her standards from. Certain things were right and certain things were wrong. There was no grey in between those I can assure you. But she was wonderful. How she brought that family up – I've said since – since I'm old enough to know – well I can't imagine how she ever did it. She told me once she had lived on cold water for three days so that she'd have just enough to keep the children going. And charity – once at the St Mary's Church there they had a food kitchen and the bishop told her, anybody whose father wasn't working take a basin and go down to the food kitchen and there'd be some food for you. Oh, I saw her hackles rise straight away. 'Cause Grace and I were to go together so as we shouldn't spill it. 'We've got a dinner for today, we'll manage'. She resented other people knowing. I got smacked once for crying – we hadn't had any dinner that particular day. I think it was towards the end of the week and she hadn't got her money. And she said, 'What are you crying for?'

I said, 'I'm ever so hungry. Could I just have a slice of bread?'

She said, 'You know there's no bread there till we can go and get some. You be patient.'

And I went into another child's house to play and they were sitting down to a gorgeous dinner. And of course we'd all been told what were good manners, you came out immediately they have a meal. And I got to the door and of course, only being a kid, I was sniffing and this lady, she was a Welsh lady, she was good, she said, 'What's the matter Annie?'

I said, 'I'm hungry.'

'Well, come along then,' she said 'There's plenty here, sit down.'

'Mother won't let me.'

And she went and told me mother.

'Oh you won't go in there again to play. You'll play in the yard.'

You see. I don't know where she got this immense pride from. She'd got a standard and she wasn't going to let anyone know that she fell below that standard. But it was only her own efforts. Dad didn't care.

She treated him like a lord. You know, the newspaper at night – if by any chance you picked it up. 'Put that down, your father's not seen it.' And he had all the best cuts, when there was a joint to cut: 'Your father'll cut that.' And he had the best of everything. I couldn't have done – I've said since I've been married, I should have said 'No, you don't have a blinking bit, you haven't done a thing towards it.' She never made him lose his manhood. She paid everything. She wouldn't be in debt. Debt was abhorrent to her. We used to think she was so harsh, always seeing other children's mothers giving them a penny – go and buy some sweets from the shop and that kind of thing. And we'd look but we daren't say anything, we mustn't say we never had one. Only a ha'penny from Dad on Saturday. And she must have given him that.

We were quite a contented family. We had very little, 'cause Father never earned any money really. However they lived I don't know. It was mother – we didn't go without food and she was a wonderful needlewoman. She could make any old thing look nice you know. Oh she was wonderful; I wished I could have done what she did but of course I wasn't clever enough. Where we lived first in this Silverwood Place we used to go to St Mary's church. They were very good to us there. And there was always jumble sales or something. And mother made a point of going, she'd got a knowing eye and she would look them over. They came from better class people. Well I could just give you an example. Being the littlest I never got a new dress. I had to have one turned up a bit from me sisters you see. And she saw a grey flannel dressing gown, a long one. It was in good condition. She washed it, cut it, unpicked it, turned it inside out and pressed it and she made me the most wonderful frock I ever had for Sunday. Well, that was the kind of woman she was. And down Hockley, it was still there then, the cheapest of the drapers shops were. She used to say, 'Only wish I'd got fourpence to spare.'

I said, 'What for?'

She said, 'You want some new vests.' You could get calico for two three a yard she called it.

I said, 'What does two three mean, Mum?'

'Just twopence three farthings a yard.'

And she'd cut the neck out and would crochet it. She taught me how to crochet too and would crochet round the neck and the armholes. And then when we wanted to be ever so fine – we were posh you know – we decided, our dresses, won't they look nice with some needlework. You could buy it from one of the shops, just about that width you know and sew it on by hand.

I never had a pair of new shoes. None of us did. I can always remember they used to take us round Sneinton market when you could barely walk and there was always a stall that sold second-hand ones, for a few coppers. Mother had to pay just what she could until we began to grow up and one or two of the elder ones went out to work. And there was a little shop when we lived on Union Road and I was sent with a message to her and she looked at me feet, this lady did. She says, 'They're poor shoes – they don't even fit you.' And of course I was so proud, you know.

I said, 'My mother bought them me.'

So she said, 'Who is your mother?' So I told her.

She said, 'Have you lived here long?'

I said, 'Oh quite a while now.'

She said, 'Ask Mummy to come and have a word with me will you?'

And I've never forgotten this. This has stuck in my mind. So mother went.

She said, 'What do you want to see me for?'

She says, 'You're crippling that child – and in somebody else's shoes if you don't mind me saying so.'

She says, 'We can't afford to buy them new ones. There's so many of them.'

So she said, 'Well, I'd like to make a bargain with you.' She says. 'If you pay me so much a week – and I won't be hard on you – I'll refit them all out.' And we all had new shoes. And just before mother died she paid the last money off that shoe bill.

Mother had to come to the school on one occasion. My shoes had worn out and I'd got me feet wet every time and she couldn't afford to have them repaired. They were beyond repair. They were only secondhand really when I had them. And me feet were very wet. And I saw the headmistress there. She was a very nice woman. I liked her. She says, 'Couldn't you change your shoes, child?' And before I could think I said, 'I haven't got any more.' So she didn't say any more to me but when I came home, 'Would you give this little note to your mother?'

I said, 'Yes, I will.'

And of course when I gave it to her she said, 'You'd better read it.' You see because she wasn't sure of herself. And it said was it possible to get that child another pair of shoes, she's going to get a very bad cold getting her feet wet like that. And mother started to cry and that upset me.

I said, 'I wish she'd never looked at me feet now.' I've managed before you see. I don't know whether she asked one of the other girls – my eldest sister was going to work – there was a sort of a market where they'd got secondhand goods. Next day I think they must have been and bought a pair. Wouldn't have cost very few coppers. At least they wouldn't let the feet get wet. So I said, 'Can I show them to the headmistress, she'll be pleased I haven't got these others on again?'

So mother said, 'Well it would be good manners to tell her that I say thank you. . . .'

As soon as you could do little jobs you'd each one got a job to do.

The big girls used to come home from work on a Friday and we had to blacklead the grate. There was a little old chimney fireplace with a steel fender. Oh and I loathed them. And if a spot of water dropped on it it rusted. It would take you hours to do this. But it had got to be just so. Red tiled floors that were scrubbed. They had to be scrubbed Saturday and Sunday. We had white tablecloths on but we'd never any polished top. We had to scrub the top. Everything had to be scrubbed. We used to have to scrub the stairs down, plain wood. They had to be white. We shared. If there was one got rather more than another, or if one got done first, and you sort of got a plan – you wanted to get done quick and go out, they'd say, 'Oh I'll help you to do that,' you see.

Mother did the washing. We wore lots of blouses in those days (needleworkers we used to call them) and underwear. And oh – the ironing! Hours and hours of it. If you wanted to go anywhere in particular and wanted to iron a blouse you'd got to do it yourself you see. And we always made the bed. Mother only made her own bed. But when we were cleaning our bedrooms we cleaned mother's in with it because – how could she! We didn't mind it. We didn't think we were hard done to. Imagine washing for ten in an old dolly tub. It was a dolly tub and a ponch and she'd count them. If you said, 'I'll dolly for you, Mum.' 'Yes, but just remember how many times I want it turning,' and you had got to remember. Old fashioned wringers. We used to fold them and turn the wheel. But I learned – in fact I enjoyed life. And she was a beautiful washer. I'm ashamed to say I'm nothing like her at washing. Did everything so thorough you know. And when I first got married she said, 'I'll teach you to wash properly my girl.'

She wouldn't let you touch the food. She cooked the dinner. She did cook a lovely midday dinner. We'd have broth you know, root vegetables and perhaps a bit of breast of mutton. Made a good one. Then she'd make us meat and potato pie. We loved those – and a rice pudding was delicious. She would make a lovely rice pudding or a Yorkshire pudding. But Yorkshire puddings were saved for Sundays. They were a treat you see. And sometimes she'd make us a steamed pudding with currants in you know or jam on. And we all loved the treacle ones. But she said it was too messy some days, and she wouldn't do it. We had to go to the butcher's and the greengrocer's and we got into the way of going and we didn't mind it, those that were at school, and she'd cook it and it was all ready when we got home from school and she'd stack everything up in the sink and then when we'd had our tea in the evening we'd all the washing up to do and that kind of thing. One'd wipe and one'd wash – we didn't make hard work of it. We were used to it. And then she had to rest. I never thought that she was ever so strong because she always told me, 'If I don't have that little rest in the afternoon I'm no good.' And my little mind couldn't take it. And yet she always seemed robust.

I only once in all me life known her to stay in bed. She used to look terrible sometimes but she wouldn't stay in bed. 'I'm a very strong woman. I shall get over it.' Of course I can't remember the babies being born because I should only be about three when the other three came along – the other elder girls were telling me – they were so annoyed about it. They said, 'It's not right, Father should have more consideration – dragging her down like that.' And what Father didn't do those girls had to do, and go to work and look after the other little ones. I can quite see their point. I couldn't at first but looking back on it I can see it. He always got up first, made the fire and took her a cup of tea. He used to think it was wonderful. But it wasn't really wonderful considering all she did. I tell you the only thing father ever mended was the clock.

The policeman was Harriet's husband's father. Everybody in the terrace called him Bobby Willis – because his name was Willis. A very big fat man. Well nobody was afraid of him – we all loved him I think as a matter of fact. He was more like an uncle to us. He was very kind to children. He loved children. He was very kind to me. I used to run errands for him sometimes you know. And I always remember once on a windowsill in the back yard in the summer – great meat dishes full of what looked like wizened up bone. I said, 'What are those, Mr Willis?' – nosey parker again!

He said, 'Don't you know?'

I said, 'No.'

'Well,' he says, 'They're walnuts.'

I said, 'Well what are you doing to them?'

'Well', he says, 'I'm going to pickle them.'

And I said, 'Well, why do you have to put them in the sun?'

'Well,' he said, 'I've got to soften those shells you see.'

I think I drove Mother mad, 'Could we have some pickled walnuts?'

This Bobby Willis's wife was an invalid. She had something

wrong with her legs and she used to lay on this sofa in the living room all day and he had two daughters but they weren't living at home. They were married. And he'd got great big sons and they used to do the washing and the cooking. My mother used to say she never saw anything like it. The eldest son was in the Grenadier Guards – oh he was a fine man. And when he came home on leave – that month's leave – he was singing at the top of his voice in the little scullery and doing the washing and pegging it out for his Dad. There was no disgrace in it. But that man did all that. And he did cook – most marvellous joints, thick joints, we'd never seen them. And he once said to me, 'Will you have your tea and let me give you a bit of bread and black pudding. And I did like black pudding but I'd never had it fried in the frying pan. I've never forgotten it. I said to mother, 'Why did he? – it was lovely, mother.'

She says, 'Well I've always eaten it cold.' But that's the kind of man he was. A wonderful man I thought. When you see my Dad sitting there and Mr Willis scrubbing the step or anything. And that was during his police duties, you see, being on shift he had more opportunity. He was the first man I ever saw or heard of doing anything. They used to sit back, wait for the meals to be done and then they were off out, out to the pub or the football match and so on. But they didn't think they were brought up to help in house.

She never went out. She would not leave us. I once asked her if she'd got a hat. So she said, 'Yes, of course I've got a hat.' I said, 'Oh but I've never seen you with it on.' So I says, 'Show it me will you?' And she'd got quite a nice hat. And she was telling me who bought it her – how many years – I said, 'Don't you never go out?' 'No,' she says, 'I don't – only for shopping.'

Well once this aunt came to live just round the corner from us. She'd sent me to this aunt with a message once and this aunt said, 'Tell your mother it's about time she came to see me.'

I said, 'Mother, auntie says she'd like to see you.'

'Oh,' she says, 'One day I'll go.' But I had to keep on about it you know. And then one day I said, 'Come on Mum – take me to see auntie.' And she did go. But once for all. I never went again with her. I went myself. I used to go there quite a lot. But I don't think she wanted anything else. 'Cause I said to her, 'It's a lonely life – what pleasure do you have?' And when the Hippodrome first started it used to be ninepence in the gods and we girls were getting a bit more money as we got a bit older and Grace said to me one Friday night – we'd drawn our wages and we felt like millionaires you know – she says, 'I wish we could take our Mum, I'm sure she'd love it.'

I says, 'She wouldn't come.'

She says, 'Well we haven't tried it proper yet. We've got to sort of see what we can do.' Well we went on and on and on. I says, 'I want to see you in that new hat.'

She says, 'It isn't new.'

I said, 'Never you mind. I'd like to see it.'

Well Grace says, 'Go on – she'd give you no peace you know.' 'Cause they called me the natterer. I was always on about something. Well we took her. In turns you know. Nothing very serious. She was laughing out loud in the wrong places. And Grace said, 'Mum wait till he's done before you start to laugh.'

Mother didn't believe in fancy names. You got one name. The eldest sister was Elizabeth. They were married – the first three before I can remember anything you see. Jemima the next one – there was approximately two, sometimes three years between them. Julia. Alice. And she had a girl – Harriet – that died. So the next one happened to be a boy and she called him Albert. Then the next one she had was a girl and she got Harriet because of the poor Harriet who had died. And somehow or other all we sisters we thought a special lot of Harriet. I don't know why. Mind she was a lovely girl. I used to think she was wonderful. You see she was so much older than I – about six years older. I was the one that was a little toddler. She wanted something 'Go on – you go.' But she was very kind to me when I was ill. She'd take me to bed and sing me to sleep and I've never forgotten it. And she would tag me about. And I said to her, 'Did you want to go by yourself, Harriet?'

'No,' she said, 'You're quiet so I don't mind.' I loved her because she never grumbled. I loved them all but that one I think in particular. Mother made her take me you see. She'd two babies after that and she couldn't put the babies on to Harriet as well. And then my brother John. And then I had another little sister Ruth. These two both died in infancy but I can remember them quite well. And then Arthur. He was the last one that I can remember but Mother's told me since – she used to often tell me bits – that she'd miscarried twins or something all along this line which made that she'd had actually thirteen children you see.

I remember the funerals of the last two babies. One was eighteen months – that was Ruth – she was next to John. And the other little one died when he was very small. But I was pleased about it because the lady next door gave me a piece of cake. I said to mother once – I was only very young myself – I said, 'Do you think we could have another funeral and the lady would give me some cake?' She was furious.

And if the three grown up girls were talking mother said, 'Little pigs has got big ears – go on – get out to play.' And I always knew she didn't want me to listen to what they were saying. But I wasn't interested. I was sorry for my elder brother. Because Mother and Dad and all the girls treated him as a girl. Used to make him wash up. He was terrified of Dad. He wasn't cruel to him, 'O but you get that dish cloth and you wipe up while the girls'll wash.' And he used to look like this. But he was very kind to me. He'd give me rides on his shoulders and in this Silverwood Place where we lived there were three distinct burial grounds – you won't know about the buries – and our yard came to the end of one. There was a brick wall and railings. And I'd say, 'Go on, Albert – just be my horse – just up and down.' He'd ride me on his shoulders and he'd let me hang onto the railings and look right over Nottingham. I thought he was wonderful.

And then once he got me up there and he says, 'Oh look,' he says, 'There's a fire.' He could see it over Cartergate way – quite a long way.

I said, 'Oh yes.'

He says, 'If you promise not to tell your Dad I'll take you.' It was evening time. And he did. He took me on his shoulders. He galloped along. He let me pretend to whip him and I thought he was wonderful. And it was Deacon Street factory on Congleton Road. It was absolutely gutted. And of course Albert was so interested in it all. He'd no idea of the time and of course I was too young to know. And I'll always remember Dad was a little man. I said, 'Albert how's it going on?' And Dad patted him on the shoulder. 'It's one o'clock in the morning – what do you mean,' he said 'by keeping the child out like this?' There was crowds of people there though. Of course Albert was one of the crowd. I've never forgotten that. 'I'll give you a whpping when I get you home my lad', he says, 'this poor child's falling asleep.'

'I'm not, Dad,' I said, 'I like to see it.'

'You be quiet.' Because we were the young ones, weren't supposed to be heard in that little crowd. And of course he was only like Dad. Dad liked to go and see a fire. But it was wonderful to me – the experience. I said, 'Never been up as late as that in my life, have I?'

He said, 'No dear, you haven't and you'll not be again,' he said to me.

We got on well, really, on the whole. But we did snag a lot to each other and we were very jealous of each other. You know, if we thought that mother or father was showing the slightest more interest in one than another we'd say, 'H'm' you know, and we'd be really huffy about it. But I don't think we were an antagonistic family. I played with Grace and John. Grace was two years older than I and John was two years younger. But anybody round about – we sort of played in groups. We had a big skipping rope. We stretched out across the big wide road we lived in and oh we loved that.

We played stick and goose. Have you heard of that before? Stick was just an ordinary stick and a goose was a goose. It was a little bit of wood and we used to have to get Dad or Albert to sharpen the ends and you laid it on the floor and the end stood up and you used to say, 'One, two, three' and hit one end. And it spun up into the air and they used to measure how far each of you could get it. The farther you got the goose – as we called it – you was winning the game. And we all stood in line and took it in turns to do this. And on Pancake Tuesday, as we called it, there used to be a little barber shop and he used to make us little wooden battledores and tiny little wooden shillycocks we called them. And whips and tops for the boys. She'd save a ha'penny at a time to give us. They were only about a penny each. Oh we loved them.

And we used to play marbles. If ever we could get any. But mother didn't hold with the girls getting on the floor. She said, 'You're dirtying your clothes up. You're not to do that.' But the boys did it more than we did. And we used to play tin lurky. This tin would be set up and we all gathered round it and one was on. Now he'd got to kick the tin as far as he could kick it and with his eyes shut and say, 'One, two, three – scatter!' And then we'd all got to hide. And bring the tin back you see. And the one who was left with the tin he was on, as you might say. He got the privilege of kicking the tin. Hoops were for people who'd got the money to buy them, we never had them. Unless somebody gave us an old one and we used to have huge fun with it. And running games and tick and all that kind of thing as we used to call it. You had to run like mad and tick your neighbour.

These buries that were near us there was plenty of open space. There's only gravestones in between. It was open and everybody went through it, you see – and we never touched the graves or anything. But we played on the grass. You'd have to watch yourself – see where you sat. Grace would be always looking after me in her little way. She'd say, 'You've dirtied that frock again – she'll be mad with you.' She was cross with us but not very harsh. And if there was any child that she disliked, 'I don't like you playing with those boys from down so and so', she'd say. And we just didn't have to do it. This one boy she caught him pulling my arm for something – well children do as they're a bit rough. And she said, 'Don't do that.' And this boy laughed at her. And that was the greatest insult. So when we got indoors again she said, 'You'll never play with that boy again. He's a most rude boy.' And I couldn't see because I'd pulled his arm first you see. And of course she hadn't seen that.

We used to have an old cat and he died and then for many years we didn't have anything. But when we were on holiday from school I was very fond of pets and I always was on at Mum and Dad to let me have one but they sort of said, no. But during this particular year's holiday somebody that Grace knew, who used to work with her, had a baby. And I was just baby daft. And when I'd done me errands for Mother I said, 'Do you think I might go and take Mrs What'sname's baby out?'

'Oh you and these babies,' she said.

'Well I would love to.'

'Well', she says, 'You must ask her and be very careful won't you.' She says, 'You won't tip it out.'

'Oh,' I said, 'No Mum. I'm careful.'

Well I took this lady's baby out. Not every day – when Mother could spare me. During the month off school. And she'd got a little Yorkshire terrier dog and it had just had puppies. Well I was fascinated. I'd never seen anything so tiny – lovely little puppies. And she offered me money but mother always trained us we weren't to take money. I'd offered to do it and I did it because I loved it. So when I was going to school on the following Monday, at the weekend I took the baby home and Tipsy the little doggy was playing with all the puppies and I said, 'Aren't they lovely?' She said, 'Do you like doggies?'

'Oh,' I said, 'Yes.'

So she said, 'I bet your mother wouldn't let you have one?'

So I said, 'Well I could ask. Are they a lot of money?' 'Cause first thing in your mind when you're like that 'Is it a lot of money?' and then it was put out of your mind completely if you think it is.

She says, 'No, but I was going to give you one because you've been such a good girl and helped me with the baby. You've taken him out while I've got on with me work.'

Well I was oh so full of joy. I run every bit of the way home. It wasn't far and Dad was up in the front room and there was only Mum in. I stood there and she says, 'What are you standing there for?'

I says, 'You know the lady I take the baby for – I've told you about the puppies haven't I?'

So she says, 'Yes, you have.'

I says, 'She's given me one – do say I can have it!'

'I've got enough to do with you lot' – straight away. And as we're saying this Father's coming down the stairs. And that silly thing me started to cry. He said, 'What are you shouting at her now for?' Because Mum just started raising her voice then.

So I says, 'I can have a little puppy as a present to me but Mum says, no.'

And she says, 'Is it only a little one?'

'Oh,' I says, 'His mother's only like that.' And it was a thoroughbred. So he looked at mother, he looked at me, 'Go on Liz,' he says, 'let her have it. She's been a good girl. She's not played much this holiday. She's had that baby out every day.' So Dad says, 'What does she want you to pay for it?' I said, 'No, she's giving it me as a present!' Oh dear – me feet never touched the ground. Mother found an old piece of shawl. 'Wrap it up carefully – it's only a baby.' I said was it old enough to be taken from its mother? But they knew it was. And we had him years. And do you know Mother and Dad loved that dog. He was no bigger than that, you know, that shaggy they brushed him religiously. He never went on the streets. We got a yard. There was one gate for two houses and we used to yell at the people next door, 'Don't leave that gate open' you see. And he knew every word that was said.

He had his own special little bit of an old cushion and if you went in with sweets in your pocket and you rustled the paper he never left you. And I believe my father loved him as much – more than anybody. When Dad sat down on the sofa he'd push his mat just to the side of him and presently Mick'd have his nose across Dad's knee. Yes, that was one of the joys of my childhood.

With Dad's ha'penny we were wealthy. Farthing everlasting strip – I don't know if you've ever heard of them. It was like caramel. In a long thin strip. It wouldn't be more than an inch wide but it was so long. Yes, it lasted and lasted and lasted. That's why we bought them really. And aniseed balls. I loved aniseed balls. I think we got about four for a farthing. So me ha'penny went a long way you see. And very, very rare we could afford a bit of chocolate. But if I'd got one or two pennies perhaps I'd been saving. And I did love chocolate.

We all had our weekend little chores to do. Nothing very much you know – 'cause many hands get rid of it quickly. And often at school they'd ask us to take boxes for the Lifeboatmen and Dr Barnardo's and all those kind of things and we were allowed to go for so many hours if mother could spare us, and she usually did, and I loved doing that. And we'd play about the streets and that. 'Cause there was no pictures till a long time after.

The first pictures that I ever saw – it was where the Scala is now. It was on Market Street, at the top there. And they used to charge tuppence for children on a Saturday afternoon for a couple of hours. And if I'd perhaps run an errand for some other old lady up these streets and then I got tuppence and the other girl that I used to run about with a lot, she'd got plenty of pocket money, she said, 'Come along, I'll take us.'

'No I must pay my ticket,' you see.

And Mother says, 'It's disgraceful. What do you want to go to pictures for?'

I said, 'Well I would like to see what they look like Mum.' They weren't talkies of course, they were silent. And this girl took me. And I never forgot it. But I never went again though. Until they opened a place on – what was that street where the fire station is? You'd think I'd remember that. And as we were coming out the lace market, this was when we were working, a man used to stand with a lot of what looked like raffle tickets. Give me a penny for the ticket and you can go to the pictures tonight. But these weren't talkies. These were silent. And we all used to crowd round and the poor man never had enough. But I've been there and I did enjoy it very much.

Mother and Dad never went to church. But they were quite sure it was right for us to go. We always had to go to Sunday school. Sometimes she made us go to church on Sunday morning if we'd been a bit unruly, and she wanted us from under her feet. One of the ladies – Sunday school teachers – she lived in the Park, and I think there were eight of us little girls in her class and she said, 'I'm going to ask your mother if you may come with me and I'm going to take you home for your tea.' I didn't even know there was a Park then but of course she took us. And in the evening – while we lived down there – there was a church mission on Neatherley Street – there was a church mission and we were all very fond of it. They used to have a church hall. The Captain and his lady made the services so that we enjoyed them. We had a flower service and we used to go and sing at a very poor part – they called it the Marsh. We'd go and recite to them or sing to them. They trained us to do this kind of thing. And we did love that. But we had to go. The only way you got out of it you'd got to be ill and she knew whether you were shamming or not. You couldn't get away with it.

Our vicar at St Mark's he was getting on and some of the boys were a bit unruly and he would not have us in the church. He said it distracted the other people. So the Captain said, 'Well I think I can manage them.' He was young – and you know we loved that man. He didn't sort of make us think we were being made to do these things. 'Now come on dear, shall we do so and so?' And you did try. We had flower services, we had concerts. Oh I loved that little mission.

If there was anything a bit better that you had that was your Sunday clothes and that was sacred and you could not put it on for anything else in the week. You had to keep it. It had to be taken off and brushed and put away and just put on on Sunday. We weren't allowed to play games on Sunday. We weren't allowed even to read books. Mother just let us look at these two religious books – I think it was *Home Companion* or *Family Circle* – something like *Woman* only not so big, not so flamboyant either. It was all in plain print. And she liked them and we had to ask if we may look at them. But when we was knitting crazy or anything like that and I once brought some knitting out and she said, 'Have you forgotten what day it is?'

And I said, 'No Mother, it's Sunday.' You see, I hadn't registered her so me mind was just concentrated on doing it. So she said, 'Well you'll put that away until then. What you don't get done in the week you won't do on Sunday.' We weren't allowed to do any housework. It was well done at the weekend and it had got to last. We just did the washing up.

You prayed only privately to yourself. Mother would always say, 'Good-night God bless you. But don't forget to say your prayers.' We sort of followed on after the older ones. We copied them all the time you see. And of course – the Captain – we went there for years. He used to say, 'Now even if you don't say them out loud you just kneel down and say them.' And we thought we was doing something clever because we were pleasing him.

We belonged to the Band of Hope and each little Band of Hope – all of them from Nottingham – went to the Circus Street Hall. Circus Street Hall it then was. And they would sing, for prizes you see, and recite and give readings and all that kind of thing. We really looked forward to it. It was a red-letter day and it was a great honour for the mission if you won anything. I once won first prize for recitation. I've forgotten the title but 'A schoolboy at school once more sedate than the rest, had once his integrity put to the test.' I can't follow it all but I know how it starts. And I always remember why they gave me the prize. I couldn't understand it. 'Cause I said it wasn't really interesting. I didn't want to have it but it was a set piece. And I had to do it. But the judges said it was the clearest – he meant I said it straightforwardly and he said you could follow every word. And they gave me the first prize. I had to stand up at the mission and they all clapped when we got back.

Every Goose Fair Father took us down Saturday afternoon. And Bostock and Wombwells they always had a big menagerie. You've seen the pictures of it. Well it was always drawn up there when the Old Exchange was there. There was a brass band on the front and there was either a couple of monkeys or a bear or something all chained up. Oh you used to stand fascinated. But it was wonderful. We thought we'd seen all there was. And the band and that. And then he'd take us to the stall. For very few coppers he bought us all one of those little sticks of brandy snaps. It was Grace, John and I. Harriet had gone to work so of course she didn't come. And then he bought a pound of russet apples. And he'd take you there and just bring you round the outskirts and take you back. Well we thought we were queens and everything else.

And I think it was King George V came to the throne – there was going to be a big celebration on the Forest. And I said, 'Wouldn't you like to come Dad – take us?'

'I don't want to go,' he said.

'Come on!' Grace and John and Dad – Mother wouldn't come. But he took us onto the Forest and we heard the bands playing and we were quite thrilled with it. We'd been from the school but that wasn't quite like going with your own people.

Mother took us twice with an auntie of mine to Wilford Roundhouse one summer. And it was me auntie who kidded Mother on. She said, 'Go on – take 'em out. They never get out with you.' Oh and it was wonderful. She put some tea in bottles and bread and butter packed up in sandwiches and we crossed. I'd never been across the toll bridge before. We walked along this lane after we'd crossed the bridge into a sort of a farmhouse yard. There was a long trestle table and the lady came round and asked us if we'd like hot water. If we'd got the tea with us. Oh it was lovely. It was out of doors. It was such an exception to anything we'd done before.

And once Mother said to Harriet, the next but one to me, 'Take them for a walk this morning, this Sunday morning – take them to see Uncle Sam and Aunt somebody.' I've forgotten the names now. And they lived in this little cottage in Jenner Street. That was Mother's brother. And then I went to see this other aunt who lived near us. Uncle Herbert, Dad's brother, used to come sometimes and I liked him. He was a man who talked to children and I used to tell me Dad I liked him. And me Dad didn't like it. And then one of his daughters came one day and said that her Dad was very poorly and he'd like to see Dad. So he looked round at Mother, he says, 'I'd better take her with me, hadn't I?' And I was thrilled because he took me.

When my sister Harriet started courting the boy next door, the policeman's son, he used to ask me to go errands for him. I think it was threepence he used to send to the Post Office Savings Bank. He said, 'Go and take me this threepence up to the Bank.' Right. Off I'd go. I treated him like a brother because he lived next door to us. And he was talking to me when I got back and gave him his book and that and he says, 'I'm going the seaside.'

I said, 'Are you?'

'Yes,' he said, 'Aren't you allowed to come?'

'Oh no,' I said, 'I can't come.'

'Why not?'

'Well I says, me Mum and Dad couldn't afford it, love.'

So he says, 'Oh well,' he says, 'we're only going to Skegness.' It was a half crown trip in the evening.

And of course he would come and he asked Mother – they only lived next door – and she was always very careful. She said, 'You'll take care of her won't you?'

And he said, 'Yes of course, Mother. I will.' Have you been to Skegness recently? Have you seen it at all? Well I might have been twelve or something like that, but the clock tower is the key point and he sat with my back up against this clock tower and the sea dabbled at my feet and I was terrified of it. I said, 'Oh look at it, Arthur. It doesn't stop!' I couldn't imagine where this water all went.

'Well,' he says, 'I bring you all this way to see the sea and you're frightened of it.' He said, 'Come on – paddle!'

'Oh no – I'll stop here.'

She didn't stick to any hard and fast rules about bed-time. But if the other ones were going to go out, then get these children to bed before you go sort of business. And we wouldn't think it was any hardship. We used to lay and talk to each other if we didn't go to sleep. Oh we never stayed up late, not ever so late. When we were old enough to go to work and go out for a little while you had to be in at ten on Saturdays without fail and nine on Sundays. And of course we had to just have whatever there was – a cup of cocoa or something and go straight to bed. The other children would put us to bed – or sometimes Dad did. When I was young Dad always carried me to bed and I loved that. No, not Mother. She never did. We all used to say the same thing, 'You don't kiss us good-night, Mother, do you? We always kiss you.'

So she says, 'But I think of you just the same.'

If there was anything you don't want her to tell the family you couldn't tell her because the first time you did anything that she didn't like out it would all come. And you did say, 'Oh Mum – you wouldn't tell them.' But I must tell you that funny little bit. I'd had bronchitis and I wanted to pass me test at the swimming at school. And she says, 'You're not going to go to those swimming baths.

Every time you go to the swimming baths you get cold.' Me teacher was saying, 'You've only got two more lessons for your test and you'll be all right.' Well I had to get that bathing costume. I didn't know what to do. And our Grace says to me, 'Put it underneath your clothes. She'll not know.' That was all. Well I passed the test and I was so bubbling in good spirits but of course I daren't tell her. And by the time I got home with a wet bathing costume and all me clothes, I was shaking from head to foot. 'You've got another cold coming on and that's after I warned you. Now my girl you'll go to bed.' And I said, 'Please Mother, don't come upstairs. Let me get up there.' I got away with it. She never knew. Because I got Grace to take me bathing costume and run round the street with it to dry. Oh we've laughed over this many a time.

She was always very friendly with the neighbours. But she wouldn't have one inside. She went out to the toilet and it was across the yard and if another lady was passing she'd speak through the entry sort of business but she made no special effort. When I got married she says, 'Don't make neighbours. Bane of your life. And you don't want to tell everybody your business.' She was very reserved. When I look back I wonder where she'd got it from. I can't think. There was one old lady. 'Mrs How's the nipper' we called her. She used to wear such a lovely black cape with all jet beads on it and I think she was an old chevenner. But I'm not quite sure about that. But occasionally she came to see Mother and she sent me to the door and she says, 'I'm Mrs Maltby. Is Liz in?' She'd call her Liz. And that would infuriate Mother in any case. Mother says, 'Tell her to come in then.' And she'd sit one side of the fire and she smoked a clay pipe the whole time she was there. And of course, my father never smoked or anything like that. Well they never had any money. And everything she started to say, 'Well – how's the nipper?' And my eye caught Gracie's and it went round to all – and in the end we were all laughing. And oh my mother was infuriated. When she'd gone she said, 'One of these days I'll give you all a thorough good hiding. Where's your manners? She may be an old lady but there's nothing wrong in that.'

This man used to come – Mr Thornelow, the President of the Trades Council. Dad used to speak a lot about this man. And I used to think, Oh Dad must think a lot about him. Dad used to go to this Trades Council periodically – he belonged to something belonging to his work. Mr Thornelow sort of used what Dad told him when he made his report. And sometimes this Mr Thornelow would come to our house and there'd be one or two of the men from the workshop when Dad was working for his father and they'd sit and discuss and say what they thought was right and what was wrong and so on. And I was all ears. It interested me – very much so. And of course, we was all threatened to keep quiet and not to speak when me father was speaking or any of these gentlemen. We were made to have good manners. We wouldn't be allowed to talk if your parents were speaking. You'd wait until you got a chance and there's nobody speaking. But I really did like it. 'Cause when we got into the last form at Huntingdon Street, we had debates. And I loved it. On all sorts of different things. And I didn't know much about politics but I used to read the *Post* and that kind of thing.

Father always used to say he was a Conservative but he never took any personal interest. He'd read the paper and talk about it as men do. But I never knew him take any personal interest. When he worked for his craft for his father there was a trades council, a very crude affair from what I could gather, and what I can remember the President of this trades council, Mr Thornelow, used to take Dad with him. He said, 'You can't write, Pop, but you can speak.' So he liked to take him for the workmen's point of view in this trades council and Dad looked forward very much to that. It only happened perhaps once in three months. But he took no personal interest in the affairs.

I was just about three when I first went to school. The church schools took you if you could speak plainly. I doubt whether I was three. I loved school though. And it didn't matter if there was other children in the house. I believe they thought it did help the mother, you see. And it was not far from where we were living at that time in Silverwood Place, we'd only got to cross the bay and I was at St Mary's school. I went at nine o'clock and came back at twelve o'clock. It must have been half past three when we came home in the afternoon. It really wasn't far but it would be for little legs 'cause our yard was a big one as we came down, then we'd got to cut across Bellargate, up this flight of steps into the bay and the school was the top of the bay you see. If she was a bit afraid of us crossing the road there when I was little, I can always remember her hurrying Grace, 'Go on – take this child across the road – see she's safe.' You see.

There were odd teachers that I didn't seem to get on with at all. We had one that was very sarcastic and I used to think when she sort of walked down the rows and looked I thought she was sneering at me – that's the idea I got – the woman may not have been. I couldn't bear that one. I never did any good for her. But with the others I was perfectly all right. But I was so dead keen to learn. Good manners were most important. And to be truthful in all things. And tidy in your person. And if ever you got a tear in your clothes she'd say, 'It's high time you learned to sew, you see.' They sort of instilled a personal pride in you. I would be talking to the other girl and not paying attention to the lesson. She'd tell me once then the next time she'd say, 'You'll have the cane.' She'd say, 'Come on – just on the hand.' It wasn't hard.

I must impress on you that we were all terrified of teachers you know. 'You wait till you get to school. The teacher'll soon straighten you out', if you'd been naughty at home you see. And you went to school in fear. But you see you were so tiny. You were sort of brought up with it and it didn't impress you as it would have later on. As a child they did take an interest. They did help you know. And they once asked us if we'd be willing to give up our playtime – they worked very hard with us. We used to sometimes do songs, learn songs and things and it took a long time. 'Cos we got quite a lot of Welsh people lived in Silverwood Place and people from all over. There were very few real Nottingham people. And it must have been very difficult for them.

I had to leave St Mary's because we moved house. Went from Silverwood Place to Gordon Road because Albert was getting a big boy and Mother said he must have at least an attic to himself. And John was growing up and she had to do this so we went to this house on Gordon Road. Well it was much too far for John and I to go right to St Mary's. But at the bottom of Gordon Road we only had to cut across the Victoria Park and Bath Street School was there and I was taken there. And I stayed until – I forget how old I was.

We had to take an examination to see if we were clever enough to go for a scholarship for Huntingdon Street school where they had to pay you see. It wasn't like the scholarships there are today. Huntingdon Street school had the boys and girls of better class people, business people mostly, and if they'd got one or two vacancies they'd let them in from the board schools. The fees weren't heavy fees. One or two of the girls used to tell me, 'My father pays so much a year for us.' You got in free you see because you'd been top of your class. I'd been in the top class at Bath Street so long they were getting tired of me. I shouldn't be quite ten when I went there. And I stayed there until I was thirteen and could leave.

Before I went to Huntingdon Street school I can remember our children in my class we were made to make a dress or whatever we got on last so very long, we weren't allowed to come to the table without a white pinafore on. And you had to wear one. And Mother wouldn't let me go to Huntingdon Street without a pinafore. And I can hear the gasp when I walked in with this. It was quite a nice pinafore. It was white. And the teacher said to me 'You could have hung your pinafore up in the cloakroom, Annie.'

I said, 'But Mother wouldn't let me – I'd soil my dress perhaps,' You see.

She said, 'Well it's the rules here we don't have you in here with a pinafore.' A lot of snobbishness there was. And so of course I was made to – in fact I rolled it up in a bundle and put it in me school-book bag when I got towards school so that I wouldn't have to be immolated again. But Mother was very cross about it. I told Grace and somehow or other it came out. She didn't mean it to do. So she says, 'You'd better not take them any more. If that's the regulations.' She said, 'I wonder what the dresses look like underneath.'

We all had our own pegs in the cloakroom. And I'd hung me hat up on this my own peg. And they were very long cloakrooms. And as I got to the bottom that hat hit me on the back – it had been thrown at me – my hat. And I heard this girl say, 'I'm not going to put mine with the dirty Bath Street lot' and you couldn't live it down. And the headmistress was a snob. I always remember her name, Mrs Thorn. And I heard her once say, some little thing we'd done – 'What would you expect from that place.' Quite a few of the girls who were fairly comfortable, had good positions and got lovely clothes and that kind of thing and – they'd sort of pull aside, they wouldn't pass you on the stairs if they could help it. And they used to look at us as if we were tramps in the street. And of course it used to get my back up a bit and I said to one girl, I said, 'Well, I shan't contaminate you and I'm not a tramp either.'

Father thought all book learning was piffle. But mother said, 'Well – they really can't learn too much.' But they didn't know that it'd be like it is today. You're lacking if you haven't had some

93

kind of training, aren't you? Well that never occurred, you see. When you left school at thirteen you got any job you could get because you was going to take five shillings home and it was gold to you. But you always got to be clean and tidy. At night before you went to bed your shoes – they'd got to be cleaned ready for school in the morning. They'd got a wonderful standard, you know, from that. And if you were trying to evade something and you didn't say quite what was true, Mother would say, 'It's no good – I know you're lying to me. That'll do. Now when you're prepared to tell the truth I'll listen.'

I read a lot of books on the sly I did – I will tell you that. I borrowed them from school. I remember one and I shall never forget it. It was all about a farm and this family. I can't remember the title. And I had to hide it because you see reading was a vice. You've got something better to do than put your nose in a book. That was the expression you see. But I did love it. And me sisters when they went to the musical comedy once at the theatre they bought the pictures in a big book. Oh I devoured them. They gave them to me. And they'd hum the tune and I knew the words from these books. Oh I did love it. We'd read in bed. We were allowed a candle. We'd no light upstairs. And she'd open the stair foot door periodically – 'That candle's been on a long while. Just put it out. It's time you were asleep,' sort of business.

The only books in the house was the Bible. Mother and Dad's Bible that I told you about. They were on the sideboard. And she paid for one paper – *Home Companion* or something – or *Sunday Circle*. I forget exactly. And they had the *Evening Post*. But there was no proper reading. You see at first they could not read. Grace and I between us we taught them both. 'Cause Mother couldn't sign the name Elizabeth Wilson. I said, 'Well you can put a cross, Mum.' But that wasn't right for her. I guided her hand for a long while – showing her how. She wanted to read. There was a story in this book. The *Sunday Companion* or something like that. And she said to me one day, 'I should love to read it.'

So I said, 'Well you can soon read it if you try hard.'

Our Grace said, 'I'll help you.' I'd perhaps start it off and Grace would take it over when she came in and by the end they could both read the bits in the big headlines in the *Post*. And they could read this story. And she lived for the day when that book came. I believe it was the highlight of her life. And she could sign her name. I taught her how to put Elizabeth Wilson. The one luxury was the *Post* of the evening and these two Sunday books.

Sometimes Mum and Dad would talk and sometimes they'd tell us bits about the old things when they were children. Especially if we'd been naughty. And Mother said, 'When I was such and such an age I was working and doing this and doing that.' And she must have been only about a child eight years old. And Father said, 'I can't remember when I didn't work.' And he didn't say it as if he'd got a grudge against it for it was just everybody else did the same. I used to say to her, 'The Captain says, "Do you want to come to the Bright Hour or something once a week, Mother?" He would like to meet you.' And he hadn't time to go and visit everybody. So she said, 'I've got no time – I've got my work to do.' You see, every spare minute she was at the chevenning because it was her livelihood.

When I left school I wasn't quite thirteen. Because I should have waited till the March when I was thirteen – but Dad had to go to the Education Offices to say that I was thirteen – he went a few days before – he didn't mean me to miss the chance for getting a job. And he got the wrong date. And I went and got this job. And they made me go back to school again for another week because I'd gone a few days before. The schools didn't have everybody leaving at a certain time. You left when you was thirteen. I believe we went down on the Friday afternoon, the girl next door and I, and we both got these jobs – we was to start on the Monday.

There was always a label out 'Errand girl wanted' or something like that. Or someone would tell you. And I did anything the machinists asked me to do and all sorts of errands within the factory. They used a little sort of hand thing to wind cord and stuff that they put on the lace for edgings and you'd keep all the bobbins with the numbers tidy in boxes so that when the machinist came out and over to the box – they called it pearl – it was like the edge of the lace you see. And they'd come and ask me for a certain number and I'd know just where to give it 'em. Or I would wind them some more off the card – but couldn't put the cards on the machines – had to be wound on bobbins.

I worked mostly from half past eight until half past five. Always Saturdays. Always till twelve noon. Five shillings pay – it was the standard rate for an errand girl. We thought we were rich. Five shillings was an enormous amount of money. We gave it to Mother and she always gave us threepence to start off – that was our pocket money. She couldn't have managed otherwise you see, with all the other girls, they paid their board. That meant just for their food and that but they bought all their own clothing, but until I could earn enough to pay me clothing – and the others – Mother had to find our clothes, but we always tipped up – gave her our packet just as we got it.

When I was an errand girl, there was just odd ones that were a bit erratic. One or two you know. Well I was a child you know and every little thing, 'Blame it onto her.' So everything went wrong that they could get a go at me they did. But I didn't let them bully me because I liked the other girls and they liked me. Just an odd one or two. I liked the indoor part but I loathed taking this cat out. It was the overlooker's pet. She bought it herself as a little one – but they were very pleased she did because you'd go some days and on the benches where lace had been left when the machinist got up – it's been all dirt from mice – and rats too. On the lace. And they had to sort of try to scrub it clean. And it smelt. 'Oh open the door!' sometimes. You could smell it.

Oh and they were so huge these long rooms. They went right across the top of the factory. It was five floors up. I think it's pulled right down now if I remember rightly. And there was the machines all in this room. The far room the clippers and scallopers used to sit in little groups and work in there and there was no machinery in there so that you could shout your head off in that room and nobody would hear you in this room. And I had to put big sheets of brown paper down near the hoist – one of those hand hoist things that you pull up – for the cat to use as a lavatory. And I had to fill it with sawdust and take it up each day and carry it down all these flights of stairs. There was no lift or anything – to the dustbin so it wouldn't smell or anything. That was the part I didn't like.

The overlooker – she used to make me take this cat for walks. And I did resent it 'cos all the lads round about going for the errands, 'There's the cat girl coming!' you know. And as I passed this Redgates – it was just at the top of Heathcote Street leading on to – is it Hockley I think – yes, it would be Hockley. And I saw this notice outside. It said, 'Smart Girl wanted.' So I thought, 'Oh the overlooker at Hamburgers likes me cards that I write out for the dinners – I don't know about the reckoning.' But then I didn't get any mess-ups with the money. I thought, 'Perhaps I will.'

And we didn't have to be at Hamburgers till nearly nine o'clock because the errand girls couldn't go before the main staff were in. And if they were on short time we were on short time. So I called at the Redgate and I saw the manager and I told him. I said, 'I've come in answer to your advert for a girl.' He looked at me. I was very small.

So he says, 'What can you do? What have you been doing?'

I said, 'An errand girl.'

He said, 'Hm that won't make me think any the better of you. Anyway,' he says (he brought a piece of paper) 'Write your name and address on here.' He says, 'Do that and I'll pass this on to Mr Redgate when he comes.' He was the boss. He said, 'And what wages are you getting?'

I said, 'Well you know what errand girls get – five shillings.'

'Oh well,' he says, 'That won't do for a clerk, we shall have to have you as a clerk I think.' Oh I couldn't believe this was true. And he said, 'Call in again.'

I don't think I went the next day. I think it was the day after. 'Can you come at the same time and I'll have a talk with Mr Redgate about you and we'll see if he thinks you'll do.'

'Course when I went and they took me into Mr Redgate's private office then he says, 'You look a bright girl.'

I said, 'I try to be, Sir.'

So he said, 'Very well then,' he said, 'how would you like to be an order room clerk?'

I said, 'No errands?'

He said, 'No – it would be a waste of time you doing errands!' And I loved it from the beginning. I was not quite fifteen when I went to Redgate's. And I was there for over seven years.

I'd got one girl at work – if Grace didn't want to go out – perhaps Grace had other interests you see and she said, 'I'm not going out now.' I'd say, 'Oh well I'll go and fetch Florrie Smith then and go with her.' And I didn't have a lot of friends. But we went out. And the embankment was our second home. And I used to walk often from there to Radcliffe-on-Trent and walk back again. We loved it all. Sometimes she'd come to tea on a Sunday and I used to go to her house on a Sunday. And we'd go for walks sometimes on a Sunday. I'd say, 'Could I bring Florrie, Mum?' And she'd say, 'Oh my goodness that's another.' But she didn't say it nastily. And I would say again, 'Well can I?'

She'd say, 'Yes, all right then.' Mind you we had nothing any different, bread and butter and Hartley's blackcurrant jam. But she was such a nice girl. They were just a working family like we were – and she'd got a lot of brothers and sisters.

After work I was very much interested in playing round. Used to play round a lamp – we got an old bat and we used to go up there and play – about four or five of us. We started to learn dancing and one night a week we went dancing. And if there was something on at either the Hippodrome or the Empire it was only ninepence in the gods and we'd save up 'til we'd got this ninepence to go. 'Cause we liked it. And then in the weekday if you went to the pictures or the Hippodrome or anywhere like that as a special occasion, we couldn't get in the first house because we'd be washing up, so it was later. You was allowed till ten. And we had to run all the way down Union Road. But were we to be a little later – 'Where have you been to this time of night?' 'We've been walking – we've been talking.' Oh I've seen her look at me Dad as much as to say, 'You'll not get anything out of them – they won't say.'

Dad was – how can I say – jolly. Either he was morose and wouldn't speak at all to you and you had to sort of look to see what his face looked like. But sometimes he'd be very funny, 'specially when he talked about these funny old men he worked with. And he made us die with laughing. I was scared of him in a way. And I think we all were because he didn't never hit us or he did me but not the others – but he shouted at us. And it was his voice that did it. We had to be good and obedient – do as you're told. And that kind of thing. I once grumbled about washing pots up. I was only about thirteen. I wanted to go out when I'd been to school and I said, 'Always got the damned pots to wash up.' Me father says, 'You should be very grateful to be able to do it for your mother.'

I said, 'Well it's not right.' I wanted to go somewhere, you see. And I said, 'Well if you don't let me I shall leave home.'

And what really threw the spanner in the works and made me decide I was going to leave home was that I went to this place at Redgate and I was an ordering clerk there and the boss said to me, 'You know you could improve yourself, Anne,' he said, 'why don't you go to night school?'

I said, 'I would love to.' And so I went to Huntingdon Street night school. I looked in the paper and it said you'd to go and sort of register. And they said the fee would be half a crown. And I had got some money so I paid it and of course they gave me this receipt. I never even thought – I was so pleased to tell them – I thought they'd be pleased. And I said, 'Look Mum, I'm going to go two nights a week to Huntingdon Street night school. I'm going to take English and shorthand and typing.' I see Father looking thunderclouds at me, so I said, 'What's the matter with that?' He said, 'And what did that cost you?'

'Oh,' I said, 'We had to pay half a crown entrance fee.'

He said, 'Yes, and your mother could well have done with that for some dinner.' Oh I never felt so guilty in my life. I ought to have given it to her, he said.

And of course I was very incensed. I said, 'Well I do try to – I want to do something better in the world, Dad. I want to get a good job with some money attached to it.' He said, 'You always did.' He said, 'You're all right as you are. You're getting good money now and you've got a good boss.'

I said, 'Yes I know I have but,' I said, 'I want to get on.'

He said, 'You stop where you are my girl, you're better there.'

But you see – I'd had a bad example set me. Four of me sisters had left home because Mother was going to have another baby and they'd had too much, I could quite see their point of view. They said, 'It's nothing but babies and kiddies and you're expected to do this and you're expected to do the other,' and they were quite young and they wanted to get on and get jobs and all the money had to be tipped up and so on till they got so fed up. When I knew the true facts of it I realized why. And yet I thought it was awful hard on Mother, you see. And I wanted to – I tried when I was just turned fifteen. Me boss gave me a raise and I thought, 'Well I think I could manage on this.' And I went to one of me sisters and she said, 'You mother won't like it but,' she said, 'if you're really keen on coming', she says, 'I'll have you.'

Well I'd only got a little cardboard box affair – stuffed in what few bits of things I'd got – very little. And I had to pack it in the morning so that when I went home at night I could pick it up and shift out as I thought. Of course, when I went upstairs me box wasn't there. And when I came down Dad gave me such a – 'It's no good looking for it – you're not going.' I said, 'But Dad,' I said, 'I'm not happy,' I said, 'You get on to me – I can't do any more than I do do.' I said, 'I want to leave home.'

'You're not going!' And I broke my heart about it. Because I thought – well I could have been better, you see – because you always felt you'd got so much of the responsibility.

My elder brother Albert ran away into the Army. I knew he'd gone, he told me he should. He'd had just sufficient he said. He wasn't treated like a man. And he was turned eighteen. And then one day when we got home from school Mother was crying and Albert was coming home at five for his tea. I said, 'Where's Albert, he's late?' She says, 'He's not coming home, he's run away!' Oh I thought that was the biggest tragedy I'd ever met. And it was quite a long while before we found out he'd joined the Army and he was in Ireland. And he wrote to one of me older sisters. And Mother was furious because he wrote to her – 'Why couldn't he write to me?' She couldn't have read the letter if he'd have written it to her, you see. But it was taking Mother's place. But anyway they smoothed things over. And then he used to write letters to Mother. And then he asked could he bring this orphan boy home. They had a month's furlough every so often.

Me Dad says, 'Well it'll be a pal for Albert to go with.' He remembered Albert was one of all those girls see, 'cause John was too tiny to count. And of course George came with him. He was a Londoner. I was fascinated by his London speech. We all tried to do it. 'Have you come all the way from London. George.' Oh he was furious!

'Yes,' he said, 'I speak just as well as you.'

I said, 'You don't – you can't say salt.'

He said, 'I can – salt.'

I said, 'That's not it.'

Well of course he stayed in our house for a month. And then he did say once when we were all sitting talking you know, he says, 'I never had a letter.' Mind you he was telling us a lie. We didn't realize till afterwards, till we found out.

I said, 'Never had a letter?'

He said, 'No.'

'Well if it comes to that I don't think I have,' I said, 'but you'll have – I'll send you one every day when you get back.' 'Course we was only doing it for fun but he believed me. I said, 'No not every day, George, can't have that.' But I did write to him. Well of course when the letter came home it was delivered while I was at work and I'd never seen his handwriting. I said, 'Who's the letter for?'

Mum says, 'It's yours.' And when I opened it, of course I'm too impulsive, I couldn't keep it in me own mind. I said, 'Oh it's from George!'

'That's going to stop.'

I should only be not much more than sixteen. And she wrote to me brother – she got one of me sisters to write to me brother and tell him. I was only a kid and she wasn't going to have no nonsense – he wasn't to write to me again. But anyway he did write to me. And I'd taken him once to a girlfriend who I worked with and she says, 'I'll take your letters for you.' And this was the first big thing I did wrong, you see. George used to write to this girl under cover for me. And that's how we kept it up. They didn't know for ages and ages 'cause I never told them, you see. But I was very, very fond of him, I was. But after a while I told her once, 'George wants to get engaged to me.'

She says, 'You're only a child.' Oh I shouldn't be eighteen I don't think – no.

So she says, 'Plenty of time enough.'

I said, 'No, the war's on.' And he was always saying he wanted a home. He'd never been in a house like ours with all our family and he'd enjoyed it – we did have lots of fun. We did, strange as it may seem, but we did.

4

Florence Atherton

Florence Atherton was born in Queen Street, Farnworth in Lancashire in 1898.[1] Her parents who were born about 1860 had ten children but lost four of these in childhood. Two boys and four girls grew up, but one boy was killed in the First World War and a girl died at the age of nineteen. Florence's parents were both Farnworth people and lived all their lives in Farnworth, except for a brief period when they moved to Bolton to be nearer Mr Atherton's work. Mrs Atherton was unable to settle in Bolton and the family returned to Farnworth, where there were homes in King Street and Church Street before they moved to Preston Street, where they lived for many years in a four roomed house. The dining room was used as the living room, Mrs Atherton's dress-making work occupied the front room, one bedroom was used by the girls and the other by the parents and boys, a screen separating the beds.

In Florence's childhood her parents seem almost to have exchanged the roles of mother and father. Mr Atherton is remembered as motherly and demonstrative, with more time for children than his wife who was preoccupied with work. His work as an insurance agent who sold pictures as a side-line, freed him from long hours of work outside the home during the children's waking hours and enabled him to spend time on household tasks. He visited the children's school to enquire about their progress, put them to bed, took them out, made breakfast, served dinner, did the washing up and most of the housework, kneaded bread, repaired shoes and helped his wife with the washing. Many Edwardian fathers took an interest in family life and gave their wives a helping hand, but an involvement to this degree is extremely rare. Why was Mr Atherton thus? Let us look at four of the factors which would account for his attitude to his home and family: his personality, the family's social class and the class from which he and his wife respectively originated, the region of Britain he lived in and his relationship with his kin. These are of course not discrete factors but will interact and affect each other.

Mr Atherton's personality lacked those qualities popularly regarded as masculine. There was nothing of 'the guv'nor' or Mr Barrett about him. He was gentle and kind rather than forceful or dominating. Possibly his being an only child may have freed him from the need to fight for a position in the family or to keep younger siblings in order. An only child may also experience less pressure to conform to a stereotyped gender role, as he or she must fulfil the parents' needs for both sons and daughters.

The class position of the family is complex. Florence described herself as respectable working class but said that her father was middle class and that this 'showed in the way he cared for us'. Mr Atherton's family, who disinherited him when he married a Catholic girl, do seem to have been middle class. They were Tory, Church of England, property owners, probably in business; they were likely to have kept at least one servant and Mr Atherton's father almost certainly did no domestic work. His mother too probably did very little and with an only child would not have been very hard-worked, even if she had cared for her child herself. A man differently constituted might have modelled himself on his father and turned his wife into a servant, but Mr Atherton may have felt guilt and regret at his wife's burden of dressmaking and childbearing, and therefore tried to lighten it as much as he could.

Mrs Atherton may well have worked in a textile mill before she had children, for Farnworth was a cotton town. While husbands were expected to go out and earn the money and wives to stay home and manage it, marriage was seen very much as a partnership in the Lancashire cotton towns and when married women went out to work their menfolk were expected to help with the chores. Boys and girls were therefore brought up to do housework and there was a less marked division than there was in areas where there were few opportunities for factory work for women. In some areas of heavy industry where there were fewer jobs for women, less than half of the female population were employed according to the 1901 census, and less than one in ten of these women were married or widowed. In the cotton towns however, Burnley, Preston, Blackburn, Oldham, Bury and Bolton between 70 per cent and 77 per cent of women were employed and a much higher proportion of these were married or widowed women. In Burnley, Preston and Blackburn for example one in three women workers was married or widowed, in Oldham and Bury one in four and in Bolton three out of twenty.[2]

Although Florence considered herself working class, the family's life style and values were essentially lower middle class. In the Edwardian period this was a life style that had much in common with the skilled, respectable working class but there was one marked difference. The lower middle class kept aloof from neighbours and brought up their children to do the same. Florence remembered that her parents did not 'neighbour' and she did not play in the street with neighbours' children, but on some ground at the back with her brothers and sisters. 'An essential principle of the working-class "neighbourhood" was that status and recognition were accorded to all those who accepted the local mores and did not make themselves conspicuously unpleasant to those around them. White collar respectability required that they be fussier. Neighbours posed a double threat: on the one hand, they might infect the household with inferior standards in cleanliness, language and so on; on the other hand they might come to spy on the often rather pinched reality behind the more prosperous facade.' Respectability was not only a cause of pride; it was the basis of the white collar worker's livelihood. An insurance firm would expect an employee to have a dress and manner that would inspire confidence in clients.[3] It was usually easier to achieve this in poor circumstances if the privacy of the home was maintained. Mrs Atherton for example dressed her children well and 'no one knew we were poor'. Had they gone into the home however, they would have seen her unpicking an old coat in order to make a new one because 'one year we were so poor'.

Let us now consider the fourth factor, Mr Atherton's relationship with his kin. The schism with his family would have intensified Mr Atherton's social isolation, the companionship of neighbourhood and pub would not have attracted a man of his background and status, nor was he able to enjoy the society and affection of his relations. With no money or taste for other pursuits, the care of his children and the companionship and support of his wife were his only remaining sources of self-expression.[4]

Mr Atherton was fifty-four when he died and his widow lived

until the age of eighty, nursed at home during the last fourteen years of her life by Florence and her sister. She used to say, 'Don't think I don't know the sacrifice you have made for me. God will reward you.' Florence did not marry; she took up hand sewing after the Second World War, following her mother in the trade her mother had hoped she would avoid. In 1957, following a kidney operation she retired and now lives in an Abbeyfield Home in Farnworth. She is unfortunately in very poor health but, like her mother, uncomplaining and grateful for the help of her nieces and nephews who visit her often.

NOTES

1 Florence Atherton was interviewed by Anne Burke in 1971.
2 Elizabeth Roberts, 'Working class Women in the North West', *Oral History*, vol. 5, no. 2, pp. 12, 18, 29. Robert Roberts, *The Classic Slum* (London, 1971), p. 200.
3 Hugh McLeod, 'White Collar Values and the Role of Religion' in *The Lower Middle Class in Britain*, ed. Geoffrey Crossick (London, 1977), p. 70.
4 'There are sociological questions about how and why working-class men and women adopted such segregated conjugal roles. Elizabeth Bott in *Family and Social Network* (1971) while describing an investigation into families in the 1950s, postulates a theory which has a wider application. She argues that the degree of segregation of conjugal roles is related to the degree of connectedness in the total network of the family; those families which had a high degree of segregation in the role-relationship of husband and wife also having a close-knit network, many of their friends, neighbours and relatives knowing one another. Certainly the great majority of families in the sample in Barrow and Lancaster had these close-knit networks, and this is possibly one reason for the clearly segregated roles of working class husbands and wives in both towns.' Elizabeth Roberts, op. cit., p. 21.

My mother was a dressmaker and she always kept us nicely dressed and no one knew we were poor. And we were very poor. On the machine all the time, soon as one baby was born she's back on the machine again. She made a lovely wedding dress for five shillings. Mind you, that was a long time ago. Five shillings – those were dresses those days, you know, long trains too. She had a model. My father had a brass plate on the door for his insurance and mother had a brass plate underneath for her dressmaking. Dad helped a lot. I had one of the kindest fathers you could wish to have. Mother was always busy on the machine, but my father used to take a big interest in us. He was beautiful, kindness itself, and he always had one of us on his knee. Yes, it's a lovely memory and I was only fifteen when he died but I've never forgotten him.

My father put us to bed, always in bed nine o'clock. We had a large tin bath and we used to have it in the kitchen, in front of the kitchen fire. As one was bathed she went upstairs to bed and another went in. It was every week but we had to wash our hands and face every night before we went to bed, we hadn't to go to bed with dirty face or hands. We didn't have one special change of clothes. I don't think we had a right lot to change you know. We never could have them you know, not a lot of clothes. We got dirty, we changed, but my father used to see to that. Never sent us to school untidy or anything.

I know one year we were so poor. She's got an old coat given to her, someone that's going to have a new coat made. She's unpicked that coat and made us a new coat, turned it, washed it and made a new coat out of it. I don't think I had a new coat till I started work at fourteen. I was always dressed right through making things do. She made us lovely white dresses to walk in. We always dressed nice then and on Sundays we had all our best clothes put on and put them away, special clothes for Sunday, special shoes for Sunday. I'll tell you what Mother used to do, she had a friend that kept a shoe shop, and instead of Mother paying the money for our shoes, she used to do all the sewing. So we got our shoes that way. So she earned them before we wore them. Dad repaired them, he used to repair all our shoes, clean them all, clean all our shoes. And we had a long dresser with a white top on, Mother used to cut all the food on it and on Sunday morning all the shoes used to be ready for us to change to put on to go to Mass. And then Mother and Father used to go to the last Mass. My father was more like a mother beside Mother. He was a good father as gentle as a lamb.

Mother and Father between them did the washing. Though we weren't well-to-do we always had a nice clean home and always dressed nice. Our mother would even make clothes for other women's children so they'd have something to walk in the Whit Walk with. My mother's made the poor children sets of frocks and knickers to walk in so they wouldn't feel out of it. She used to buy her materials at Rossers, in a shop called Rossers in Market Street and she used to pay for all of the children, they knew her quite well because she used to sew for them. She used to make shirts for them to sell in the shop, and another place called Walworth's in Bradford Street. And she used to get all her materials from there. Mother used to get them cheap sometimes. Now she saw a little child there very poor and no clothes and she'd say, 'She can't walk, Mother, she's no dress.' And we'd say, 'Oh, she'll walk.' And Mother sent for them and made them little white dresses. I've been told by a friend of the woman that lives round here and she knew me, 'I'll always remember your mother's kindness to us. We've walked with the Whit Walk when we couldn't have walked at all, through your mother.' That were the type of mother I had.

I belong to the working class but the respectable working class that have been brought up with a good mother and father, and taught how to behave ourselves. My father wasn't a rough man. He was very particular who we played with. We weren't allowed to be bothered with anyone that was rough and we weren't allowed to bother with anyone that had a fight or anything and we weren't allowed to go down certain streets. Kent Street, where mostly Irish people lived, they were always fighting at weekends. Well we weren't allowed to go down that street. Even though we were working class we were what you call a sheltered working class. We didn't know any of the wrong that those rough ones knew and we never heard of immorality. We weren't allowed to hear it. That is to say we're sheltered and I think it's a big shock to you when you get to know all these things later on in life.

We never came in contact with a policeman. Used to see them in Market Street when we passed the police station going to school but they never came hear the house. They had no need really. Oh we never came in contact with a policeman, we very seldom saw them coming down the street. Fights were in the streets further on, Kent Street. Oh that was a terrible street. The policemen always seemed to be passing their time on there, therefore we had to keep away. Always on there, yes. Because you see they were mostly Irish immigrants and they all liked beer. They all went out and they'd come back and their children would be half dressed and the wives would have no money to buy food but still their husbands go out drinking and then street fighting. Then the policeman had to go there. You see we got none of that. The policeman would start with his baton then. I've heard about it 'cause the girls have told us at school. Now that's why I'm telling you my father protected us. We were sheltered from all that, never would let us come in contact with it and we used to feel delighted if we could away in to watch it. If I could just sneak away to watch it and I used to run home.

I can't tell you much about the real poverty 'cause I didn't deal with a lot of the real poverty, but I've seen the girls in school and I've seen some of the boys who've come with one shoe and one clog on. And they've had their trousers torn. Well I noticed that. Now we were kept apart from them. The working class had different kinds of homes, some were rough, some were nice, some were poor, some didn't care tuppence what became of the children. You can go in different houses and see difference in people's ways, in life. I remember going in one house after school and they were called Kellen. They lived a street further up. They were very poor and they were some of the children that Mother made dresses for and I remember the tea was ready and they had a big pan on the fender, potatoes in their jackets. And they had a white scrubbed table, no cloth on. And the children went and got a potato and sit at the table with no cloth on. Now I came home and said to my mother, 'Ooh Kellens have no cloth on the table and they're eating potatoes out of a pan.' I said, 'Can we do that?'

Father said, 'No you can't.' But I used to slip out many a time. I used to go to Kellens. I used to run out and go and knock on the door, 'Can I have a potato please out of the pan?' All that you know I remember, all that.

I didn't do very much housework because I had four or five sisters other than myself and I was always the smallest, so I got more sympathy. But I was one of the quickest. I didn't like being small but I'll tell you what I did like – when they all used to be borrowing my mother's gloves and shoes and blouses to go out to a dance or anything like that I used to say, 'Well, I'm glad I'm small, you can't wear mine.' And my mother used to go out on the market Saturday with father, with two big shopping bags and the elder ones used to have to go with them and help them to carry the groceries for the week. I used to learn sewing and cooking and work you know on canvas – embroidery – I can do that now. But I always liked sewing because I used to watch Mother you see. But she never would put us to it because she said it was a hard life sewing for other people. She didn't want us to have that hard life.

He used to wash up because she always had to keep her fingers pliable to sew you see. He used to do nearly all the housework, and cut all the bread and butter up, bring it through on a great big tray. He'd help Mother to bath us too and Saturday night, he didn't drink he didn't smoke, he used to spend all his time helping Mother to get us ready for church on Sunday morning. And on Sunday Mother used to make us a good dinner and we had a nice tea. And then my Father would play the piano accordion and we had one of those accordians and after tea when we lived in Queen Street I can see it now, he used to sit down and have us all round him and he'd play the accordion while we sang. They didn't do any work on Sunday, didn't do any work on Sunday, just the washing up, weren't allowed to do any crocheting or knitting or cleaning. Everything had to be done. You could play games but no work. Mother wasn't narrow minded nor father, narrow minded about games. Play as long as we were happy. It didn't matter.

We used to come home from school twelve o'clock. My father's there. He used to have the dinner ready. Mother used to prepare the potato pie or whatever it was – a pie in the oven. Mother used to put the crust and then we used to all sit round the table waiting for it to be served. Our father used to serve that, he used to wash up after. The eldest was served first. We all had our own place at table, you daren't take one another's place. We all had our special place and the eldest came first. Same at Christmas. When we were waiting to see what we had in our stocking, used to stand at the bottom of the stairs, the eldest came down first. We used to come down, down, down. Well Christmas Day was the happiest day of the year. And Mother always made a big Christmas pudding and a nice dinner, turkey and everything else and me father used to come out with the Christmas spirit and we used to have a branch of holly and he used to have a little drop of brandy in a glass and he used to set fire to the holly and pour the brandy over it. I remember that quite plain. Yes we had a lovely Christmas Day and all had a present. Father used to play the piano and play the accordion and we used to be singing quite happy and we used to have all a white pinafore on Mother had made with lace round, tied at the back with a bow. We got presents. I got a doll at ten years old. I used to be always making dolls' clothes, painting and sewing little bits of things, you know.

Father never punished us. He used to leave it to Mother. Mother had a little strap but she didn't hit us with it. She used to hit the table with it. She'd threaten us and that was all. I remember being sent to bed once in my life and that was for going down the market in the dark and I wanted to see this circus. I think it was called Clark's and they had a baby on show. It wasn't a nice baby, what they call an unnatural kind of child. There was something wrong with it. Freak of nature they called it. And they had it in a big glass case. It was preserved. So my father knew about this and he'd forbidden us to go. And he stood at the gate waiting for me. So he said, 'Where have you been?'

I said, 'I've been to the circus.'

He said, 'Well, didn't I tell you not to go on the market in the dark?' he said, 'Upstairs to bed without supper.'

So I just remember that. The first time Father was ever angry. I cried, oh I cried, because my father had done it you see. Never lifted his hand to one of us. Mother sent him up with a cup of milk. I was only twelve years old then.

Mother had not time to be as affectionate as my father because she was always busy, but she did her best for us. She loved us but she hadn't time to pet us. My father did the petting. I always remember us playing hopscotch with my brother at my side and I've often heard the neighbours say, 'She's not like the others, is she? Isn't she little?' And I went and I said to Mother, 'Mother, am I yours?'

She said, 'Of course you are love, Who says you're not?'

I said, 'Oh she said I'm not like the others. She said I was more like a little rabbit.'

And my mother got hold of me, she said, 'You know, you're only a remnant, but you'll outlast the lot.' And I am. Isn't that strange?

Father working in the Royal Liver he didn't start till he wanted, probably about half past nine or ten, therefore he had time to get us some good breakfast ready. I'll tell you what we used to have. A little bit of bacon, a tomato and half an egg each. We had meat nearly every day if we could get it, rabbit pie, hot-pot, Lancashire potato pie with a crust on and kidney in. And sometimes a pan of broth on front of the fire. It had herbs in. I was always on the shy side. My mother said to me one day, she said, 'Will you go to see Fielden, love, and ask him for a pound of rump steak!' I thought that was very rude. So I kept thinking, I don't like asking for rump steak. So I got to Mr Fielden and said, 'Mr Fielden, a pound of bottom steak for my mother.'

On Sundays we'd always have home made apple pies and cakes, jellies, fruit and it was all on the table. It was a nice sight to see. My father used to go out of the kitchen with this tray with roses on. I can see it now. A big tray with roses on. Father always put roses on the tray with cut bread on Sunday. She bought vegetables of course. But she never bought anything out of a chip shop. Made all of her own. Father did really. My father kneaded the bread and wouldn't buy anything in tins. And she wouldn't buy a cake out of the shops to put on the table. Sponge cake with all them eggs in, in a big roasting tin – and toffee, her own toffee. She made hop beer and she made stout. She used to buy from Berry's drug store. She used to get the real malt in the jar to put in the stout, the beer. It used to smell lovely. We used to have a big mug with it in. We used to have to keep taking the top off. And she used to make us drink the top because of the yeast. So say they had very little education, they were clever. They were clever in many ways. And they could make a pound go where today they won't be able to make ten pounds go. She could make her money go without getting in debt.

We went to the cinema occasionally but Mother would never let us go to a theatre or music hall. She was always afraid of a fire, always dreaded a fire. Sometimes I think she cared for us too much. You can do, you know. You can be too sheltered and then when you come to face the world you get a shock. I think I found that out. We weren't brought up rough and I think myself my father was too gentle. He was kind and gentle. I think that's how he made us. Too sheltered. Mother didn't domineer us like in a way but she used to 'Now tell me where you're going, who you're going with.' And I'd be all right. But we weren't to go anywhere unless we told her who we was going with and where we went. We weren't allowed to go out and please ourselves where we went or what we did.

They had good neighbours, good friends and neighbours, yes. My father was well liked. Everybody was welcome at weekend. No we didn't go out visiting much but they used to come to us. They just called in when they wanted. She went to the church and church meetings and she went to the Ladies' Guild and she sewed for the bazaars and she helped at the parties therefore she had a lot of friends. We had friends but we didn't neighbour much. But friends and relatives yes, mother's relatives.

When he came home from work he had a lot of clerical work to do. He used to leave that till we'd all got in bed at night. So that used to take a lot of his time up. Then he had this other side line, used to go out after and pick some money up you know, when he's sold his goods and that. And that's the way we lived. He didn't go out on his own, no. Always with my mother. Well I think they mostly used to go to the concerts and the operas and at school and church concerts they was always together. They never went to the pictures. He used to like watching cricket matches because he's taken us to watch the cricket. He loved watching cricket matches. I always remember them spending their time with us. Always with us.

The clergy they came to our house a lot. Nearly every day of the week one or two'd come 'cause I think they liked watching the children and we were churchgoers and we worked hard for the church and my mother was a nice good woman so I think that drew them to us more. And then my father loved music and my sister being in the opera I think that's the way they used to come to our house a lot more than perhaps they went to someone else. The church had a lovely opera society, there was three of our family in, and a dramatic society and we had socials, oh and whist drives. I used to attend them all. All of those parties. Mother used to do all the cutting up with all the other ladies behind the scenes you know. We used to go to these social evenings and these dances in the hall and then used to have a guild and go there and they used to have a special night for their dancing. There was always a night for something. Always. We belonged to the church you see. Used to help the church a lot. We used to find a lot of pleasure in doing that. We never used to think about going out, going mad or anything like that.

Agnes my sister that died, the eldest sister, was a lovely singer. She was in the operas. Oh mother sang, but not as good as my sister. My sister was also a trained singer in the end. My mother did afford to have her voice trained and eventually she got married and started bringing a family up. My father could play the piano. Used to have evenings together and my eldest sister was in the opera society and we used to have nice evenings at night you know, learning all the opera songs. And Father Whitman what was over the opera used to come and have a nice night you know, train them, have a nice time.

Grace was every time we sat down, before and after meals. I remember once Joseph was having porridge for his breakfast 'cause she couldn't give us anything that day. And he said, 'Well come on Joseph, what do you say before you leave the table?' He said, 'Have I to say prayers for porridge?' We had to kneel down before we went up stairs and say a few prayers before mother's knee. And my father used to take us all upstairs and used to separate in the rooms and we used to sing that

> There are four angels round my bed.
> Every corner an angel spreads.
> One to sing, one to pray,
> And two to carry my soul away.

And I said, 'Oh I don't want anyone to carry my soul away!' You don't find anything like that now do you? My father were a nice singer. My elder sister had a beautiful voice. We used to sing something different every night you know. At the top of the stairs so we could all hear.

Mother was a Catholic but he wasn't. He never missed church. He used to go with her morning and afternoon on Sunday. Take us all with him. But of course my mother and father didn't tell us, and I didn't know he wasn't a Catholic, till he was dying and he asked could he die in the Catholic faith. And they brought the priest and the priest wouldn't believe he wasn't a Catholic. He'd always seen him in church with my mother, with us all trailing behind him. There was a lot of trouble when he married my mother over religion. They didn't want him to marry my mother because she was a Catholic and he was the only child and there was money and my father didn't get a penny. It was the religion that broke up the family. Even his own father turned against him. My father's family rejected him altogether because of religion. His own father passed him on the street, just because he married my mother, a Catholic, see. And I think sometimes that's why my father never became a Catholic on account of it. In Heywood this aunt, she was an undertaker, she buried him. She bought his coffin, had his coffin made and everything and she was the only one that came near.

Only two cousins came the day after he was buried and had been to the cemetery to see where he was buried. And because he was buried on the Catholic ground they said to my mother, 'We can't help you, Lucy, you know why.' Mother said, 'Yes,' she said 'and I don't want any help. You haven't helped up to now, I'll manage please God, I'll manage.' And that were the last time I saw them. I remember two of his cousins coming once and they looked like two real ladies. And I remember them asking Father to take Mother and us to her for tea and we went and they had a beautiful home and all I can remember it was up Dunscar because I was only three or four, and they had property. And all I remember is going to this big house and Amelia, my sister, was going and she was playing the piano for us. And I always have that in my mind and that was the only time that I remember ever seeing my father's relatives.

I've stood beside eight death beds. My little brother died and I went to his funeral and that were the first one. That was 1910 I think. Then my father died and I went to his. My father died 1912, he was fifty-four. I wore a black hat but Mother wouldn't let us wear black clothes, we had to have a black armband, a band on our arm. We went to Father's funeral, wouldn't let us have black on. She let us wear a black hat. And my brother didn't have mass then. Well you can have one now but you see we didn't have those because we didn't have Requiem Mass then and we buried him in the afternoon and we all went and there's four carriages with plumes on, Belgian horses. It was lovely.

I started school at five. I left at fourteen, because I was too small to leave at thirteen. I was thirteen, and as I was too small mother let me go twelve months extra. It was a Catholic school. All of us went to the same school. We all went with each other. The eldest looked after the young ones. The boys and girls were separate, the boys upstairs and the girls were down. But it wasn't a school that punished children a lot. I have seen girls caned for being late, for being untidy, or not doing their sums. I only got the cane once in my life. I'll tell you, now listen. The teacher sent me for some Beecham's Pills. Used to sell them in little packets – threepence a packet. So she said, would I go to the chemist shop and bring her these pills. Well in the meantime she'd be doing our homework paper and I'd done mine wrong. So when I came back I gave her the pills. So she said I hadn't done the work that I ought to have done so she gave me the cane. So I just said, 'There Miss Sullivan, I won't bring you any more Beecham Pills.'

Children used to come to St Gregory's from Hollins Home workhouse. Now these children were pathetic. All their hair was cropped and they had thick clogs, thick caps and all their hair was almost shaved off. Now they were something apart. We could tell they were something different. Well I think myself they felt it. They felt it. But the teachers didn't punish them. But they were always at one side. We knew they were workhouse children but we didn't bother with them because we didn't understand what those children were feeling. We didn't know, we had a good mother and father, see. They had what they call a mother, bringing them and taking them back you see, and I was always in the concerts and used to sing and go on the stage. But the poor workhouse children had to go home.

Then before I left school there was to be a social and we had to pay tuppence. Used to get a small pie and a cup of tea, and then we could dance after. For all those as were leaving school. So I was going that year so Mother said I could have me best dress, have a white dress. So she put me this white dress on. I had beautiful hair, I could sit on my plaits. It's true I could sit on them. And they made me nice. Father put me some clean shoes on. So I noticed my mother, she'd been cooking some beetroot and left it on the dresser to cool. She hadn't put vinegar on. And I thought (I was a little pasty thing), I thought, 'ooh I wish I had red cheeks!' So I said to Mother, 'I'll go out the back way. I'm meeting Maggie.' She said, 'All right,' and she said, 'Come straight home after.'

I said, 'Yes'.

So as I was going out I got a piece of this beetroot and I rubbed my cheeks with it. I thought, I'll have red cheeks too. When I got to the school, Miss Wynne was the teacher, she said, 'Florrie, has your mother seen you?'

I said, 'Yes.' I said, 'She's got me ready.'

She said, 'Where'd you get your rouge from?'

I said, 'It isn't rouge, Miss Wynne.'

'Oh Florrie,' she said, 'I'm surprised at you telling a lie.' She said, 'Your father . . .'

I said, 'It isn't rouge.'

She said, 'Well take my towel and soap and go and wash it off,' which I did and when I came back, 'No' she said, 'It isn't rouge.'

I said, 'It was beetroot.'

So she had a good laugh and gave me sixpence.

The teachers seemed to do a lot for us after school hours. Always something going on, socials, dances, teaching us, going to school after school hours and showing us how to do things. We used to go to one teacher's house for music – you know to sing. She used to play the organ, and they had a rabbit and soon as you got in this front room they used to learn the singing. She used to say, 'Now, listen!' And as soon as she's played a few notes there's scratching on the door. The rabbit wants to come in. And it was stood like that all the time. She was called Mrs Kelly and she used to teach us how to sing in the choir. The headmistress at St Gregory's she was called Miss Kelly and she was a real born lady. She was beautiful and she never used to cane us and we loved to misbehave ourselves, and she'd help those that were down. She always watched the children and if she thought they were very poor she used to help them. And when she left school – ooh she had some beautiful presents the children bought her. She was a real little lady. And she lived till she was eighty. As I grew up she saw me in the street once, she said (she used to call me Florence) 'Florence, my word, you have got to be a young woman.' Yes, she was a nice lady.

I liked going to school very much but I didn't learn enough. I always wanted to learn more. But we were too poor to be sent anywhere else. I was always quick at a lot of things, I never missed a class. But I always remember those – their parents were teachers and they had a good job. Now those were the children that always won the scholarship. If they got a scholarship they went to Mount

St Joseph's. They had to pay so much because my niece won and her father had to pay for her. Well I longed to go but my mother and father was too poor, they couldn't have us going there. I have known a lot of people get to the top if they've been educated. Always through education. And I think that's the greatest thing you can have if you want to get on in the world, but get on in the proper manner, not be a snob. I think it's the best thing out.

When I left school we had to go to work and some of these girls that had won scholarships and got on and had a good education they'd broke away from us. They went on their own, they didn't seem to come to us like they used to do before they went to these high schools. They broke away. I noticed there was some kind of distinction between the girls who went to a high school and those that had to go out working for a living. I've always wanted to go to a nice school and wear uniform. Its strange that, isn't it?

I went in the mill to learn weaving with my sister at fourteen. And I worked in the mill thirty-six years when I went to hand sew after the war – the Second War. My sisters all went. And they got each other on you see. And the manager knew us and he knew they were steady workers. So we all got jobs under the same manager. When I started work at the mill first they started six o'clock. And then they had half-an-hour for breakfast and we started again at half past eight till half past twelve. Used to go home for dinner then. We used to have to work till half past five at night. I only remember working Saturdays for a few months, but after that we'd Saturdays off. Then I'd only be there about twelve month because the First World War broke out. And then they put the hours less you see. So I really had a better time than my elder sisters, and I got more money. I remember giving Mother my first wage, my half crown. Because I went to learn that was all. Then I got five shillings, then I was to get two looms, then you got four. Out of that half crown she used to give us tuppence back. And every year we got older till we got about twenty-one she used to give us a penny in the shilling. And we used to have to buy our own gloves out of that.

We were really too young to realize the hard life we were having you see. It was only through the war that we got wakened up. People got better wages and they started going further afield and learning things. They got better wages, see, so I think that in itself got poor people out of a rut, and it made them think more. The manager was a very strict, severe man. He was rather a cruel man in some ways; he didn't understand people. But I got through all right. He used to watch and see if you let a little thing drop and he used to pick it up and then used to have them in the office and shout at them. If you was to make a mistake in the cloth, used to get fined sixpence and that was taken out of your wage. Yes, they'd fine you sixpence but they stopped all that during the First World War you see. Started giving us good wages.

I didn't like the manager because I tell you when I was young I was very happy natured, and a girl and I always went out together and we used to be singing. I liked singing. And we used to be singing and he'd come through once when I was singing so I didn't take much notice of him. I went on. I was then about sixteen. So he sent in the office for me, and he said, 'I'm going to move you.' He was a man that nobody liked. He wouldn't mix with anyone. And they always said he came from Germany. And he'd four sons. But he was a tyrant the manager, Everybody seemed afraid of him. And I've always remembered that man but I wasn't under him very long before he died. But he was a tyrant. Well then things changed, seemed to go a lot better. But he was a very harsh man. You'd be frightened to death making a mistake. My eldest sister went into him once and said, 'Do you know, Mr Day,' she said, 'You're only short of a whip!'

He said, 'Do you know who you're speaking to?'

'Yes, I'm speaking to you', she said, 'You can give me the sack if you like.'

He told her to go back to work.

I wanted to get out of the mill but you see with the war being on I couldn't. They wouldn't let me leave because they wanted people in the mill. They closed down Farnworth, then I went to work in Bury with me sister seven years. A special kind of weaving we did, velvet, and they closed down there. Then I came and got a mill where Mr Hesketh was manager so I worked for him ten years. And as soon as the war was over I was off as soon as I could and went to a tailor's shop doing all the hand sewing.

It was harder learning weaving than sewing. It's more brain work. It's a very hard job. It was then. I tell you what I did notice, if you were a weaver you was considered high up, but if you worked in what they call the cardroom, a little doffer and that, oh you was down below [The worker who changes the empty bobbins for full ones on a power loom]. They treated you different. They had a tap of their own to make their tea. The weavers seemed to be the better dressed and came from a different type of home than the other side, a lot of poverty those days. A lot of poverty. Sixteen I joined the union and I was shop steward when I was at Prestwich's, about ten years, before the last world war. Some of them would leave it all to you. They'd come to you with their troubles and ask you to go to see if they'd put them right. And when you asked them to be there, they weren't there. They stayed away then and you had to face it all on your own. Employers did use the workers for their own ends those days. They got as much out of you for as little as possible. Now today it's gone the other length, hasn't it?

I was sad because I had to go to work because I liked school. I liked the people and I used to help them, the young ones used to help the old ones. And with brothers and sisters there too I had to behave myself.

I've told you all I do remember really, about us being all together, having our hard times, our hardships and having a lot of happiness. And best of all having a good mother and father and growing up in a good home. And poverty didn't matter because it wasn't a grinding poverty, and it wasn't a rough poverty. It was what you call a genteel poverty. Nice to be happy and protected. I think poverty can be poor in many ways. You can be poor with being short of something that you want to get on, but you see other people getting without effort – there's something you wanted and being too big a family to get it and mother wouldn't let one be better than the other.

5
Geoffrey Brady

Geoffrey Brady's account of childhood is of especial interest because it shows the enormous importance of the education system in enabling a child to keep his options of a place in the middle class open after his father's business had failed.[1] The pressure on him to work hard for a scholarship to Stockport Grammar School and succeed academically is a peculiarly modern pressure, one associated more with the growth of the direct grant school system and selection at eleven plus, post Second World War developments. There is an ironic twist to the story of Geoffrey's success because his hard work led to his being in the sixth form when he was fourteen, and therefore able to leave school when an opportunity to learn the flour importing business occurred. This killed his hopes of going to university in the days before grants from local authorities.

Geoffrey's childhood would have been typical of childhoods in the upper stratum of the provincial middle class had it not been for the collapse of his father's business when he was ten. The Bradys conformed to a pattern familiar to anyone who has studied this class. They went regularly to church but preferred to teach their children religion at home rather than sending them as middle and working class parents did, to Sunday school. They took an English seaside holiday, kept a cook and housemaid and part-time people to do the garden and washing, read the standard English classics (nothing *avant-garde* like Hardy), played golf and tennis and belonged to clubs for these purposes. Mrs Brady paid and received calls on At Home days and employed a governess for her son before he went to school. They were careful about their children's manners. Their financial reversals may have made them extra careful, but manners were very important in the middle class as Lord Percy born in 1887 remembered, 'Attentive readers of *Pride and Prejudice* will have observed that, even in 1813, a country gentle-woman like Miss Austen evidently preferred the manners of Mr Gardiner, the City merchant, to those of either Mr Bennet or Mr Darcy. Three or four generations later, when the two strains had had time to mature or run to seed, there could be no doubt that Mr Gardiner's descendants, wherever they had remained faithful to their urban origins, usually in provincial cities like Birmingham or Liverpool, and had resisted the temptation to become country gentlemen, had the advantage over Darcy's, not only in company manners, but also in a cultivated taste for the amenities of life, for food and wine and books and conversation.'[2] Lord Percy's parents 'impressed on me constantly, with however little success, the superiority of English "middle-class" manners'.

But of course Geoffrey's childhood was exceptional because suddenly many of the essential features of the middle-class life disappeared. They could not even keep one servant and without a servant a family could have no pretensions to middle-class status. Social life disintegrated because though provincial middle-class recreation was not expensive, tennis and golf costing a great deal less than racing or yachting, yet subscriptions to clubs had to be maintained, invitations to tennis parties repaid with refreshments served. Calling too was impossible without a servant to answer the door. There could be no social life without reciprocity and the Bradys could not afford to reciprocate. They could hardly afford at times to feed themselves. Geoffrey's friendships were affected too. There was now no tennis lawn and with only a penny a week pocket money cycling, a solitary pastime, was about all that was left.

It must have been a bitterly lonely time for the young boy. He had to work very hard, there was no money for outings or holidays, and his parents were preoccupied with a new baby. Yet he bore it all stoically, identifying with his parents' belief in honesty and hard work and the deferment of gratification for long term ends, exchanging the drudgery of school for the drudgery of the counting house at the age of fourteen. He had kept his place in the middle class; his education would lead to fifty years in business. Although it was not what he wanted he bore it uncomplainingly, stifling his hopes of a broader future.

Geoffrey was demobilized in 1919 and in the 1920s he tried to set up on his own with a partner, but the venture failed and he was reduced to commercial travelling, selling sweets and chocolates to shops until he got a position with a leading firm of Grain Brokers in the City. He had come south in 1926 and met his wife in 1934. The following year they married and had a son and a daughter. In 1947 having longed for years to get away from the City, he bought a nursery garden in Surrey. The hard winter of 1947–8 was a disaster for the business and Geoffrey, being the sort of man he was, kept all the men on full time. The set back and slow start proved too much to be overcome; an attack of whooping cough left his heart weak, and he was forced to sell up at a loss and return once more to the City. He retired at the onset of his last illness in 1966 and died in 1968.

NOTES

1 Elizabeth Sloane interviewed Geoffrey Brady in 1967.
2 Eustace Percy, *Some Memories* (London, 1958), p. 20.

I was born in 1898 in Stockport and I continued to live in Stockport or on the borders of Stockport until I was twenty-seven. Stockport is a manufacturing town and the centre of town is mills and railways and factories and round that, as you find, rows of small houses and then beyond that again the suburban area where you get the professional people and the people with executive positions and things like that. The house I was actually born in I can't tell you much about as we moved out of it when I was about two. But I have seen the house since. It was a semi-detached brick-built house, I should imagine with two living rooms and possibly three bedrooms. My father then was fairly prosperous; he was the owner of a cotton mill which came down to him from my grandfather, might even have been my great-grandfather. I don't know. But it was in the family. And I suppose he was doing fairly comfortably and we moved to another house in another suburb of Stockport which was an altogether bigger house. I don't know whether it had more rooms; there was a dining room and a drawing room we used to call it, and a kitchen, a big scullery and cellars downstairs for coal and things like that. Upstairs I think there were four bedrooms, certainly three, and above that an attic, typical of its kind, quite a large garden with a drive leading up to the front door, and a conservatory round it. Of course no garage because nobody much had cars and things.

I was the second child. The first one was a girl who died before I was born and then my mother had a daughter, nine years after me, a long gap in between us and there were just the two of us, my sister and myself. The nine year gap was a big one. I don't quite know whether it was by design or accident. And quite suddenly my mother and father who had been good companions to me were suddenly occupied for some years looking after a small baby. When she was four or five I was thirteen or fourteen and if we went for summer holidays I would have liked to have been learning to play golf with my father, instead of that I was sitting on the beach making sand castles to amuse my sister and things like that. I don't think I was ever so to speak jealous. I helped to look after her and so on, and we were good friends, but I was even more on my own and for the reasons I mentioned before I had to lead a rather lonely life anyway. There was no diminution in their kindness and care for me. They just had less time. They hadn't got time to play games with me. They were busy with this small girl.

There was a very well defined sort of class structure in those days. Now my father and mother and their fathers and mothers and all my uncles and aunts and so on (because they were both from very large families) they were all professional people, solicitors, auctioneers, engineers and people like that, or else in the case of my father he owned this cotton mill, and they were all of that type. They were, of course, in a town like Stockport very limited in number. You just didn't attempt to mix with people either higher or lower. What we called county people i.e. landed gentry and the lesser aristocracy out in Cheshire would never have made friends with the professional people, and mill owners in the towns. It didn't worry us in the slightest. Similarly, although we were perfectly polite and friendly towards local shopkeepers, and respected them immensely as 'honest tradesmen', we didn't ask them to come and play whist or tennis, and I am sure they would have been astonished and embarrassed if we had done so.

My father's greatest friend was also our doctor, two or three solicitors he was friendly with, the local clergy, and the wives used to visit each other's houses and so on. But they never mixed with, shall we say, a successful shopkeeper or a mill manager, anything like that. They were just that grade lower down, and I don't think anybody minded you know in those days. I went to the local grammar school and my friends were really of two types, children of friends of my parents, and cousins (both families lived near Stockport), and friends which I made at school whom I didn't know otherwise. But there my parents, as they would be in those days, were very selective. If I came home and said, 'I like Smith' well they'd make enquiries as to what sort of a home Smith came from. And if he came from a home like ours, 'All right – we'll have him for tea.' But if he didn't – 'Well I don't think he's quite – quite the sort of boy we want you to be friendly with.' It all sounds terribly snobbish now but that's as it was.

First of all I had a nursery governess when I was six. I had her for two years. She used to come in every morning, teach me right away, from the rudiments upwards, mainly the three Rs, and take me for a walk and generally look after me for the morning. And I had two years of that; and then they sent me to Stockport Grammar School at the age of eight and I was ahead of most of the other boys of eight because I had a few weeks in the lowest form and then I moved up to the next form. I didn't find school days very wonderful. The thing which was peculiar to us and which affected me in a lot of ways is that about two years after I'd started school my father's business collapsed. He lost all his money, partly through fraud, partly because he was keeping out of the business his mother, his sisters and so on, which made a terrific drain on the business and there was one of the cotton trade's periodic slumps. And I was too young to know much about it, but all our little world collapsed in ruins around us when I was about ten. And it was put to me bluntly that I might not be able to stay on even at the Grammar School.

You see, the sort of grammar school I was at was rather different from the county grammar school; it was a very old foundation that went back to the 1400s, and apart from a few scholarships you only got in if you passed good enough exams. And I don't know but there may have been a certain amount of social streaming as well. You had to have interviews with the headmaster. He may have picked as many as he could of the sort of middle class, but some of my contemporaries there were the sons of shopkeepers, mill managers, senior clerks and things like that. I don't remember anybody at school with me who belonged to what I call real working class, people who turned out to the mills at six o'clock in the morning; their children just didn't get to the grammar school at all because they didn't get the preliminary education to enable them to pass the entrance exam.

I was told that I might have to go to a county school. My one chance was that I might get a scholarship. So at a very early age I was faced with the idea of slogging away at homework whether I liked it or not, as hard as I could, and even at that age I realized that the only school in the neighbourhood of anything like that type was the school where I was. And I did; I worked very hard and I was given the one annual scholarship which was awarded to the hardest working boy in the school. I got that and because I got it I was able to stay on at the Grammar School for the rest of my education. But if not I should have had to leave and go to the Education Authority school and of course in those days that was very different.

And so all the time I was at school I was pursued by this damned scholarship because if ever I skipped my homework or didn't do very well in one term or something like that I might be sent for by the head, 'Look here, you were fourteenth in Latin this year, not what we expect from a boy with a scholarship you know.' So that and the fact of our suddenly having become very hard up at home meant there was a continual pressure on work. At the Grammar School of course I did meet a good many boys who were so to speak rather of a lower level socially and I don't think that amongst us all together at school that it made any difference. At school we mixed together very much on level terms. I could hear even at that age that they spoke badly and perhaps behaved roughly and things like that. But if they were good sorts and friendly I don't think it mattered in the least. I think this sort of snobbishness we had was very much induced and brought about from one to another. I don't think it was a sort of natural phenomenon at all. As I say at school in school hours, playing games, everybody was very much on a level. The boy who was looked down on was the boy who sneaked or cheated or something like that, in that there was quite a strict moral code, a school boy code if you like, but that was amongst ourselves. But if you left all your aitches out and spoke with a broad accent that didn't matter a bit. If you played a good game of football or something like that you were a little hero. It was outside school where the differences came in.

I suppose one of the biggest dividing lines at a younger age was actually speech, accent, because of course you know all the northern districts have a fairly marked accent. My parents were very strict about how they spoke and I very soon learned to pick out those other boys and girls who didn't speak so well probably because their parents in their turn didn't either. And then of course as you got higher up in school, of course having a grammar school education did tend to differentiate you a little bit from those who went to the other schools. By the time I was in the sixth I had quite a fair smattering of Latin, I could speak French moderately, things which just weren't taught in the technical schools, the secondary schools and so on. And in your conversation, well things like that cropped up. I used to read French books for pleasure, well if I mixed with other boys who didn't know a word of French there wasn't the contact. It wasn't a deliberate choosing. It was just that you weren't on the same ground. And although I stayed on at school until I was in the sixth, a good number of my friends who started with me left at the age of eleven or twelve and went to public schools. Two of my best friends went to Charterhouse; well I still kept in friendly contact with them although I didn't manage to go anywhere like that. But there was all the difference in the world between meeting those people at the age of fourteen or fifteen and meeting the boys from the local technical school. The differences were, I should say, far greater than they are now.

This school, and I think it was perhaps typical of local grammar schools in those days, didn't think much about sport. Work – it was good. Looking back at other people who were better off and went to public schools and so on I didn't do too badly, Latin, French and science and so on, all quite good. But they just made you work. Sport hardly counted for anything. I used to try hard at football and cricket but was not particularly good and anyway I was always being pressed to do anything up to three hours' homework every evening and so on. And so school to me was a rather slogging effort. It was the only school I went to so I have no standards of comparison, but I wouldn't say it was unduly strict. We never felt that we were being treated too harshly. Some teachers were stricter than others, and you had to behave yourself. You soon got a hundred lines if you didn't.

If you were persistently obstreperous you were sent up to the head and about the second time you would get a caning which (I was never caned) nobody thought very badly of in those days. They used to make rather a joke of it. My parents were both really better educated than I was. My father went to what is now a public school up in Lancaster and my mother was educated mainly privately and, well, they came from families where they didn't necessarily go to universities but good education was taken for granted, that everybody should have that. They were very careful over things, like for example, speaking properly. They were very strict about that. They were not unkind but strict over work for the reasons I've mentioned. They kept my nose to the grindstone pretty well, I would say in fairness out of encouragement more than strictness. I think they were very strict on what you might call morals, telling fibs or anything like that. They'd come down on you like a ton of coal. Strict truthfulness and all that sort of thing was insisted upon but without wanting to sound like a little hero I don't think I found that very difficult. I think they mixed strictness and kindness very well.

My parents would insist on what they considered the correct way to hold your knife and fork, waiting until everybody had finished before there was a second round of things, not talking as a small child unless I was myself spoken to, and not using your table implements the wrong way. You must hold your fork this way up, you musn't scrape round the last bit of gravy off your plate, all that sort of thing they were very strict about. And of course they did that thing themselves and one falls into the habit of it. It wasn't pointed out as much in strictness as much as in conversation you know. And of course children imitate their parents and one took to it naturally enough. We were always I think a very happy family. I recollect very few rows with my parents or anything like that; I was punished no more I'm sure than any child has to be punished. We were always a very united crowd.

My father was churchwarden for many years and my mother used to do quite a lot of sort of church work and I was taken to church nearly every Sunday of my life. But rather gently led forward rather than pushed into it. In those days I think, again it's rather a question of class distinction, I don't remember my friends at our sort of social level going to Sunday school. Sunday schools were very well patronized, Stockport used to boast it had the largest Sunday school in the world, children who went were nearly all children of the less well educated or working-class people. I think the middle-class people, thought, rightly or wrongly, that they knew enough about it themselves to teach their own children.

At a fairly early age my mother took me in hand on Sunday afternoons and gave me what I could call Bible stories, no more than theological instruction in any way and that continued perhaps getting a litle bit more advanced, but it was nearly all a matter of reading the Bible, getting me to learn sections of it, explaining any odd questions I asked, but not much attempt ever to preach to me so to speak. But I was taken to church very regularly and I didn't go to children's services, I went to the grown-up services and I do remember that very often the sermons were miles above my head; but I had to go and I had to sit still and attend, say my prayers every night before I went to bed. Gradually of course as you got older the services began to mean more. But after I went to school, apart from the fact that I'd had it drilled into me that I should go to church every Sunday or nearly every Sunday, I wouldn't say that they were not interested but they left it really to my instruction at school and regular churchgoing rather than attempting themselves.

In those days there was so much more leisure. That is of course one of the things which was greatly changed when my father lost all his money. Until this crash came we kept two maids, it wasn't a very big house. I can't think what my mother did all day long with two maids to do all the work and a gardener one day a week or something like that, and a washerwoman who came every Monday to do all the washing. So they had a great deal of free time. Out of doors they both played tennis, my father used to play for the local club, and then in middle age my father took up golf and he played for the local club in golf also. My mother by that time wasn't playing much in the way of games but in the big house we lived in we hadn't got a tennis lawn, they used to play croquet with their friends at the weekends a bit. My grandparents had a big house with a tennis lawn, we used to go there to play tennis.

Indoors they played whist and bridge, I remember it sort of coming in. They used to have musical evenings too to some extent. My mother played the piano competently, my father sang a little bit, not very well. But they'd ask half a dozen friends in and they'd sit round the piano and take it in turns to sing a song, play a duet or that sort of thing. That used to happen during the winter. Then there used to be a certain number of rather formal dances during the winter which my parents used to go to. But not a great deal of that. My father used to go at times to a man's club in the district, he wasn't a member but he knew a lot of people who were. They played cards and billiards and things like that.

A social custom which we were well in, which has gone right out now, amongst the married women of the place of the middle class was 'calling'. Every woman had her own day, her 'At Home' day. I think ours was the third Thursday in the month. Well on the third Thursday of the month the maid would have a clean bib and tucker and a nice tea laid on, everything like that, various other married women would walk in or be driven in in hansoms or something like that. They'd all come in and they'd sit around and chat and have tea and then perhaps go on to some other house. There might be some other person who also had the third Thursday and you'd do a round of them. Mother had her book, called it her 'calling book' in which she had the names and addresses of all these friends and against each one was the name of their 'At Home' day. So about two or three times a year she would go to each house in turn but if you got a fair-sized circle of friends that would fill in, if you wanted it to, two or three days a week. Of course as a small boy I didn't see very much of it.

I remember all these people being grandly shown in and putting cards in a silver tray in the hall and things like that and being ushered into the drawing room. Occasionally I was allowed in for a few minutes. 'This is my little boy' sort of thing. But that was a great feature of social life in those days.

They both read a good deal, I would say, the better class of novelist of the day, H. G. Wells, Arnold Bennett, Trollope. We had huge bookshelves with bound leather volumes of Dickens and Thackeray and Walter Scott. Well my parents had read all those I suppose in their youth and I was more or less compelled to read some in my youth, some of which I liked and some I didn't. They were members of a library, W. H. Smith or something like that, and used to take books out, the better class of novels and biography probably. We were faithful adherents to the *Manchester Guardian* as everybody would be, although my father was a Conservative in politics. For business and for general news there was nothing to touch the *Guardian*. *The Times* hardly circulated up there and if you took any intelligent interest in affairs at all you took the *Guardian*. You might as a Conservative hate it for its Liberalism but there just wasn't anything to touch it. The evening papers were the *Evening News* and the *Evening Chronicle*, neither of which was up to much. My father used to get them sometimes.

Apart from what I, so to speak, had to read, I read a good deal of Dickens, a good deal of Walter Scott, H. G. Wells, Arnold Bennett. I think those were the ones that made the most impression on me particularly Bennett and Wells. I think I read Dickens and Scott and a little bit of Thackeray. Thackeray bored me stiff, I soon gave up Thackeray, but the other two were partly because – well everybody read them. I was given various volumes of Kipling for

Christmas presents by aunts and uncles to bring me up in the right way of the time. I liked Kipling. We were always at school given a book to read over the holiday which we were examined on afterwards, very dull they were too. *Life of Nelson* and that sort of thing. They just had to be ploughed through, but I don't think I enjoyed them very much.

We went to Christmas pantomimes occasionally, mostly in Manchester, Stockport wasn't very much. It had a theatre but it was a poor sort of place and I think there was a music hall too. Manchester then had four theatres. We used to go to Belle Vue regularly. Belle Vue in those days was much more of a zoological garden and less of a general sort of entertainment place than it is now. I used to be taken there most summers. Once in the summer generally. They used to have great fireworks displays in the evenings. I as a small child used to go out often for tea with cousins and other boys and girls. We made our own games, played in the garden. I used to make an effort to play both football, cricket, lacrosse, which was a great game round Stockport, not very successfully; but I kept struggling along. I was always very fond of cycling. I had an ancient rusty old bicycle at a fairly early age and I was always a little bit of a lone wolf even at a small age. I used to go off by myself on my bike for half the day or get some sandwiches and go off for the day sometimes. And cycling then was a good deal safer than it is now, but on the other hand the roads were totally different and after five miles you were simply white with dust from head to foot. I got to know the beginnings of Derbyshire and right down to the other end of Cheshire.

Of course school was six days a week; we worked Saturday mornings so there was six days' homework to be packed in. Sundays there was church and Saturday afternoon very often I'd go out to friends or friends would come in to me and we'd play about in the garden. We used to play ball games and then when our financial crash came I had a very quiet time for some years after that because I just hadn't got the pocket money or the facilities or anything like that. It made rather a mess of things in that way. We moved down to a tiny little house with hardly any garden at all and there just wasn't the money for hobbies, games and things, and I think that's where my love of cycling was cultivated. It's one of the cheapest things there is.

I remember once going to spend the afternoon with a friend of mine, a school friend, about my level. We used to sit next to each other at school always and he had a nice house and garden and a paddock at the back with a pony. And I said something about how much it must have cost and all, lots of things he used to have. And he said well he'd like to have a lot more but he only had half a crown a week pocket money. Well my pocket money was a penny, literally a Saturday penny. Every Saturday I was presented with a penny. You could buy a quarter of sweets for a penny but you didn't do much on a penny a week. So that was rather the position between me and my friends which made life a little bit difficult.

I had very great kindness after the crash. One family in particular used to take me to the theatre in Manchester and the opera once or twice and things like that. They even had me away with them for a week once for a holiday and things like that, and never expected any sort of return. They realized perfectly well that there was nothing much I could do. The other fellow was about my age and used to come round to our house a bit sometimes. But there was nothing much for us to do at our tiny house compared to the big place he had. He had a tennis lawn and things like that. It was perhaps fortunate that I think it was generally realized that my father's failure was not due to any, what shall I say, dishonesty or hanky-panky or anything like that. Just due to bad business, perhaps to bad judgment, nothing that he need be ashamed of and so, both myself as a child and them as grown-ups, we did get a lot of help in all sorts of ways.

They had to give up outdoor things. I think my father gave up being a member of the golf club for some years. Eventually, he joined again when things were a little better; and they just didn't attempt to go out socially for bridge or things like that because if one did it meant having people back again and they just hadn't got the money to do these things. We really were for a few years, very hard up, very hard up indeed. I've known my father go out and I remember him going out once and selling his watch in order to buy us some food.

Servants? No, for a lot of the time we didn't. Then I remember for a few years we did have one maid. But I think really because no one else would employ her. I think she'd been into the local lunatic asylum once or twice. She was a big strong hefty woman, I remember quite well, one tooth sticking out of her mouth, not at all intelligent, used to do the most appalling things sometimes through lack of intelligence, very willing and very loyal and she would carry big buckets of coal and keep the kitchen clean, do the washing up and things like that. She did do the rough work and took it off mother's hands. Of course, even in this tiny house we moved into, it had a cellar downstairs and an attic upstairs with a ton of coal down the cellar and coal fires everywhere, three bedrooms and an attic bedroom as well where the maid used to sleep. We paid her, I suppose, very very little probably but I think for a woman in her position she was thankful to get a home. She was kept warm and comfortable and mother paid for her uniform; I think she realized the world was a bit harsh, and we had this oldish woman for quite a long time.

There was a lot of rough work and of course in a town like Stockport everything got dirty. All the factories were pouring out coal smoke and I don't think people, particularly down south, realize what it was like then. And we were living in a fairly pleasant suburb; and if you had your window open for a quarter of an hour you had to go round with a duster afterwards to clean up the smuts and things like that. Curtains were being washed continuously and one's clothes, handkerchieves, collars and things like that were quite filthy by the end of the day. So the amount of work of that sort was very considerable. But of course when we were better off we had two, what you might call well-trained maids. One was a cook and the other was called a nurse-housemaid to look after me and do the sort of housemaid job. She used to take me out for walks in the afternoon sometimes, things like that, play with me a bit. I think she was sometimes a little bit strict but I suppose like all small boys I probably needed it. I was no particular paragon I don't think. She was quite kindly and the cook was a typical cook, rather a fat old thing, I suppose living on all the titbits. She used to allow me in the kitchen, that was a great treat, and feed me up on a few bits of cake. But of course although they treated me as a child if I didn't behave myself I was always to them 'the young master'. I called them I think 'nurse' and 'cook'. I think my mother used to call them by their Christian names, but I know the cook's name was Alice. I've forgotten what the nurse's name was. It was just nurse and cook to me. I think, in fact I'm pretty sure, they were treated kindly and considerately and were paid, I suppose, sufficient for those days. But they were the maids and my mother was the mistress, and there was a great gulf between them. Not so much as a matter of strictness; it was almost automatic on both sides. They didn't expect to be treated as anywhere near equals; they expected to be treated kindly and that sort of thing but my mother and father took a sort of interest in their personal affairs. But there was no attempt to break down the big social barriers between them at all. They were quite simply separate.

Until we were too hard up we used to go regularly for a fortnight's holiday, generally to North Wales, which is the sort of holiday ground for the north of England, either there or to places like St Anne's or Blackpool on the Lancashire coast. I don't remember ever getting any further afield than that, generally North Wales, we went round there quite a lot. Of course we had no car – one or two of our friends had cars, mostly doctors who needed it for the job, but we never thought of having a car even when perhaps we could have afforded it. So one went down by train. But during the hard up period, well I used to go occasionally and stay with uncles and aunts and things like that but we virtually didn't have a holiday.

Apart from that visiting friends and relatives, if you hadn't got a car it was not so easy to get about; you could go by train but I don't think we ever did very much except for the seaside holiday or going into Manchester. I think people in those days were more self-sufficient, amongst our sort of middle class people, either in the individual household or by combining with other households as for example the musical evenings my parents used to have. We had a succession of dogs, we nearly always had a dog of some sort or another. And at one time we had a cat as well. I had some greatly beloved rabbits, for some years; I had a rabbit hutch just outside the back door. And a bowl of goldfish. I never remember when we didn't have a dog. I don't know whether we were unique in that way, but we rather took it for granted that every household had a dog. I think most of my friends used to have a dog too actually. Just one of the English habits.

I was only fourteen when I left school and went to business. Looking back on it now I'm quite certain that it was a mistake, but a mistake in good faith. My father was a business man and his father before him and so on. And to him business was the thing unless you went into the professions. And at the age of fourteen through some friends I was offered the entry into a very wealthy and very good class firm of flour merchants in Manchester. They wanted a youngster to go to them as an apprentice and they wanted him at once. Well, they knew something of my father through mutual friends, they also went to the headmaster of the school and said would he recommend anyone and he said, 'Well, there's a lad named Brady', or something like that and they said 'Oh yes, we know of him already', and so the two things converging settled it for me. Well, I wasn't given much option about it. My ambition in those days (my interest was in science) was to struggle along and get a scholarship if I could to Oxford or Cambridge. But my father came to me, and of course I knew what our financial position was, and said 'Here you are, the opportunity of a lifetime to start with a firm like that. You're made for life if you start with anyone as good as this', and so on. 'I think you ought to go and you can't start too early. The more business training you have the better. And these people could train you'.

And so I left school one Saturday morning and started work on the Monday morning and worked for fifty odd years after that. But I think really it was too young. I know lots of boys did but I think for anyone with a background as we had, to leave school at fourteen was a great mistake. Unfortunately for me I'd reached the sixth whereas most of the boys in the sixth were fifteen or sixteen while I was only fourteen. If I hadn't got to the sixth I probably shouldn't have been recommended for this job. So in fact my hard work and pushing on in that way rather let me down because it pushed me out into the world too young. It seems odd to think at the age of fourteen going off to Manchester in a hard bowler hat and a little grey suit and so on to start business. And I continued with this firm, well till early in the 1920s.

The firm were a firm of grain and flour importers, an international firm in those days, with four or five branches in this country, branches in the Argentine, North America, India. And they and another firm were regarded as two of the sort of giants of the business. They were private firms. They weren't limited companies. They handled millions of pounds worth of imports of grain and that sort of thing. My first day, I think I was given a typewriter and told I'd got to teach myself how to type, stuck on a lot of stamps. I was told to keep the fire going in the partners' room, like all the fires right throughout the office, and I was told it was time all the inkwells were washed out and I got all the ink bowls and washed all the ink bowls out. Everything was done in pen and ink those days. Letters were typed for other people and the first year or so I did very little except gradually I learned to type.

Everything that went out of the office had to be copied in an old fashioned copying press with a big handle you turn round and damp sheets. I was given charge of the postage book, every penny had to be recorded in that. And I worked a small telephone switchboard. I added up columns of figures for other people, ran errands for the partners and things like that. I was the lowest thing in the office. I never finished my five years because the war came but all the time I was gradually being taught something about the business. They were perfectly fair, I certainly had to start at the bottom and really stoking the fires was about the most regular job I had. But as I say I was gradually shown and I was told to 'Come and see, Brady, how we do this, come and write a letter to So-and-so as you would write and I'll tell you how it ought to be written.' I was treated gradually as a youngster who was going to move up into the important positions in the firm.

The firm consisted of, first of all, one of the partners who was partly based in Liverpool. He used to come to Manchester one or two days a week. Then there was a manager. Then this junior salesman and myself. We were in so to speak the top grade. And then there were two clerks and eventually a girl who were doing clerical work. Well the clerks showed me how to keep all the books and things. I don't think they particularly wanted to; they were told they had to because part of my training I had to learn how to post ledgers and make up balance sheets. I was taught to do it and used to help them to do it although I was never given it to do as a full time job myself. It was their job but I used to help take on some of the work and so on.

I think they were all very friendly. They may have thought, though they never said it, that this youngster's one day going to be our boss. There was this differentiation. But they were always very friendly and nice. The man whom I didn't get on with was the manager of the place. He was a bit of a swank really. He used to order me about as though I was a little bit of dirt. I suppose it was just his manner. The senior partner when he came down was very charming indeed. But of course one looked on him with sort of reverence, big noise like that. He was very kind. There were all kinds of strictness about office life. For example nobody was allowed to smoke at all till six o'clock. If you worked after six you were allowed to smoke, six was the closing hour so to speak, nine till six. And if you worked after half past six you were sent out to tea at the firm's expense, given one and sixpence and told to go out and have some tea. We used to work sometimes till seven and half past. But hours were very strict.

Again because I lived outside Manchester I was given a little concession. I was allowed to arrive up to five past nine instead of nine, because there'd be a train that fitted for that. But if I came in at ten past nine the question would be raised at once, 'Why are you late this morning, Brady? Train late? Couldn't you get here quicker?' And they were very strict over lunch. My lunch hour was twelve to one but if I went to the bank with the firm's cheques which I very often did, it was quite out of my way. I was allowed five minutes extra. But if I came in at seven minutes past I'd see the manager, 'Busy today, Brady, busy at the bank?' He was very strict on the work too. I learned to type as I told you but nothing was ever allowed to go out of the office that had been altered. I used to get away with it sometimes. I found ways of using a hard rubber with great care. Nothing ever left the office that was not quite perfect.

The next man immediately above me who was just out of his apprenticeship was a salesman. I used to go into his office and listen to him telephoning to customers, writing letters, to see how it was done. Well, if I'd been just a clerk I shouldn't. I'd have been out in the general office entering up ledgers. But I was shown how. Once or twice to my great joy if he was off ill, I was allowed to do a little bit of telephoning myself and so on and gradually I was taught how a merchant business like that runs and I suppose if it hadn't been for the war I should have gone up the ladder in that way.

It was perfectly true what my father said, they were a first class firm. During all my career of course I've been able to say, 'Well of course I started my career with So-and-so.' It's a firm everybody knows. And I suppose in a way that's some small advantage but like a lot of very good firms the mere fact of being there was looked on almost as an honour. So they didn't bother to pay you very much. The idea that you were going to get any money out of it didn't bother them very much. I went to them on a five year apprenticeship. There again this class system comes into it. If you were working for a firm as an apprentice you worked for very little for five years and you were taught the business. And after that you then became a junior salesman or something like that and the way was open right up to becoming a senior partner if you were good enough. If you went in as a clerk you might become a senior clerk but a clerk you always were. You never got away from a desk and books and things. You never had any executive powers, you never mixed with any other people. You were just an office man. And there you were, the two separate grades. If you went as an apprentice it was with all these dazzling prospects of what you might someday be. They paid me specially generous terms because I lived outside Manchester. So the first year I was paid £15, next year £20, next year £25, £35 I think it added up to £125 spread out over five years and that was £5 a year more than the other apprentices got, to cover me for my railway fare, even in those days £15 a year wasn't very much. I was paid quarterly so at the end of the first month I remember very tentatively and tactfully suggest-ing to some other fairly junior person in the office, 'When do I get any sort of pay?' 'End of the quarter.' And at the end of the quarter I got a cheque for £3 5*s*.

Of course I didn't go anywhere very much. Obviously my parents kept me at home and helped me out with the cost of clothes and things. But it was a very low level to start. I opened my first banking account at the age of fourteen. My father again, a business man, said, 'You ought to have your own banking account', so I was given an introduction to a bank manager in Manchester. I think I used to pay for my own midday meal in Manchester which was I remember 10*d*., café near the office. And then I paid something towards my season ticket but there just wasn't enough money to pay for it all and so I think my father used to make up the rest of that. I think they used to pay for my clothes because again, it was so little it just didn't exist. And I'd get a shilling or two a week pocket money and that was all.

I used to read a lot in the evenings, go out with friends a bit, not very much because going out cost money. It was the beginning of the pictures, very extraordinary flickering pictures in an old hall where you sat on long wooden benches. I used to go there at the cost, I think, of sixpence when I could. In the summer I still stuck to cycling, did a little bit of fishing occasionally, walked, used to go long walks with myself and the dog. Occasionally I got a little bit of tennis or a little bit of golf if someone was kind enough to sort of take me under their wing, but I wasn't much good as I didn't get practice and I couldn't afford to join the golf club. A lot of time spent very quietly really. If you are hard up there isn't very much you can do really. I used to go to Stockport library and borrow books a lot, the Public Library. That was a great help because of course it didn't cost anything. I used to very occasionally go to the Hallé promenade concerts, and it used to cost a shilling to go and stand on the promenade, a great joy occasionally during the winter. Again you see if you have very little money it restricts you right away because if I stayed to go to a Hallé concert I had to have some sort of a meal. Normally of course I went home and had my meal and it didn't cost me anything.

Anything that cost half a crown was an expensive evening out. Most of my friends were still at school. That gave me another spell of rather loneliness, cut off-ness. Those of them that went to boarding school were away and some of my very good friends were at the grammar school, stayed on there a year or two. And I soon found that going to business cut me off from them a lot. I don't mean intentionally on either part but I was suddenly transported into a different world though I used to go to classes in the evening for shorthand and accountancy and things like that. I used to go in the winter one or two evenings a week to classes and things like that. And so I began to get into a different world of my own.

I was too young to join up. I was only sixteen when war broke out and they didn't take anyone under eighteen. There was very great feeling in those days about volunteering for the army. All what you might call the best people, quite regardless of social class, the best sorts, volunteered to go. And I have had some unhappy moments because I suppose I looked old for my age when I was seventeen and travelling up and down to business and looking like, I suppose, a young business man. I was once presented with a white feather in a railway carriage. Unpleasant remarks about 'Isn't it about time some people started to do their duty' and things like that and it was rather unpleasant. And so as soon as I was eighteen I volunteered. I wasn't going to be labelled a conscript. You were registered and given a shilling, the King's shilling to show you were enrolled. And then they sent for you when they wanted you and I was called up when I was eighteen and seven months, something like that. A lot of young men got commissions. They got them without any military training at all, to begin with certainly. A cousin of my mother's was colonel of the local infantry battalion and if I'd have liked to go to him, I've no doubt I'd have got a commission quite easily. But I was a bit conscientious so I never pulled any strings. I was demobilized in March 1919.

6
Henry Vigne

Henry Vigne's family was descended from a Huguenot officer in the army of King William III whose son Thomas, born in 1699 married the daughter of another Huguenot, the city merchant Robert Myré. Thomas became a partner in his father-in-law's firm later to be known as Myré, Vigne and Luard of Threadneedle street. His son Robert was able to provide very well for the family before retiring from the city to Much Hadham in Hertfordshire, near the border with Essex. The next generation established the Essex connection with the eldest son, Thomas Vigne, of the Oaks Woodford, a celebrated sportsman of the time and his son Henry Vigne at Churchill Priory, Walthamstow then in rural Essex. Henry came into the firm as did his sons John and Felix. They seemed more interested in the city than leading the lives of country gentlemen and moved to Notting Hill after their father's death. The firm was then called H. Vigne & Sons, Stockbrokers, Old Jewry.

John's son, John Henry, became the senior partner in the firm. He lived at Eweland Hall, Margaretting and Writtle Wick near Chelmsford where his youngest son Henry Verrier d'Olier was born in 1898. Henry too joined the family firm after serving in the First World War and planting rubber in Malaya. 'I wanted to see other countries. I was determined not to go into business in the City of London if I could possibly avoid it. My father wanted me to and I knew if I stayed in England that I should have to go there. And I did have to go there in the end but I'd had my little fling abroad by then.' Henry Vigne married Joyce, daughter of Douglas Reid of Saffi, Morocco in 1927. They have been happily married for over fifty years and have a son and a daughter. Their home in Essex is near Henry's childhood home and apart from his years abroad Henry has always lived in Essex.[1]

Although the nineteenth century Vignes had married into baronetcies and the families of peers' younger sons, Henry's father was considered a bad match for the daughter of a London doctor because he was a stockbroker. Although city men were accepted in London society more easily than doctors in the Edwardian period, there were grave doubts about the new aristocracy of money round the court of Edward VII, and a doctor aspiring to social equality with men in the traditional trinity of Army, Church and Law, would therefore be particularly likely to keep his distance from a stockbroker. Professions in England were valued according to their remunerativeness, influence and recognition by the state. Remunerativeness was not purely a question of scale; it was also important that the money earned should have a stable basis. Here the stockbroker was vulnerable, 'His social position is so sudden that it cannot yet be looked upon as assured,' his 'wealth, though great, has the garish hue of luck, and the glories associated with which may dissolve themselves at any moment into thin air, like Aladdin's palace, and who himself is popularly supposed to be more or less on the tenterhooks of expectation and anxiety from morning to night.'[2]

In addition, the stockbroker was thought by some to be so absorbed in the affairs of his business as to be unable to devote as much time as necessary to the pursuits of society and the affairs of the county. His influence was therefore likely to be less than a merchant, and he was much less likely to be a member of parliament. Recognition by the state through the honours system would probably not come his way. The élite status of the professions of Church, Army and Law was intimately bound up with the conferment of honours and titles on their most successful members.[3]

But Mr Vigne was not interested in London society, preferring to live in the country. Nor was he immensely rich for we learn that had Henry not won a scholarship to Harrow, he would not have been able to go there. In fact, Henry's childhood was fairly free from reminders of class distinction. He learned the local dialect and played freely with farm labourers' children, as socially secure as any landed gentleman's son. Not until he went away to school was he made aware that class was to some minds an indicator of a person's value as a human being. Until then his attitude was like that of Sir Lawrence Jones, who grew up on a Norfolk estate in the

1880s, 'We are not class-conscious, because class was something that was there, like the rest of the phenomenal world; moreover they were all our respected friends who simply happened to be "the poor", and consequently could not expect to dine like ourselves, off turkey and plum-pudding.'[4]

Henry's relationship with his father during his childhood and youth was distant, and became warm only when they worked together in the firm. This is typical of father-son relationships in many professional and business families, where long hours of work took the father out of the home and the presence of servants and wife and nurses relieved him of any household or family duties when he was there. There was no work in shop or field or garden for Henry to help him with, and no estate for him to teach Henry about, for the countryside did not provide their livelihood as it did the families of labourers, farmers and gentry. It was more from his older brothers that Henry received training in manners. His mother, as was typical of a professional or upper-class mother, was responsible for his religious upbringing. Sundays were more strictly kept than in some Edwardian households but that is to be expected when parents have done most of their family building in the Victorian period.

Henry enjoyed the interest and companionship of a large family but it was very different from the experience of a working-class child with six brothers and sisters; boarding school, the navy and the army kept the other family members away for long periods, and though the family life was not oppressive, displaying no features of the 'stifling fortress of emotional bonding' in which Lawrence Stone believes many bourgeois children grew up in the nineteenth century, Henry longed to get away.[5] This seems to have been because he lacked companions. The house was two and a half miles from Writtle and he had no friends near at hand. The education he received, in company with three or four girls, was not very exciting and so he persuaded his parents to let him go to a school in Eastbourne when he was not yet seven.

This early separation from his family caused Henry only a few moments' distress. He welcomed the change and had 'a very cheerful time' at school. The practice of sending young children away to school is considered by many to be a peculiarly cold, English form of barbarism and it is worth noting that a child might choose to leave home by seven and begin the apprenticeship to a professional man's life where 'getting on with other people' was so important. Children leaving home young is not merely a feature of preparatory school life, it has a long history. In the Middle Ages childhood was thought to end at seven and a boy was a page from seven to fourteen, a squire from fourteen to twenty-one and a knight from twenty-one onwards. In England in the seventeenth century many children of the gentry lived away from home learning their place in noble households, while sons of nobles in seventeenth-century France joined the army at eleven or twelve.[6] In the nineteenth-century and Edwardian period the children of the poor would be expected to earn from a young age though they could not support themselves unless they were living-in servants of home, farm or shop; most of this labour was female. This meant that many girls went away at thirteen or fourteen to live in middle-class homes while their brothers stayed at home. A. L. Bowley and A. R. Burnett Hurst state in *Livelihood and Poverty* that as late as 1914 10 per cent of families in some English communities had no other source of income but their children.[7]

Although Henry's education was a classical education typical of public schools of the day, he was not a typical public school boy. He was a scholar, and carried his scholarship lightly. Most boys left public school after years of labour at Latin and Greek unable in Sir Lawrence Jones's words, 'to construe an inscription on a memorial tablet, let alone to read with enjoyment an Ode of Horace or a Greek epigram.'[8] But Henry was one of the few to whom the classical authors became a source of pleasure, a pleasure he retains to this day.

NOTES

1 Henry Vigne was interviewed by Ann Jungmann in 1974.
2 T. H. S. Escott, *London: Its People, Polity and Pursuits*, vol. II (London, 1879?), pp. 39–42, 47.
3 Ibid.
4 L. E. Jones, *A Victorian Boyhood* (London, 1955), p. 70.
5 Lawrence Stone, *The Family, Sex and Marriage in England 1500–1800* (London, 1977), p. 669.
6 Peter Burke, 'The Discovery of Childhood', pp. 5, 16. This was due to appear in the History Workshop Series on *Childhood*.

7 A. L. Bowley and A. R. Burnett Hurst, *Livelihood and Poverty* (London, 1914), pp. 110, 111, 200.
8 Jones, op. cit., p. 214. Jones was at Eton. For an account of a classical education at Harrow in the 1890s see Stephen Tallents, *Man and Boy* (London, 1943), p. 106.

At Writtle Wick there was a big billiard room, dining room, withdrawing room and a schoolroom and a sort of open hall with some curtains you could pull round where we used to sit a lot in the winter. And then there was one – two, three, four, five, six, seven – eight bedrooms altogether. There were no bathrooms of course. By the time I was born there was an indoor loo. But only one. That was kept for the small children and ladies. The men went down the garden in the good old fashioned way. How you kept clean I don't know, we always used to have a bath every day, everybody in a hip bath in the room. The water was boiled downstairs and brought up in cans. Then in 1910 my people went to Margaretting which is three miles the other side of Chelmsford and we lived there officially till 1927 but of course I was away at school most of the time and then in the army you see, so I hardly knew very much about it. It was a biggish house. Beastly uncomfortable I always thought. I hated the place. I liked the area but I loathed the house. We were very fond of the original house but the original house was a tragedy. You see it was offered to Father for £2,000 which was quite a lot of money in those days I know, but the fellow who bought it sold ten acres of the sixty acres that went with it for £200,000 a little bit later on. Terrible, isn't it? So inflation's nothing new you see! It was going on then. We always lived in a rented house. He never owned a house in his life. He had a horror of owning property; I don't know why.

I had three sisters and three brothers. I'm the youngest. All the boys were at Harrow. It was the done thing at the moment. My eldest brother John left Harrow to go to the South African War in the Imperial Yeomanry. He was seventeen years older than me to the day almost. He stayed in the Army. He died in India in 1904, he got enteric and he was in the Thirteenth Hussars then. My eldest sister Dorothy was a year younger than the oldest brother. She was the only member of the family who was not hale and hearty; she had a dicky heart. She was a darling and she stayed at home and did all mother's housework you know, looked after the place generally, 'cos mother was not very well, as Victorian ladies weren't after their eighth, tenth or twelfth child as a rule. She married eventually and had one child. Then after her was another sister who was the lively member of the family. She was, I think, two years younger than Dorothy and she married and had two children. And then a year younger than her was a brother who went into the Navy and he was the one who was very different to all the rest of us, he was pure Waggett – my mother's family, not a sign of Vigne about him, but he was senior parner in our family firm later on in the city and I worked very closely with him. Then there was a gap, how many's that? That four we've had? That's the four eldest. Well they were all more or less grown up you see when I was a child. Then the ones who were with me as children were – one sister who was eight years older than me, I can sort of remember her as at a gawky schoolgirl state you see, and my brother who was just three years older than me. So I was very much the odd man out.

At Writtle Wick there was a cook and housemaid, a parlourmaid and a kitchenmaid and the two indeterminate ones. I think one was a sort of underhousemaid and the other was a general dogsbody. I suppose the housemaid probably got fifteen pounds a year and the underhousemaid seven or eight, dreadful to think of isn't it? But on the other hand they were very happy I think. Of course it's jolly hard to tell as a child, but I can't remember any sort of squabbles or rows ever. They were mostly the daughters of neighbouring people that we knew you know, farm labourers and so on. Father wasn't rich you know, but it's amazing what you could do on quite modest earnings in those days.

They had three bedrooms. Quite nice rooms. They ate in the servants' hall which was really a kitchen, do you know what I mean? It had been as a kitchen and a scullery. The scullery was the old farmhouse kitchen. Then the next room had been made into a kitchen and then I don't know whether it was done before we got there but it had been made back into quite a nice sitting room servants' hall, and all the cooking, brewing tea or something was all done in the scullery part. Occasionally one was honoured by being invited to a meal in the servants' hall – a great thing. Of course, later on I realized it was a damned good way of getting rid of me when mother was entertaining someone else. They all mucked in together. Cook was always known as Mrs, didn't matter what she was. Everybody else went by a Christian name. There was a very large kitchen garden with a nice sort of sitting place where we used to go and have tea and that sort of thing as kids very often. There was a big orchard which they could use, and just in front of the house they didn't come; but they could wander around the rest of the garden if they wanted to in their time off. They had the freedom of the grounds but wouldn't sit in the front by the drawing room.

There were two gardeners and a garden boy, and there was a coachman and usually two grooms. The coachman lived in the farm cottage at the back of the house, didn't join on but just across the back yard; the others came from outside. The two gardeners were called Mr So-and-so by the children; when you were annoyed with them you'd call them without the Mr, and the boy was called George or whatever his name was. He was a very temporary person. I mean he did knives and boots and helped in the garden, or if William who was the coachman. He was always called William, he had started as garden boy. If he wanted help in the stables he would say, 'I want so-and-so to-day can I have him?' and he went there and helped muck out or whatever it was you see. I think I got on awfully well with all of 'em. We always liked them all. One gardener we didn't like, or his family, they were rather foul but most of the people we liked very well.

The first nurse they had was called Nanna. I never knew her. But we three younger ones had this girl Nindoo who came as a nursemaid. She was a darling. She married a fellow down at Thames Ditton and we used to go and see her occasionally. And then she got ill poor woman and died fairly young and never had any children. But she was awfully nice. The underhousemaid used to assist. If Nindoo was busy I mean the underhousemaid would see that we boys washed in the bath, that sort of thing you see. She was a charmer. She was an awfully nice person. By the time she left I was four or five, we got a room of our own my brother and I, it had been the day nursery which was now no longer wanted you see. So it became our room. We used to roast sparrows over candles and that sort of thing in it you know. You know the sort of things small boys get up to. Awful things we did!

In the morning one got up and one was supposed to wash, which you didn't very much. And from the age of four or five we came down to breakfast always. Father used to say good morning and then he used to rush off to the station. And we used to have breakfast. We had Force, those cereals of different sorts, bread and jam. And if we could possibly scrounge any sausages or buttered egg or kippers or something of that, that's what my mother and father had, and there was a couple of entrée dishes on the sideboard and when we were a little bit older you see we used to help ourselves. I always liked to be last 'cause then you could scoff what remained. Lunch was I think rather simple, one dish and some bread and cheese or something of that sort. We wouldn't eat an awful lot. And then I think unless there was something special on we used to be shooed off into the garden to amuse ourselves which we did very thoroughly. We had a sort of garden door, from there about twenty yards was a shrubbery, an old fashioned shrubbery, all laurels and things and it was a lovely sort of place, you could dive into it. And the first thing you did when you left the house of course was to hare off and dive under the bushes and go and sit in there and discuss what you were going to do, because you were safe there from grown-up interference. We had a four-acre meadow, and an orchard and the house and garden.

We had to behave decently downstairs – we must have been taught how to use utensils by our nurse I think. I can just remember not a baby's high chair, but having a chair rather high so I could sit up to table and not spill things; and I must have been what – four then I suppose – or five. Tea was a hefty meal. Masses of carbohydrates: scones, buns, cake, bread and butter. We used to have a lovely chant – 'I've had two pieces of bread and butter may I have some cake.' But we were always strictly disciplined you see. I mean however nice a cake was you weren't allowed that until you'd eaten your proper meal of bread and butter. Looking back I realize now it was in order to make the cake last longer. I had two older sisters living in the house, I mean they were seventeen and eighteen; they had supper downstairs in the evening with the old people you see. I had it when I went to a public school, when I was about thirteen or fourteen I think. Not before that. And we didn't attend a dinner party then or anything like that. We went to bed at seven; Mother always said good night to us, Father not very often. He usually used to see us having supper. We used to have cocoa and bread and butter or something of that sort in the nursery.

Mother's family had a vague Irish connection (the family as a family were most frightful snobs and my grandfather was a nasty old man), one never heard much about 'em but my uncles and aunts were very nice. They weren't snobby but the old man was quite impossible. I mean there was an awful row because my mother married such a common awful person as a stockbroker you see. And when her younger sister wanted to get engaged to father's brother that was the end, you know what I mean. It was stamped on. She was almost put into a nunnery I mean. It didn't come to pass and poor old Bob went off and married somebody else.

Mother didn't go out much. She was a pretty seedy woman and she had a leg that she could not bend. And it hurt her an awful lot. But there was absolutely nothing wrong with it whatever, I think it was purely mental. But it did prevent her doing things. And I mean there's no question it hurt her. It did hurt her. Badly. She used to have a lot of pain. I can remember her quite well at about forty-eight or fifty, and I mean she no longer played tennis and she walked very sedately and slowly and pottered about generally. I mean we kids used to be awfully annoyed – 'Oh God, Mother's coming out for a walk with us, we shall dawdle along,' sort of thing you know. We were very fond of her. We were a very united family. She did a certain amount of good works you know – I mean NSPCC (known as Waifs and Strays then wasn't it), and things of that sort. She was a sort of collector you know in the area. I don't think people did very much in those days. There wasn't quite the same need probably. She used to read a certain amount to me. I don't think she did an awful lot for me really. You know house-keeping was an awful business then. We could always see her any old time. She was always about. We used to go shopping with her sometimes; of course what we really liked was going to the market on Friday. That was a great joy.

I really knew Father very very little till I was grown up. In six months after the war I got to know Father very well indeed, got very fond of him. Before that I was quite indifferent to him. I mean he was very busy. He used to come back rather tired in the evening about half past six, and used to just sort of say good evening to us and that was that. Saturday he might have gone shooting, he might have gone out somewhere, he might go out hunting. I didn't see him much. Sunday no; he probably slept all the afternoon on Sunday.

I think they used to go out a good bit in the evening – go to dinner parties and things which you did in those days. Dinner parties by the way were a great joy in the house. I daresay you noticed a little thing like a rabbit hutch outside here did you, a little black table? Well that stood outside the dining-room door and the stairs went straight up opposite it and our room was just at the top of the stairs and if there was a dinner party on in between courses one used to nip down the stairs and see if there was anything there you see – pinch things you know, sausages from round the roast chicken and that sort of thing.

I think Father was a member of MCC as far as I remember. But I don't think anything else. He was not what you'd call a club man at all. He never dined at his club or anything. He went out to masonic meetings occasionally. I think he belonged to Chelmsford golf club, I'm not quite sure. He had been quite a reasonable cricketer, I think, in a minor way when he was young. Belonged to I. Zingari for a time and played there, when he lived in London that was. He hunted, and he shot a little. He tried to teach me to ride and shoot but I knew far more about it than he did. My brother and I and my sisters were all much better natural horsemen than my father. He was a bit of a tinker on a horse quite honestly. I don't think he sort of went to Newmarket or anything of that sort. He'd go to the local hunt, point to points and that sort of thing you know. The local hunt, point to points were very much a social event even then. They weren't just making money like they are now. They really were where you met all the country people of all classes. There used to be Galleywood races in those days too which were right on our doorstep. We used to make a party usually and go. Yes, Mother'd probably go on those occasions.

I think they were always kind and nice and I mean there was no reason to be frightened of them. Why should one be? They never repressed us. I mean if they wanted us to stop doing something they'd probably say, 'Oh do stop doing that dear, I'm busy,' or something of that sort and that was the end of it. You just stopped you see. It sounds as though we were horrid little brutes doesn't it? I think à propos of that you know – having a big family the older children did an awful lot of the educating of the younger children. And also they were about so you weren't bored, and weren't importuning your mother or your father as you might have done as a single child you see, because there was nobody else to talk to. At meals we chattered away. We talked quite decent standard English I suppose you'd call it, in the house. But I also talked broad Essex because I spent a lot of time with farm labourers' children and that sort of thing and I still talk broad Essex when the occasion demands it, and I'm not a bit ashamed of it. I think people ought to talk their local language. I don't remember any of the men about the place ever swearing. I don't think countrymen do swear much you know. And they were all country folk you see.

We had Sunday books I remember and when I was quite small we used to have to learn the collect for the day and repeat it to our mother after lunch. And we went to church in the morning; we never went to church twice a day thank the Lord. We had to be tidy on Sunday morning and we got into what they call working clothes in the afternoon and Mother used to always give us what I suppose amounted to a Sunday school session really in the afternoon. Things like cards we didn't do and nothing that caused any of the servants or employees to do anything. I mean I could ride a pony on Sunday afternoon if I wanted to, but I jolly well had to do everything myself; I mean I mustn't ask one of the men to do a thing. Sunday was a day off where they did the minimum. I mean the men in the stable saw the horses were watered and fed and cleaned out and that sort of thing but nothing extra, nothing beyond that. As a matter of fact that applied all through, I mean if I rode any time when I was young I always had to get my pony ready myself, and had to clean him up after I came home, and clean the saddlery. I've no doubt the men went over it all afterwards to see it was properly done, but nevertheless I'd done it all.

Religion meant going to church and trying to behave decently, I think – two things. And Mother I think was genuinely a devout churchwoman. Father I think was simply a conforming churchman. I don't mean he wasn't a Christian, he was; but I mean I don't think he cared two hoots about what sort of service it was or anything of that sort. I mean the respectable thing to do was to go to a Church of England Church – so he went, you know. We liked hymns and things in church. I had an uncle who was a great divine and so naturally one paid a little attention. Writtle has a big church. It's got a north aisle, a south aisle and a very big nave with seats, two sided seats in the central part of course; and then there's a little chapel which was a chantry originally, which the Usbornes appropriated and sat in always, must have been rather nice, you couldn't possibly have heard anything that was going on in there so you could sleep peacefully through it you see.

We sat about the second row back on the side. First and second rows we had on one side, and the Roffeys who were maltsters by trade they had the first and second pews the other side. Those were the front two pews. They were on the parson's side, we were on the pulpit side, which was very annoying because you couldn't go to sleep very easily. The village shopkeeper, the local butcher or the baker and people of that sort, they all had pews all the way back, and one or two of the bigger farmers had pews they stuck to. And then some of the girls were supposed to be able to sing. They couldn't. They used to sit up just behind the choir and join in. No females in the choir; they weren't considered quite nice.

We went to church on Christmas morning and we had an enormous meal. And I think we were driven out or I used to go for a walk in the afternoon, probably on the excuse that the dogs had to have exercise. And what happened later on? Oh we probably played charades and things of that sort, possibly some neighbours came in. I can remember sitting in a fairly high chair you know with cushions and eating turkey. We used to have stockings always, one or two other presents, not many. I think the servants had a jolly good meal which we sort of assisted them in getting ready, and we used to sort of decorate for them and things of that sort. That's about all I fancy. I think the old man used to do 'em pretty well at Christmas.

I liked breeding ferrets and ratting and that sort of thing and fishing a lot, coarse fishing. I always had dogs and rabbits and guinea pigs and you can imagine all the type of things. Had a bike when I was fairly young. Let's think – I borrowed my sister's bike and learned to ride on it and wrecked it. I must have been about six then. [Billiards?] Actually I was just beginning to play billiards when the old boy sold the table. Well we moved you see when I was about eleven years old. Croquet I think Mother used to play fairly seriously and we used to fool about occasionally. There was a lawn and tennis court as well.

We had a cricket pitch up in our meadow and we used to have sort of rather mixed cricket games you know occasionally in the summer. A lot of local families we used to play. Probably they would play indoor games in the house, or possibly cricket people used to come, next door village people. We had at least two houses within a couple of miles where we could walk in when we wanted to. We used to sort of say, 'Well I wonder what So-and-so's are doing, let's walk up and see,' you see. You probably found when you arrived there you were offered tea and played something or other you know, grab patience or something of that sort. One of these things. I think all our amusements were what they call home made. Roller skating was a great thing of course, loved roller skating. We used to go down to a roller skating place in the town, pay tuppence I think. And then we skated at my prep school. We had a lovely concrete area we used to skate and play hockey and all sort of games on skates, great fun. But that was school rather than home you see.

Mother and the sisters used to read books, one of them used to read while the others worked, needlework you know, mending and that sort of thing. But apart from that I don't think they read a lot. Now let's see, we used to have *Punch*, the *Strand Magazine* and the *Field*. That's about all I think. I used to read to 'em sometimes when they were mending socks or darning towels, all that sort of thing you know; Kipling, not Wells I think, Seton Merriman. Do these mean anything to you? Seton Merriman wrote rather good romances, like Ethel M. Dell but not so damned silly.

[Poetry?] Oh yes, one used to recite the 'Wreck of the Hesperus' and that sort of thing but I mean no serious reading of poetry. Father was mad on Dickens and I conceived a complete hatred of all his works from that. And I've never been able to get over it. I think generally as a boy I found all the classics too long-winded. I didn't discover the joy of them till I was much older. I liked shorter stories. I think I was really brought up and grew up myself on Kipling largely, and Wells you see, all short story stuff, in which I could take in the whole thing and which I didn't understand of course.

I even read Elinor Glynn's *Three Weeks* at the height of the horrors about it – 1906 or 1907. I thought it was quite a good yarn. I mean all the sex part passed me by naturally, except you see, being a country child I was perfectly aware of sex. I do remember being terribly shocked at a sexy joke made by a boy at my prep school, about twelve years old. Well it shocked me that anybody could think there was anything funny about sex whatever. I knew all about that sort of thing from a very early age I think, I suppose odd casual remarks about it, cocks in the farmyard and bulls and that sort of thing. And I didn't think there was anything interesting about it; I mean I never gave it another thought. I mean it was all part of the world.

Mother wouldn't receive a divorced woman in her house until it happened to my elder brother (and entirely not his fault as a matter of fact but still, that doesn't matter) but she then realized that one just couldn't be a judge in these matters, it was a private matter. And I think if she'd known that a woman was a scandalous liver she'd have refused to receive her, but just because she'd got divorced, no. This change came about 1920.

I called Mother Mummy; later on I always called her Mother when I was a bit more grown. We used to refer to the old man as the guv'nor of course. When I was at school I would have called him Sir. We got accustomed to it at school you see, calling a grown up man Sir. Most men much older than myself I would call Sir, probably anybody over about thirty-five or so, certainly all middle aged men. We could be quite natural but we were expected to be polite, and they weren't demanding parents in the way of affection – but we gave 'em affection because we were genuinely fond of them you see. Cleanliness, honesty, decent manners were important, kindness. I should put it all under the label of courtesy I think. I think I learned more from my older brothers about my behaviour as a boy, but general behaviour from Mother. When we were very small we might get beaten with probably her slipper I think. Perhaps once a year or something. I can remember being choked off by Father but no physical punishment. It conveyed to me that people were rather annoyed with me for a time and I think I forgot about it in a day. So I don't think it worried me a lot.

Relations would talk about their own jobs but they didn't suggest that you were suitable for this, that or the other at all. It was always assumed I think that you went into one of the respectable jobs you see, I mean Army, Navy, Church, Law. But if you wanted to run a corner shop in Springfield you were frowned upon heavily. I should love to have been a small shopkeeper you know. I never tried either; I daresay I'd have hated it if I'd done it. As children we didn't know any of the town people at all but we knew an awful lot of farm labourers and that sort of thing, and liked 'em and got on well with 'em. I think the two lots, us and them, went their own paths and were of course still quite friendly but they didn't envy us I don't think in any way and we certainly didn't envy them. I think it was always impressed on me that people who might be my inferiors in some way or other had got to be treated especially politely. I was first made aware of 'class' at school. I thought it rather odd. I thought it was rather odd that one should feel aloof and different to 'em quite frankly.

I suppose I dropped out of playing with local children when I went to school. I was never told not to play with them, no. I mean if she might say, 'What are you going to do?' I'd say, 'Oh well, I'm going to go and play with Maude and Jack.' 'Right oh, well come in for lunch in good time.' I was always quite happy. I was rather a solitary child, always have been. I still am a solitary you know. I mean I don't find company necessary to my welfare at all. I'd be quite content to walk on the moor all day long without speaking to a soul, though I'd enjoy it more if I met somebody interesting to talk to of course.

I was the odd man out and I had to be got rid of at times when people were busy. I used to be sent off then, but not very often. I once went to stay with a school friend in Scarborough and loathed it. But I went. Father had shingles and he and Mother went off to Switzerland and I was shut away with this boy I didn't like very much anyhow. And I couldn't – I was rather a shy sensitive child and the bluff Yorkshire people didn't go down at all well with me.

When we were small we used to go to Felixstowe. I suppose summer holiday time it would have been, a fortnight, three weeks. I think we used to go every year until I was about eight or nine. Father and Mother used to go. They used to stay in a hotel and we used to stay in a boarding house. The two elder girls stayed in the hotel with Father and Mother, and three younger ones stayed in a boarding house. I think we used to stay in a lodging house which was kept by a relative of our nurse. We fished occasionally and we played on the sand – had boat trips. But later on we used to hire a sailing boat down at Mersea Island here and also spend a week or a fortnight down there which was great fun, just going off with a horse caravan. It was fun; the biggest journey we ever did was up to Newark, Nottinghamshire. I think two of my sisters and myself, a brother and a friend went and two dogs. I think I was about twelve then. It was a good holiday but you see the roads were quite decent then. My sisters would have been grown up; they'd have been about twenty then you see, or twenty-two or twenty-three.

There was no difference in Saturday than any other day when I was quite small. But later on we very often used to go out rabbiting or something of that sort with a neighbouring farmer. Actually we had a lot of racking rights all round the country. We had a gun and the dogs and ferrets and we used to have a very good time, especially in the winter holidays. Summer holidays we used to fish violently every spare minute. We didn't go to the theatre a great deal not till I was considerably older when I was sort of getting on towards my teens, and we started on musical comedies, *The Merry Widow* and *The Arcadians*, and adored them. I fell in love with Yvonne Arnaud in *The Girl in the Taxi* at a very young age, I suppose about eleven. I can't remember who we used to go with – various friends used to sort of make up a party, 'We're going to the theatre will you join us?' sort of thing. I think Mother took me to *Peter Pan* on at least one occasion.

We used to go to parties a lot which I loathed. But we had two or three neighbours all with children where we had sort of open house. I mean you walked over to see them if you felt inclined. They did ditto. We went mostly on our own, I mean I can't say I went very far until I was ten or twelve myself. But you see we had neighbours who were sort of one mile and a half that way at Writtle, another one just up the road at Chignell, about three quarters of a mile; two more another quarter of a mile or so beyond that, and it was all quiet country road or across the fields so it didn't matter.

By the time I was five I was reading quite fluently, and my elder sister taught me to read because I think she was bored stiff with having me hanging around her skirts all day. I think I rather cramped her style with her boyfriends you see so she set about teaching me to read. I read Wells and Kipling at five. The older children had a governess. By the time I came on the scene she'd ceased to be. My sisters all went away to boarding schools after a bit. I don't think they ever wanted to go on anywhere, I mean they weren't brainy at all.

I went to a little school run by a doctor's wife and then I went on to the village schoolmaster and his wife at Writtle. There were four of us there; she was quite good. I learned a little bit of Latin there and things of that sort, and I enjoyed that immensely. I used to ride a pony over and put it in the local pub and then walk round to their house and then half past twelve or whatever time it was, no later I think – about one – I used to leave them and used to ride home, escorting two girls, who poor things, had to walk. There were only five of us I think; we were all friends. One was a doctor's daughter, two were daughters of the maltster and there was a Woodhouse child I think. We did English, spelling, a little bit of history I suppose, a little bit of Latin, arithmetic.

I got so bored with all this that I clamoured and clamoured and got sent away to a school; I went away to a boarding school when I was just under seven. I still think it was a very good plan. You got used to being away from home early on. I was bored you see at home. I was all alone, other children were at school. It was a school down at Eastbourne; it was called Warren Hill, defunct now, a nice school. My eldest brother had been there – presumably seventeen years before. Then the other two brothers went to another school at Broadstairs. They didn't believe in two boys going together to the same school when they were young. Separated us. It was a custom to separate brothers at prep school. I think it was quite a good thing. It taught us to stand on our own feet a bit you see. I mean there were a couple of boys from South Africa I remember called Bourke. Now they were together at my prep school and they were again together at Harrow in the same house, well they must have spent all that long time together. Well surely it'd have been better for 'em to have to fit themselves in with other people a bit more. They were very nice fellows.

We used to go by train to school. I think the school had a coach at Victoria as far as I remember. Parents all collected there and chucked their children in. Mother or somebody used to take me there. We used to go and have tea somewhere and then she used to take me along, chuck me over to the master who was collecting 'em. I had a very cheerful time at school. I thoroughly enjoyed it. I remember feeling a bit upset you know just before the train left, but once I got there I liked it. A chap called Slade was the most well qualified of all the staff, and he was at least three hundred per cent the best teacher in the place. He was a dear; he was very ugly, a charming man and a brilliant teacher, really brilliant. He taught most things; classics and English, not mathematics at all. And also quite a lot of English literature and that sort of thing he interested one in. You weren't just stuffed with Scott and Dickens; he fished out all sorts of things for you. Fletcher; taught me to appreciate Shakespeare and Milton and Malory. Not all just stock things, all sorts of people. Browning he was rather keen about.

I think at my prep school I had tuppence a week, which was a lot of money. When I got to Harrow I used to have five pounds in the summer term and three pounds in the two winter terms. I spent it on all sorts of oddments; books occasionally, a certain amount of food. No I was never a great person for sweets. I did earn a lot of money breeding ferrets actually. They were quite valuable. You used to get about seven and eight bob for a ferret. My father and I used to breed 'em, get quite a nice stock up and sell 'em off in the autumn.

I was seven years at my prep school and I was only three at Harrow; it made much more impression on me. You see I was growing up by then; I took things in rather more. At Harrow there is no junior house at all. Nobody went till they were nearly fourteen. You had to pass a common entrance. Actually I took a scholarship because my father told me he couldn't afford to send me there unless I got a scholarship so I worked jolly hard and got a scholarship; I don't know what – some absurd sum of fifty pounds a year or something, which was quite a lot you see then. I suppose the fees then were about seventy pounds a year, with your boarding fees on top.

At Harrow it was much more your personal character that made you popular or unpopular. [Games?] Yes you were in the limelight if you were good at games but you weren't necessarily liked. The importance was not on your standing; the importance was on your manners, behaviour and general conduct. I know my housemaster for instance, he was much more concerned at you telling a lie than he would have been about you going into a pub and having a couple of bottles of beer. He'd have probably beaten you for that but if you told him lies about it he was really upset about it, you see what I mean; that's the sort of standard. Mind you, he was a good old drunkard himself, so perhaps he sympathized with that sort of thing a bit!

You met all sorts of people. I mean you met the country squire's son, who probably did nothing, knew nothing except farming – living in the country. And you also met what I call the sort of international set and rich business people, and as I say a lot of foreigners. But they were all rather inclined to be out of the top drawer. When John Lyon founded the school it was for local boys, and there were always places available, but they were seldom taken up. The only case I can remember is Turnbull who later became Captain of Glamorgan County Cricket Club, and he came there. He was a policeman's son from Ilford or Highgate, and he did extremely well at school, not sure whether he became head of the school; he was certainly captain of cricket.

We swallowed the roughnecks quite happily and we also swallowed the super snobs quite happily, but we laughed at 'em generally. I think Harrow is very catholic in its tastes and always was, I mean turning out people who would be useful as administrators and things of that sort, turning out decent people for the Army, a certain amount of literary people. [The aim of the school?] I think it was turning out quite a good standard of not too hidebound people with decent manners and so on. We were very cosmopolitan you know at Harrow. I mean people always think of English public schools as being awfully stiff and that sort of thing. I think they were always very aware of class which was a very real thing in those days, but there was absolutely no colour prejudice or anything of that sort as far as I know. I never came across it. I mean, we had Indians in our house, and one Chinese and various people. If a person was dark you'd call him a Nig but only if you liked him. You wouldn't have said it if you didn't like him.

There was one house that was full of Jews, a lot of 'em foreign Jews; and I've sat in form next to Mr Nubar Gulbenkian. The Jews we envied very much because they didn't have to go to chapel. There was a little place we called the synagogue which was originally a practice place for music, perhaps three or four music rooms, but they gutted it and turned it into a synagogue. But they were darned lucky; they only had half an hour on Saturday or Friday (I've forgotten which day it is, Saturday isn't it?) and that's all they got. Lucky devils, they got up half an hour later than the rest of us.

You had certain houses you despised frightfully and home boarders were always looked on with grave suspicion. They lived at home altogether; their parents lived in Harrow and I suppose it was cheaper to do that than to pay for boarding fees. A chap called Pember I was very fond of. His father was Warden of All Souls, Oxford. That's the one without undergraduates, isn't it? Very academic. Pember was clever but awfully nice – very fond of him.

He was killed in the First World War. Then there was a chap called Scott whom I was rather fond of, chiefly because he was a little bit of an outsider; somehow he didn't fit in frightfully well in the house and for that reason I rather liked him. And there was an Indian fellow, not in my house, I was very fond of, Karenjit Singh – very nice fellow he was.

In the morning you waited till the bell went for going up to chapel. You then leapt out of bed and you rushed downstairs to the basement and into a cold bath. You rushed upstairs drying yourself as you went, chucked some clothes on, went off to chapel which was I think at seven-fifteen, as far as I remember, and probably later in the winter. Then you came back, had breakfast at nine. And I think the first school was at quarter to ten. But you see Harrow was run rather on what I call university lines. You lived in a house; that was your home, but everybody in the house went off in different directions to different masters, different forms, different everything you see. So it was up to you to get there. There was quite a reasonable amount of prep, every evening up till nine. Supposed to be doing prep from eight till nine but you never did prep, you chatted to your friends and played chess and that sort of thing. And then nine o'clock prayers and you said good-night to your housemaster and then rushed off and tried to scrabble through your prep for next morning.

Sunday was an awful dull day. You had chapel in the morning and an hour's scripture lesson which usually used to consist in the upper school of reading Greek Testament, which was very boring; and I don't know what the junior forms did, I can't remember. And then in the afternoon you went for a walk or something of that sort. And when I first went you had to wear your Sunday clothes the whole day. But just about the time I finished we started being allowed to wear bluers [blue flannel blazer] and straw hats instead of a tail coat and toppers; but not to go to chapel with of course.

I knew several beaks quite well, used to go to tea with them sort of thing. Oh we were very much on what I'd call university terms there, do you know what I mean? I liked my housemasters, both of 'em, very much. One was rather aloof and rather critical of one's form masters, but I mean Oily Warner was admired because he was a brilliant scholar and a very witty and amusing scholar. He was purely classics and history. Oh and Inky Stevens was classics too, he was very much admired for his mordant wit. I think he was a number one Balliol man actually; he really was brilliant. And there was old Waards whom we adored, name was Edwards. He taught mathematics and he had an extraordinary voice; always knew when Waards was coming up – out of one of the school buildings you'd hear a chorus of 'Waards! Waards! Waards!' And his famous dictum always was when he sat down in school, he said, 'I hear you boys have been trying to pull my leg. I must tell you my name is Edwaards not Edwaards.' He got squeaks of joy from everybody. He took it all in good part. I think a master at Harrow who didn't get his leg pulled occasionally would have wondered what was wrong. Oh I must say one thing, of course my form master did introduce me to Horace, which I adore still. Love his poems. They're delightful.

I was a classical scholar so I did mostly classics. I was sort of standard at classical stuff. I wasn't a sort of high class scholar exactly, but I mean after I left school I could read Greek perfectly comfortably and happily and that sort of thing. At my prep school once a week a fellow used to come and talk about stinks and gases and things, make nasty smells you know. I don't think science was very interesting then. I was keen on stinks at Harrow and when I got up to the upper fifth form one was allowed to specialize, and I dropped my classics then and went into doing stinks and mathematics because they interested me. I decided I wanted to specialize in science chiefly because I'd sort of neglected it before you see. By then I'd got up to the sixth form and I was quite good at classical stuff.

I don't know anything about the modern side. We did French and German and those things. We were compelled to do a little French, in which I succeeded in avoiding learning anything. The French set I used to belong to – I mean if you didn't want to do anything you sat at the back and read – French comic newspapers or *La Vie Parisienne* and things. Probably learned just as much French as if you were listening to the master. And eventually I thought I ought to learn some French and I asked for extra French lessons. Old Minssen who was a dear old boy used to have me over and give me coffee and a cigarette and read Victor Hugo, which I learned a lot of French from.

Some of maths were a bit grim. The purely technical maths were taught by a fellow called Russell who afterwards became head of Rossall School and he was a bit grim; he was a good teacher though. Then on what I call the more practical side, you know, ballistics and all these sort of things, old Siddons used to take that and he was a darling. Very fond of old Siddons, I used to go and have tea with him. Nice old boy. Music and painting at Harrow were thought definitely queer. Well funnily enough that's possibly why my friend Scott was a little bit sort of out of the normal run. He played the organ and he was quite a good musician and I liked him. I can remember ragging the music master, Dr Buck, because he was a Liberal. We used to pull his leg about it, but that's the only political thing I can ever remember.

The war was on so I left, but otherwise I'd have stayed on another half year. I wanted to get into something with horses you see. I heard that the father of a fellow schoolboy was in command of the Devon Yeomanry at the time, and he wanted some more young officers, supernumerary young officers, and I said, 'Oh well would he see me?' you see and arranged an interview. I was furious when the regiment went out to the Middle East with their horses and I was left behind. When I came out of the Army at the end of the war I counted up and there were only eleven people to my knowledge alive who I'd known at school. Sounds terrible, doesn't it? There were more of course but they'd disappeared. I've found some of them since.

7
Esther Stokes

Esther Mary Scott Stokes was born in 1895 at No. 2, West Drive, Streatham Park.[1] Her Stokes grandfather was the fourth son of a parson who became converted to Roman Catholicism while studying to be a clergyman. He later married and had seven children. The girls married and did not have careers; the four sons were all distinguished in their professions.[2] Philip Ffolliot Stokes, Esther's father, who was born in 1852 was a Chancery barrister, a Bencher of Lincoln's Inn. He married Mary Rapier, an only child. Her family's firm was Ransome & Rapier of Ipswich, manufacturers of agricultural machinery. There were nine children. The eldest, a daughter, died in infancy and John the second child died in 1912. There were two girls older than Esther, Judith born in 1891 and Susan born in 1893. After Esther, came Richard (1897), Anthony (1899), Mary (1900) and Margaret (1904).[3]

Marriage was the expected career of the girls and all except one of them became wives. Richard and Anthony, after fighting on the Western Front, read engineering at Cambridge and later joined the family firm; Richard in 1938 became Labour MP for Ipswich. Esther did volunteer work during the First World War and in 1920 married Charles Glyn Evans, of the Air Ministry who later became Deputy Secretary. They had three children. From 1929 to 1939 she 'slummed' in Notting Dale with the Misses Alexander. In 1951 she was made a JP and later did ten years as Essex visiting magistrate to Holloway Prison. In 1957 she was appointed to the Management Committee of the Royal Eastern Counties Hospital and served until her retirement in 1975. She was President of the Women's Institute for twelve years. Her husband was Church of England and ten years older 'but neither of these facts prevented us enjoying a long and varied life together for forty years. My greatest real triumph was to be chairman of the Governing Body of

the Church of England Controlled School in Feering, Essex. (N.B.
RC Chairman of a C of E controlled school!)' Her latest triumph
was the award on 7 June 1979 of the Bene Merenti Papal Medal by
John Paul II.

Esther Stokes herself emphasizes two notable aspects of her
childhood, its tight seclusion within the family unit and its marked
separation from adulthood. The Stokes family was a very self-
contained unit, 'almost an institution.' The girls especially, at
home and on holiday, drew on each other for companionship and
fun and seem to have had few friends outside the family. Was this,
as Esther Stokes believes, because of the family size? Obviously
children with brothers and sisters might appear to have less
incentive to make friends, but this was not usually a disincentive in
working-class families and in the professional class large families
were often very sociable. Perhaps the Stokes' social class and
minority religion separated their children from possible friendships.

Mr Stokes' profession placed him in the front rank of the upper
middle class; this would restrict his wife and children's range of
friends and acquaintances more than his own, for he might be a
golfing friend of a well-to-do shopkeeper on the one hand or a
political supporter and friend of Herbert Asquith on the other, but
his wife and daughters would not mix socially either with trade or
with London society. In addition, the suburban environment of
Streatham would not provide many suitable friends. The local
doctor was very much 'not one of the family' whereas in Kensington, where the Stokeses moved when Esther was seventeen, they
would have met doctors' families like Mary Stocks's at Queen's
Gate Terrace who were like the Stokes connected with the arts
being related to the architect Halsey Ricardo and the Wedgwoods
and Stracheys.[4] The Stokes' social sphere was restricted still
further by religious differences which at that time were keenly felt
between Catholics and Anglicans. Indeed, the only two families
with whom the Stokes were intimate were the distinguished legal
Catholic families of Lord Russell of Killowen, and Charles James
Mathew, KC. Catholicism, too, would have separated them from
vicarage families and the contact with priests and nuns did not, by
definition, bring them acquaintance with other families.

Another important consequence of the family religion was the
choice of schools for the children. The boys went to the Catholic

public school Downside which cut them off from women and girls to an even greater degree than boys in an Anglican public school, whose schoolmasters and housemasters might have wives and families. For the girls a convent school in Clapham several miles away was chosen, where they attended daily but were attached to the boarding department. Boarding schools for girls were becoming quite popular with middle and upper class girls from about fifteen in the Edwardian period, but many parents still considered it quite inappropriate to send a girl away from her home when the home was to be her life-long environment. Sport and learning would not only be useless to her, they might make her into a tomboy or bluestocking, and so less attractive as a future wife and mother. Day schools were suspect too because of contamination with girls from trade backgrounds. But the compromise reached by Esther's parents resulted in her having no local friends and, by cutting her off from the social life at school, increased her dependence on the family.

Yet she was drawn out of the family to awareness of conditions and problems in other classes by the philanthropic, radical outlook which was so very much a feature of the independent professional class. Her mother set an example of charitable acts and by taking Esther to the exhibition of sweated industries organized by the *Daily News* in 1906, opened her eyes to poverty and exploitation beyond the ministrations of private charity. In 1911 therefore she reacted differently from most people of her class to the sight of poor children cold and barefoot, being prompted to an inner affirmation of solidarity with the working class, and when she had finished her education she was introduced by the Mathew family to care-committee work. Care-committees were started by Margaret Frere, a relation of the Stracheys, to implement school meals and medical inspection in the London County Council area. Esther visited families and investigated their conditions, doing in effect voluntary social work.[5]

The separation from adults which the Stokes children experienced is very typical of that small section of the middle class which could afford to have a nanny and a nursery. This arrangement insured a geographical separation of parents and children in the house, and also separated children from the servants whose domain was the kitchen, and possibly a dining room or sitting room of their own. The children lived in the nursery and the parents in the drawing room and dining room, and the times and occasions on which children were with their parents were strictly regulated. Some mothers spent time in the nursery but it was sometimes regarded as interfering, and a mother was not expected to do so except to kiss her children good-night. Fathers were not home for the hour after tea when children always came to the drawing room and if they wished to have regular contact with their children (and many did not) they had to set aside time for seeing them in their own quarters as Mr Stokes did, or allow them to have dinner at night earlier than usual. It was in order to see more of their father that the Stokes girls had dinner downstairs at the age of twelve. In many families girls stayed in the schoolroom until they 'came out' at seventeen or eighteen while their brothers had dinner downstairs as soon as they went away to school, sometimes as young as nine, but this was more common in the upper class who would usually have a governess for their daughters. This separation made for a more formal relationship between mother and child, as the nanny was the person to whom the child would go with aches and pains and troubles. The absolute authority of parents in this class, and the formal regulation of the household, meant that incidents seldom arose requiring punishment. Families where no child was ever given even the slightest kind of corporal punishment were probably commonest in the middle and upper class in the Edwardian period. A word, a look or eventually banishment to a far off room were enough. Even in the working class, where hard-pressed parents in crowded accommodation without the help of nannies might have been expected to use their hand or an implement to discipline their children, it was not a common occurrence though it was often threatened. When it took place it was usually only once in order to teach a child who was master, a lesson that was easily learned.

NOTES

1 I interviewed Esther Stokes in 1974.
2 Adrian Stokes was a painter and academician; Sir Wilfred Stokes was an engineer, inventor of the Stokes gun and head of Ransome & Rapier of Ipswich; Leonard Stokes FRIBA was an architect, he designed the Stokes' Streatham house 'excellently proportioned, sober, early neo-Georgian, with a fine grouping of chimneys on the hipped roof'

(Nikolaus Pevsner, *The Buildings of England: London*, 1942, vol. II, p. 444).

3 Esther Stokes wished the following biographical details of her brothers to be noted, 'Richard Rapier Stokes joined the RFA, 83rd Battery aged nineteen in 1916 and served two and a half years on the Western Front without a scratch. He gained the MC and Bar and Croix de Guerre, resigning the Army as substantive Major in 1919.' He became managing director of Ransome & Rapier and was the first Labour MP for Ipswich. 'As Richard was unmarried I often acted as hostess for him when he was Minister of Works and later Lord Privy Seal. The significance of his life is that he was the first commoner RC to hold cabinet rank after 400 years (since the Reformation).'

Anthony Scott Stokes joined the Irish Guards and went out to the Western front aged nineteen and was shot in the head three months later going over the top in the Battle of the Somme, was on the danger list for three weeks and survived to the age of seventy-three years. He lived in Hintlesham where in 1950 he started a musical festival which after a hard struggle was granted trust status.

4 Mary Stocks, *My Commonplace Book* (London, 1970), pp. 12–17.

5 Ibid., pp. 57–8.

I was born in 1895 and we moved from Streatham after my eldest brother died and it was such a grief to my parents; and in those days people were tremendously affected by family circumstances, and although they'd built this beautiful house they wouldn't stay there, oh they couldn't stay there, after this precious boy had died. And that was 1912. So I was seventeen by the time I came right into London to Palace Gate, no. 5 Palace Gate up by the Broad walk there, the top of Gloucester Road. And we went to Streatham because my grandmother lived there and my mother being the only child. I think my father would have liked to move into London sooner, or move nearer, because it was such a long journey for him to Chambers, but of course my mother didn't like to leave my grandmother so the house was built near her. But it was a great journey for my father. We weren't carriage folk, we didn't keep our own stables, but we had a livery stables which looked after us and he had to drive to the station every morning, go up to Victoria, and then either get a cab or the 25 bus round to Holborn to his Chambers in Stone Buildings. And then all that weary way back again. It was tremendous. How he did it I don't really know. He was always very very tired because he worked very hard, and very seldom had time for lunch. They used to send in sandwiches from a very famous sandwich house called Sweetings. They used to send him in sandwiches to eat in his Chambers, in between his cases. But when he came back to dinner, many and many and many's the time his head has gone down, he's fallen asleep at the table. They were very courageous people you know.

He wouldn't be home in time for the younger ones to see him, but the older ones we were promoted to sit up to dinner. I think I was about twelve when I was allowed to stay up for dinner, and then we dressed you know. And so in that way we older ones would see him. But he was a very devoted father. One of my most vivid memories is that in the morning he got up very early; the kitchen maid used to knock on his door at half past six to tell him it was half past six, and being disciplined by being brought up in the seminary at Ushaw, 'cause at one time he thought he was going to be a priest, he leapt out of bed and that was it.

And soon after seven, beautifully shaven, wearing a lovely camel dressing-gown, beautifully put on, no sloppiness you know, properly put on and tied, he would make the rounds and come and see us all. He used to come and see us all as we were either still in bed or getting up. Visit us all. Every single day. And this I so vividly remember because the year that King Edward died, my father was a devoted Gilbert and Sullivan fan, and he loved *The Yeomen of the Guard* best, and we all, some of us I don't know which, were going to be taken to the Savoy Theatre for *The Yeomen of the Guard*. And he came in looking rather solemn and said, 'My dears, we shan't be going to the theatre tonight because the King has died and there will be no theatre tonight.' I remember that so well.

I don't think I was selfish about it. I don't think my first reactions were 'Oh poor us!' But I felt it was rather solemn, because my father was very very easy going. He was tremendously Catholic in that way you know, he wasn't going to let anything worry him. And my mother was a convert to Catholicism, and she had a much more austere approach to the problems of life. And if my father brought in a yet bigger pot of caviare for dinner, 'cause he was very fond of it, she'd say, 'Oh Phil, we haven't paid the school fees yet.' And he didn't mind. 'Oh,' he said, 'Not to worry! It's a poor heart that never rejoices!'

Father was very approachable in what I hesitate to call a superficial way. But I think the mark of him was that he was so tremendously simple and he hated anything (so did the artist uncle of mine) hated anything in the nature of showing off or hypocrisy, and I've often thought, I wish in a way he had talked to us more. He must have been able to talk to us a lot about this, that and the other, but out of some sort of, I thought it was a kind of simplicity, that he didn't want to impose himself, conversation and day to day things were the rule, not digging into things really. Well he was a Chancery barrister, of course their law is so much more abstruse and rare and fine, that there's nothing much that interests children really. But we used to be taken to the Law Courts. Yes, we used to be taken and then his clerk would find some little case that they thought suitable for us to go in and listen for a little while. And I've always loved the law.

Unfortunately my maternal grandfather died while I was too small to have really known him, but to have loved him. But my grandmother I was not fond of. She was a spoilt, tiresome little bejewelled creature with diamond stars all down her front, literally five diamond stars and each of us five girls got one. And she had no thought or perception of what life was really about. Not at all. And my mother was quite different. She had a very strong character and I suppose she was fairly intelligent. I don't think she was very clever, but she had a tremendous sense of what the world was all about, but always very Anglican, or really more accurately Protestant I think. She was so correct you know. I never really loved her. I had enormous respect for her and her judgment, and all she did and everything, but there was no warmth you know.

It was all the plans, and she had the two houses and the eight children and the seven maids and the gardeners, and everything to arrange for because she never had a housekeeper, and so everything really devolved on her. And she was meticulous about her own behaviour, knowing the responsibility she had of these children and the whole family set-up. She kept the most rigorous accounts. And if she went out and we went out together and we went on the bus and everything, when we got back she would want to know exactly what, she'd enter up every day, what she'd spent on the buns, on the bus fares or whatever she'd bought. It was all entered in this book. And she would wrestle with it until she got it right. She wouldn't let tuppence or threepence go. She was a tremendous person. She really was.

But she was tremendously aware of other people's troubles. In those days the poverty was something appalling. And the tramps! Down in Streatham there were a great many tramps and of course there is a kind of grapevine. They all know to tell each other where to come. And one of the things my mother did, she kept a store of paper blankets. They were sort of quilted, and when these wretched men came, she always fed them. She would let the cook send out some food for them and everything. And then she used to issue these paper blankets in the hopes that if they were sleeping rough they'd be warm. And if she saw a stray cat, do you know what she used to do (and there used to be a lot of stray cats too), she used to go the nearest shop and buy eggs and she used to break the eggs, and allow the egg to fall into the corner, wherever the cat was, so that the cat had a drink, food and drink. On top of having eight children. The control she had of the situation!

And as an example of the tremendous discipline and courage of my mother, when my little sister was going to have her appendix out and everything was all prepared and the surgeon and the anaesthetist and everybody'd arrived – this was in London. And she smelled the anaesthetic you see, and she turned in terror to my mother and said, 'Ooh they're going to do what they did to Margaret,' 'cause she hadn't been told you see. 'Don't let them take me', she said. And my mother said, 'No, Mary, I won't let them take you because you're going upstairs yourself.' And the poor little creature walked up the stairs. And I think all that made for this tremendous, in a sense, respect and also in a sense separation of a child from its parents, 'cause they were such different creatures. They didn't seem to share anything of your own experiences. I don't think I felt physically frightened. But I was in great awe.

We always went to the Academy of course to see my Uncle's pictures and then we'd go to the National Gallery and she wasn't a highbrow, we never got as far as the Soane Museum or Bethnal Green or anywhere there, but my father was very cultivated and I mean we always at meals, if something came up, a word or a little bit of history or something we didn't know, we always got a reference book and looked into it you know. They didn't go to pantomimes, they didn't like them. No, I don't remember being taken to anything other than school activities and Gilbert and Sullivan. I don't remember anything else. We rarely went to concerts. We did have dinner parties. In our case it was nearly always the family friends coming. They didn't have to do any formal entertaining. They were utterly independent. And there was no formal entertaining certainly, so they only had who they wanted. And there wasn't much of the protocol.

We had a wonderful gramophone, not a gramophone a musical box, which we loved and we used to jig along and dance to that. But my parents didn't make any music. There was no piano in Streatham but we had one in London. By that time I was particularly interested in trying to play the piano and we had a piano in the London house. We used to play croquet on the same tennis lawn we didn't have a special lawn for it. And we none of us played golf. So that was it I think. We played a great many card games. We played a lot of card games, 'cause that is a resource for a large family on a wet day, various forms of patience and simple bridge we played. I suppose whist. We never played chess, at least I don't remember, we played draughts and endless pencil and paper games that children like, consequences and lists and tele-grams. And then we loved charades. We were great ones for dressing up and playing charades at special times.

Father liked billiards. He used to go to his club and have a game pretty nearly every week. He belonged to the Arts Club in Dover Street. He used to go there on Saturday afternoons I seem to remember. And he used to take us along with him and leave us in a tea shop on the corner of Dover Street while he went and saw his old cronies. And then he came back for us. By this time I suppose we were old enough to be put in charge of the girl in the tea shop for half an hour or so. We played games more particularly in the holidays, because somehow in London, I suppose there was school and all this sort of thing going on all the time, and as we went twice a year to Cornwall we had more time there. Christmas we were in London, but then Christmas is such a busy time in itself. Except for the odd charade there isn't much time for anything else. In Cornwall we'd get up plays and act them.

Holidays were absolutely always in Cornwall. There was no alternative. Nowhere. When we lived in Streatham, Rickards, the famous bus people who still exist, used to send two small horse buses. And the family and the luggage all piled into these two buses. And the children in freshly starched pinafores were allowed to sit on the box with the coachman. There was a place beside the coachman, then there was always a little bench behind, rather like a real coach. And we used to be allowed to climb up there and drive from Streatham over Battersea Rise through Hyde Park to Paddington station to catch the express to Cornwall. And in those days if you had ten tickets they gave you a coach to yourself. It was called a saloon. Free. And they gave you this saloon. And it consisted of a double carriage with lavatories in the middle, and a long table in each. And the family used to be in the front part of this coach and the maids used to be in the back and the luggage, 'cause my father wouldn't have the luggage put into the guards van 'cause he said when we got to the other end there was such a fuss sorting it out, and he must have the luggage with him in the coach, so it was all put in the coach with him. And we were very excited about the journey for two reasons, one was that we always had tongue sandwiches and I love tongue. And the other was it was the only time we saw the maids without caps, because they wore aprons, oh yes aprons to come and serve this picnic for us, but they didn't wear their caps. And it was so exciting to see them without caps on!

All the maids went with us and then the caretakers would move into the London house, a man and his wife. And another interesting thing about family life in those days, my mother always had an extra kitchen maid, a second kitchen maid, in the summer holidays just to prepare the vegetables, because the mere fact of beans and peas and potatoes and carrots for so many, it's a morning's work. And there weren't any potato peelers or any mixers or anything. It's all had to be done by hand. In the holidays we girls had a very nice sitting room with a piano in it and we were supposed to keep that tidy. Of course it was only a question of sweeper and a duster. And we looked after this chapel which we had. We cleaned the brass and swept it out. Father Lloyd was the parish priest of Streatham. And he was the one who baptized us all and heard all our first confessions and the sacraments and came always to us for holidays and it was for him that the stable was converted into a chapel so that he wouldn't have to drive in a pony trap to say mass at the convent three miles away.

Father Corbishley was the parish priest of St Mawgan which was our parish in Cornwall and he was also the chaplain to the convent which was the Convent of the Carmelite nuns. And of course he was a friend of the family and often came to us, and we rather ragged the poor old man really. We used to play cards with him. We always said he cheated. I don't think he did really but we said he did. The boys had lots of friends to stay from Downside, they were at Downside School, and they used to bring friends home, particularly the young priests, who having taken the vows of poverty never had much opportunity for holidays. And they used to come and stay and play tennis and bathe with us and go long expeditions. And of course having the chapel was a great advantage 'cause we had daily mass. My grandmother never stayed with us. She stayed in a hotel nearby. But during the holiday times some of the favourite uncles and aunts used to come to stay. The favourite ones were the artist and his wife and the engineer and his wife. The architect one who had his own four children never came to stay. But the artist had no children and the youngest had no children. We were very fond of them. We loved them coming to stay. We thought it was tremendous fun. They'd play games with us and the engineer one helped my brothers to build a sand yacht which sort of raced along the sands.

In Cornwall I can remember that we had two very special treats. One of my sisters had a birthday in the holidays, and so we always had a special picnic for her birthday, and she always chose whether we'd go up on to the moors or whether we'd go along to one of the further beaches. And you know she chose 'cause it was her birthday. And then always for many years we used to be taken one day in the holidays to Truro which was sixteen miles, in wagon-ettes, and there put on a little steamer to go down from Truro to Falmouth, down the River Fal. And then we had lunch in the hotel there, the Green Bank, and then we came back again up the river again and then drove back home. It was quite a day.

Oh yes, we had Christmas and birthday presents but of course not toys like children have today. Not the endless toys. But otherwise we didn't have presents. And we'd save up and so on and get things. There was a famous stores in London called the Hay-market. It's like the Army and Navy only it was in the Haymarket. And they were called the Civil Service Stores in the Haymarket. And one of the treats at Christmas was to be taken up to the Haymarket stores to choose the crackers. And each one of us were allowed to choose a box of crackers. That I very well remember. I don't remember who got the presents or how. They were quite modest; we didn't have very elaborate things at all.

The house in Streatham was a neo-Georgian house built by an architect uncle. You went in through a beautiful porch into a little lobby and into a big hall. And on the right was the drawing room with a big bow window; the hall; the drawing room; then the stairs on your left; the dining room behind the drawing room with another big bow window and then the pantry and the kitchen premises at the back of that. Then upstairs there was my mother and father's room, I suppose over the hall. And the boys' room was over the gents' cloakroom, a huge place to put bicycles and coats and sticks and every sort of thing in it, it had a black and white checked marble floor. The boys' room was above that. And then

32 Geoffrey Brady's grandmother.   33 Geoffrey's grandfather.

34 Geoffrey grown up.
Probably just after the First
World War.

35 Henry Vigne at the age of about thirteen, before he went to Harrow.

36 Henry's mother.

37 Henry in the Cricket First XI at Warren Hill school. He is seated at the end of the middle row. This was his final year at Warren Hill.

38 The Stokes on the beach in Cornwall. The three girls are from left to right Mary, Esther and Susan. A friend is wearing white clothes and next to him is Anthony. Dick is in the foreground.

39 Susan Stokes aged four years.

40 Anthony Stokes in Cornwall aged seven or eight years.

41 No. 2, West Drive, Streatham Park designed by Leonard Stokes, FRIBA, Esther's uncle; the Stokes lived here until 1912.

42 The eldest and youngest Stokes girls in 1908. Judith is eighteen and
Margaret is four. The dresses were of identical blue cotton with white feather
stitching.

43 Mary Fenwick Stokes with her first born son, John. The date is about 1889.
The St Bernard dogs preceded the arrival of the first child.

44 Philip Ffolliot Stokes with two of the St Bernard dogs.

45 A view of Tregurrian House showing the chapel built on at the side. Here the Stokes family spent all their summer and Easter holidays. The house is in Watergate Bay, three miles north of Newquay in Cornwall.

46 Esther Stokes' Grandmother Rapier with Aunt Polly Jeffries on Watergate Beach, Cornwall. Besides shading their faces from the sun with hats both women carry parasols. A sunburned skin was considered very unbecoming.

47 Esther aged approximately eighteen months.

48 Jock Yorke with his mother taken at Halton Place in 1905.

49 Jock aged about three or four is mounted on Mick, a Cleveland Bay carriage horse at Halton. Jim Doyle the coachman who taught Jock to ride is holding the horse's head.

50 Jock with his younger brother Peter and their grandfather J. B. E. Stansfeld who was on a visit to Halton in about 1907–8. The bulldog was called Jimmy.

51 Joan Poynder as a child in fancy dress.

52 Joan in party clothes. Note the white gloves.

53 Bobbie Somerset, a cousin of the present Duke of Beaufort, and Joan at the beach at Filey.

54 A flight of steps leading up to the south terrace at Hartham Park, the Poynder's Wiltshire house.

55 Hartham Park, the house and its setting in 1909.

56 Joan Poynder as a bridesmaid.

the children's rooms were all round over the kitchens and over the dining room. T' nursery was over the dining room. There was another flight of stairs up to a series of rooms where the maids lived, which had these mansard windows, then a big garden with clipped hedges and formal rose beds and a tennis court. And we all had a little plot of our own, stone flagged, so we were supposed to look after it, some of us were keen and some not so keen, planting things like love-in-the-mist and all the things children grow. And lovely wide gravel paths which were great fun for bicycling. We used to race round them playing all sorts of bicycling games.

Mother would go down and see her cook in the morning, to give orders and that sort of thing. And thereafter, if she wanted to speak to her for any reason other bells were rung and the cook would come up. No mistress would ever go downstairs. She wouldn't impinge on their privacy and what they were doing after ten in the morning, whenever it was she went. We weren't allowed in the kitchen and we were never taught any cooking. The cook had a kitchen maid and she also had the outdoor man who did the sort of coals. He was a daily. Then there was the parlourmaid. Well the hierarchy was the cook and the kitchenmaid, the parlourmaid, the head housemaid, the underhousemaid and two in the nursery, the nurse and the undernurse. It made seven. My father didn't like men-servants. He didn't think that it was the right thing for men. He never liked it. Among my father's friends there were very very few men servants. Perhaps they couldn't afford them.

There was a gardener and a gardener's boy. I didn't have a governess, but the little boys, Dick and Anthony, they had a governess pre going to Downside. But they went to Downside poor little blighters when they were eight and nine, but they didn't go to a school before that, they went straight from a governess to big school. I think that was very hard on them. Terrible shock.

We had one big day nursery and then we had two night nurseries and then my eldest sister had a room to herself and the two boys had a room to themselves so there must have been four bedrooms for the children, and then the nurse I suppose slept with the baby. I'm sure she did in fact. And the undernurse would sleep upstairs, share rooms with the other maids. All our meals were in the day nursery until we were old enough to go down. We used to go down to lunch on Saturdays and Sundays 'cause my father was at home. The babies wouldn't but the bigger ones went down to lunch on

Saturdays and Sundays. And then as I say when we were about twelve I suppose we were allowed to sit up to late dinner at night.

I can't seem to remember that Mother spent time in the nursery. I seem to remember a funny character called Betty, whom I think I was fond of, she used to come in and do the ironing. I think she used to come sometimes and help put us to bed and we used to think that was rather fun. My very earliest memory was when my brother was born in 1899 when I was four and I really do remember this. It was teatime and Aggie, the old nurse said to us, 'Now, children after tea I don't want you to romp round' (there was a sort of gallery thing), 'I don't want you to romp about. I want you to be rather quiet tonight and stay in the nursery because your mother's got a bad headache and I don't want any noise.' And this was so surprising 'cause we never had this drama of Mother with a bad headache. And the next morning we were taken in to see her in the large four poster bed, and there was this baby in bed with her, this little boy, and I must have been just about four, but I really do remember it. It's not imagination. I realize now why my mother wasn't more active in playing games with us, no doubt there was another baby on the way.

And after tea of course, there's this great ceremony of nanny dressing you up into clean pinnies and things and down we went to spend the hour with my mother. I never remember Mother not being there. And my vivid recollection is that she would sit on a very big sofa and we'd sit all round her and we took turns sitting beside her so that the one who was alongside her could see the book, and she read to us. Reading was quite a feature; all the traditional things; George MacDonald and Mrs Gaskell and all those things, *Lob-lie-by-the-Fire* and *Jackanapes* and Mrs Ewing and Mrs Molesworth and the fairy tales, the Andrew Lang fairy tales were a great feature, the blue one and the red one and Grimm's and Andersen. But not books again like the children have today, I mean you didn't really have any new books for children. It was just all those books.

I'm sure bedtime was very early, I'm sure we were never allowed to sit up late, and it was all very much controlled to sort of twenty minute intervals. We'd leave you know, and we were made very responsible that we watched our own time to go. The discipline was pretty terrific really. I mean, take teatime, always bread and butter first you know. Never any jam or anything till you'd had your bread and butter first. Aggie'd watch everything. And you know the discipline in the nursery was tremendous. We had a big fire of course and a high fire guard and it was the days of button boots and Aggie'd say, 'Come along children, now we're going out for a walk', and we'd all rush to the fireguard to get our favourite button hooks to button our boots up with. I can remember that very well.

At meals we had to behave you know it was no romping. And as we got older we used to rag terribly, all young people will. And my mother sometimes used to get very exasperated and she used to say, this was particularly in the holidays, she used to say, 'All right now, this lunchtime I'm having the boys on one side and the girls on the other.' So we'd sit down with about five boys that side and five girls this side, with visitors you see. And then my mother and father at the end and we always had two joints at every meal. My father carved one and my mother the other because there was such a lot of people to feed. And we were all expected to be down in the drawing room at least five minutes before the dinner bell. It wasn't approved that we were running downstairs as the others went into meals. We'd say to each other 'You go and ask Mother need we change tonight so we can play another set of tennis.' 'Oh you go tonight. You go and ask her.' Then one of us would pluck up courage to go and ask if we could stay on playing tennis, which meant that we didn't change.

We weren't interested in visitors, not a bit. We were only interested in ourselves and our mother got desperate because the neighbours would invite us to their parties and we didn't want to go. And at last she said, 'Look please forgive me, but I've got so many children and they're so wrapped up in what they're doing and I'm very much afraid they don't like parties.' But that was such a mistake, because we didn't learn to mix easily with other people, to accept other people. That I think was a bad feature of a big family. The family was so large by the time you'd contained the staff and all that it was almost like a small institution. And there was a kind of code. I think of course we must have had moments of unhappiness and restlessness, all children do, but that's only part of the need to get away so to say, to get out of the nest. I don't think it was any feeling other than great respect and in the case of my father I was tremendously fond of him. They would never lay hands on us. And I don't think we were ever punished. We might have been punished by not having perhaps sweets after lunch, whenever it was we had them, but we were never sent supperless to bed or anything like that.

Father used to say Grace. He reduced it to an absolute minimum. Benedictus Benedicat. Let the blessed bless. That was all. Benedictus Benedicat. I can't remember and yet I imagine we must have had some sort of grace in the nursery because I'm sure Aggie was always teaching us to make the sign of the cross properly, not to be sloppy. So I expect we did. She was a very staunch Anglican, a churchgoer, and she read her Bible and she was very upright in every way, and never looked like changing. Never, never, never. In fact I think she thoroughly disapproved of us, of Catholicism.

We rather lived in a Catholic world, the Mathew family and the Russell family particularly. They were two big legal families. And you may find this difficult to believe but you must believe it, that times were very different, and if at dances your partners became inquisitive we definitely tried not to let them know we were Catholic, because if they discovered it they didn't come back for the next dance. You know we had programmes with little pencils and you booked up the dances. But on more than one occasion a young man has cut me having discovered. Oh no there was a tremendously anti-Catholic atmosphere as a child, well not as a child, as a young woman. There was no tolerance really. But I think that by the nature of things the Catholics were much to blame, because over the years since the Reformation we were always in the minority, and unless minorities band together and cling together and build the barricades they disintegrate and go. I mean you need to band together to exist. And to do that I think one became oneself very intolerant and rigid. I mean if we went to a non-Catholic wedding we were not allowed to take any part, even in a wedding, which after all is not a sacramental service. Well it is a sacrament but it's not a Eucharist or anything. We could sit at the back and we mustn't get up and kneel down and move, we could take up one position and keep to it, but not to take any part. We couldn't even say the Our Father with them, so rigid was the division.

My parents did not instruct us in the Catholic faith, I think they did it much more by example and also by seeing that we did go to Catholic schools and did have opportunities for practising our faith. I mean their emphasis on our chapel and having priests to stay and everything focused the whole of the life on the Christian way. Well, Sunday in Streatham we walked up to church and I suppose we went always to Mass and very often to what we called Benediction, the afternoon service. And in the country we just had this pony and trap and it was three miles to the convent to Mass and some walked there and some walked back. But having been to Mass and everything they were extremely liberal about what we did, you know allowed to do exactly as we liked. There was no different behaviour on the Sunday from any other day. But the grandmother, my mother's mother, disapproved of games on Sunday and as she had given us two lovely tennis courts, out of respect for her, when she was there, we never played tennis on Sundays. But I'm sorry to say that as soon as her back was turned we did. We didn't want to hurt her feelings but we thought it was very silly.

When we went to live in Kensington then we went to the Carmelites, and the Oratory of course. My father was very fond of the Oratory and the lovely singing. They used to have gorgeous choirs there in those days. At All Saints' in Streatham people tended to have their own positions. But of course there wasn't all that labelling and there wouldn't be family pews or anything. And of course in a great many Catholic churches, not so much in the suburbs but in a place like the Oratory, the men sat one side and the women the other when I was young. Catholics don't have Sunday schools you know. I think so much emphasis was laid on sending the children to Catholic schools that it quite took care of it.

My school was rather unsatisfactory, the whole thing. You see, my parents didn't like boarding schools, of that I'm sure. They wanted convent education and they didn't like the day school side of the convent because, I suppose, they thought that tradesmen's children went there; and so we were allowed to be day girls in the boarding school which was quite a mistake looking back on it, because well we never really belonged. I never felt I really belonged to the school in any sense 'cause we went away just as all the fun and games were beginning, you know the sort of tea-time and then the children play and the homework, and we went home then. So we were just quite isolated being the only day girls in a boarding school. It was in Clapham the boarding school, kept by the Notre Dame nuns and I should think they had about 150 boarders, a very fine house and wonderful grounds, a huge lake on which we used to boat. The teaching I think was very very good.

The teacher from whom I learned the most was the French teacher. I think in so far as I have any aptitude it is for languages and I enjoyed her lessons quite tremendously. I can vividly remember some of them now, when she was explaining *quelque* and *quelqu'un*. But she had no qualifications at all and suddenly the axe fell and she wasn't allowed to teach any more because she had no qualifications. Of course we tiresome little children we had our favourites you know. The music teaching I think was quite good. There was a tremendous amount of religious teaching. We started the morning with a religious lesson and we no doubt had one during the course of the day as well. The visit of the Bishop was always a great occasion, when he came to see how we were all getting on and bless us all. And we had dreadful things called religious exams when one of the appointed priests would come into each class in turn and put us through our paces. And as a little girl I well remember, I think I told you this, dreading being asked what was the resurrection 'cause I never could remember the difference between the resurrection and the incarnation. What nonsense it was! I mean we learned it all, you know, hadn't the faintest idea what it meant.

I don't think I ever learned any Latin. We had the usual algebra and geometry. I loved those. And we had a mild amount of botany, nothing very thrilling and of course a lot of needlework. I was taught a lot of needlework; I can sew very nicely, I really can, a long fine seam and embroider and that sort of thing. We spent a lot of time doing that. There are great gaps in English history that you know I never went through as a child. We seemed to go always round and round and never seemed to me that there was any plan in it. I don't know whether there was or wasn't. We never had a debate or anything like that. It was all just classrooms but I remember getting up *Everyman*. I remember having a part in *Everyman*. That's the only play I can remember them doing, but I've no doubt they did do other plays. We had a science room with some bunsen burners. I can't imagine what we did there, but I supposed we messed about with some very very elementary piece of knowledge. I simply don't remember that that was ever used as an exam subject. We took what were the then exams, they were called Oxford and Cambridge and I think they were called junior and senior, yes I think they were. We took those. And we took all the piano exams. But we never had an orchestra or anything nice like that, never seemed to be any instruments, it was just singing and piano playing, and if you couldn't pitch your voice they said, 'Well I'm afraid you can't sing' so you weren't in the choir which was very hard because I'd love to have sung.

Yes, we had lunch there and tea there. We had a presiding nun who said grace and who was in charge and she had a sort of a little desk place and if we made too much noise she'd ring a bell and say, 'Silence for the rest of the meal.' And the tables were all for about I should think for about twelve people, and there was one of the bigger girls at the head who was in charge of that table. And we got up and sat down like soldiers and it was tremendously rigid and formal. We filed in and we filed out. Everything was done by procession. And then after lunch if it was the sort of day they didn't think it was fit to be in the garden we used to go for a walk in a crocodile two by two over Clapham Common. And when we were very naughty we used to let our hats blow in the pond. We were quite naughty.

Deportment was a great thing. There was a curious kind of board, rather like a surf board, which some girls if they had weak backs used to have to spend half an hour lying on this board. And then we had another kind of board, almost like a yoke, which you would hang on. You put it like that and it kept your back up like that, with two handles. And then in a quiet way we had quite a lot of deportment. We had lovely things called Indian clubs. I used to enjoy them madly. We were quite good at swinging them, and I suppose we had marching and skipping but we didn't have any gym. We had no ropes or horses or anything like that. Dancing. Not at school. I don't think we had dancing at the school. My mother used to take us to a dancing class in the town. We had games, we had hockey and we had netball and we had some very feeble tennis because the tennis courts were so bad. Full of daisies but still . . . and there was a certain amount of boating. But that wasn't any good 'cause they didn't teach us to row. They just took turns going and being taken on the water.

I left school at fifteen. I went to Rome that very October and stayed there till May and learned Italian and learned to play the piano quite nicely. We had a very good music master there, rather a famous professor. And when the Reverend Mother was starting this school she wrote to him as being the head and said she wanted a teacher for her girls and the old Professor Gambati as his name was, said, 'I would like to teach your girls myself.' So when he came to the school the pianists all sat in the room with him and one by one you had your lesson and the others listened to the lesson. And that was quite interesting. Then we were taken sightseeing of course, with a chaperone. And then the next year after that I was sent to Cologne to learn German. I learned far more German because in Rome there were so many English girls and a number of Americans, one of whom became very great friends, except at classes and so on we really didn't get down to the Italian. But in Germany there were so few English-speaking that you really did learn. In fact I could at one time dream in German. Now it's gone because I've never kept it up unfortunately. I seem to remember that in Italy my parents had some friends who lived in Rome and we used to go to tea with them. I don't think we enjoyed it very much. And in Germany I didn't know anybody so it was just convent life. I had a sister with me in Italy, that was Susan, but in Germany I was alone. My parents came over both times, Christmas in Italy which was great fun, and in Germany my mother I seem to remember, came in the spring. It was very cold. I do remember that. But I don't think my father came, in fact I'm sure he didn't.

It never occurred to us to want to go to Oxford. But I was socially conscious, I will say that for myself, because I really came to awareness in 1911 which was a particularly desperate time for unemployment and poverty of every sort, and it was then that I joined the Labour party because I couldn't bear the sight of the barefooted children, February day, March day, hanging about outside the bakers' shops hoping that the customers would buy them bread or buns or have compassion on them. I joined it in my mind. And I remember turning to my mother and saying 'Well look, I don't know whose fault it is, but I'm on their side.' And I belonged to it with such determination! I think this historically is quite interesting, the poor had no facilities for anything. I mean they literally kept their money under the bed or in the teapot. And there was a man called Farrow, you've never heard of I suppose; he started a bank for the poor. He would take small accounts and so on. And my father by this time was making me a small dress allowance, as girls had in those days, and I put my dress allowance into Farrow's Bank.

I think my mother's reaction was very sympathetic, because, in 1906 I think it was, there was a rather exceptional thing happened in London. They had an exhibition of sweated labour. Well my mother took me; now she must have been interested because she took me. And she was very horrified at the quality of the goods. Because she said to one of the people in charge of the exhibition she said 'Well look, the sort of people who are coming to see this exhibition wouldn't *dream* of buying these things, what I want to know is how the things that I buy are made.' She said. 'Look at this blouse that I bought at Woollands and how is that made?' And he said, 'Just the same.' I can remember that perfectly well.

I was quite good with my hands. I did a lot of stitching and tapestry and that sort of thing. And we did quite a lot of church work. We made vestments for our own chapel and that sort of thing. Well I was convent trained and they do teach you to sew a fine seam. My parents didn't seek to what's called educate us. There was never any idea of us going to any further education. We went abroad of course as I told you and that sort of thing. But even with the younger ones they never went beyond their ordinary sort of course of about fifteen or sixteen. And that was it. No we looked down on the cousins who were blue stockings. We thought they were very queer. Speaking for myself which is all I can do, I felt absolutely secure in the knowledge that what I would like one day would be to be married and that that would happen, and not to worry, and just go on quietly from day to day. But the boys he wanted them to go to Cambridge and so forth which they did after the war. He was such a loving parent he didn't really like us away from him. And when my next sister was getting married which would be the third marriage in the family, I said, he was moaning a bit, I said, 'Well Father, you don't really want to grow into an old man, do you, with all these five daughters still in your house?' 'Oh yes,' he said, 'I would, my dear. I never want you to leave me, yes I would.'

8

Jock Yorke

Yorkes have been recorded in Yorkshire for five hundred years. Sir Richard Yorke was Member of Parliament for the City of York in 1472 and Lord Mayor of York in 1469 and 1482.[1] John Edward Evelyn Yorke was born in 1904 at Halton Place, Hellifield in the West Riding of Yorkshire. He was the eldest child of John Cecil and Marion Elizabeth Stansfeld.[2] He had two younger brothers, Peter born in 1906 and Michael in 1911. After Eton, Jock read agriculture at Christ Church but left after two years, persuaded by his guardian that he should learn engineering in one of Leeds' biggest firms. He did a year on the shop floor, using the same canteen and other facilities as the men, 'It was a very big jump from the House. But quite an experience, getting to know chaps. Same as being in the ranks in the army (yes, I started in the ranks) very similar in many ways. In the same way you could never have known those chaps as well from the drawing board as you could working with them all day.' Six months in the drawing office followed but Jock disliked engineering and went to London in 1925 to enter the wine trade. In 1931 he returned to Halton Place where he still lives. Apart from four years in the army during the Second World War his life has been spent looking after his estate, planting and clearing trees, fencing, etc. From 1939 to 1950 he farmed as well. He was a JP for thirty-six years and served for thirty years on the District Council. For fifty-six years he was church organist and for twenty-three years Master and Huntsman. In 1926 he married Eleanor Assheton of Downham hall. They have a son and a daughter.

By the time Jock Yorke was born the landed interest had lost its pre-eminence and land was losing many of its attractions. Many of the old landowners had become involved in business and by 1896 there were 167 noblemen, over a quarter of the peerage, holding directorships, most of them in more than one company. This was a relatively new situation for in the 1880s it was unusual for peers to hold directorships. The Yorkes, however, were not in the nobility; they belonged to the country gentry without title who made up about 90 per cent of the landed interest. They resembled the landed aristocracy except in the scale of their possessions and style of living. There were, however, two essential differences, one social and the other economic. 'The gentry were at one and the same time a more fluid class than the aristocracy, permitting easier entry and exit, and as a result of the provincial limits prescribed by their resources and way of life fundamentally a more conservative class.'[3]

Childhood in the upper middle class, country gentry and peerage had many common characteristics. There were nurses and nursery maids, day and night nurseries, governesses. Children came down after tea to be sung to and read to by their mothers, who undertook their religious instruction and led the family in hymn singing on Sunday evenings. There was promotion to dinner downstairs when boys went away to school, later usually for girls. But although Jock Yorke had a similar childhood, there is a striking difference between it and that of the son of a business or professional family on the one hand or of a landed family with social and political interests in London, on the other. For in these families the fathers were away from home and from their children a great deal but Jock's father was 'wedded to his estate'. It was his life and his home. Such government and public work as he was engaged in was local and did not take him to Westminster. Jock's mother too was active in local affairs, and there was no car to drive her out and no smart shops or dressmakers to visit. Calling, anyway, was a town custom so her afternoons were not absorbed by At Home days. There were no theatres, concert halls and drawing-rooms to provide entertainment so this took place at home. The Yorke parents were both very musical and the maids were enlisted to sing Mr Yorke's compositions. Jock was consequently in much more day-to-day contact with his parents and less formally separated from them than many children, the lack of formality being perhaps partly due to his parents' age for they were true Edwardian parents, younger by a generation than the Stokes, hence too the contrast with their household and that of the Victorian grandparents at Bewerley.

But it was not just his father's presence at home that brought him into his company and meant that although he died when Jock was eleven the boy felt he had known his father well. There was the absorbing interest in the estate to which Jock was the heir, the bond of shared concern with the condition of fields and fences and farms and tenantry; thus a walk on the estate was not just a pleasant father and son outing, it was part of Jock's apprenticeship. This apprenticeship was also served under the lesser men of the estate, the men-servants and estate workers; and Jock enjoyed many hours in their company as they taught him the things he ought to know, riding, shooting, ferreting, trapping and also taught him by their demeanour how to behave towards his social inferiors, for it was a society in which everyone knew his place and there was friendliness but not familiarity. Girls and boys in other families with estate and house servants had similar experiences. Violet, Lady Hardy remembered the kindness and beneficial influence of servants: 'An influence which was a great asset, and far more reaching than admonition and discipline from parents and teachers. I think it was because people of that class really appealed to us children. They were more approachable in daily life than our parents, good as they were. They amused and interested us and were more natural.'[4]

It was a much freer life than a town boy could have hoped to have. All the year round the Yorke boys would enjoy the countryside, especially country sports; sport played a great part in bridging the gaps between people. It was a means not only of exercise, fresh air and pleasure but of communication. Boys of all ranks played cricket and football together, professional people and gentry mixed at tennis parties, the hunt embraced men and women from a great many stations in life though labourers would not take part. Only shooting tended to set the squire and his friends apart from the village. For some boys it might have been a life less than ideal. Lionel Fielden has described in *The Natural Bent* the agony of growing up in the country with his father a passionate huntsman, when he had no taste for field sports.[5] For Jock Yorke it was a life suited to his temperament and abilities. He grew up happy with his present and future, mixing easily with people, quite free of the painful shyness so frequently suffered by nursery children.

NOTES

1 Burke's *Landed Gentry* (1965).
2 I interviewed Jock Yorke in 1974. Later he added the following information: his mother was born in 1876 and his father in 1868. His brother Peter was named after a Norton ancestor and Michael after an ancestor too.
3 F. M. L. Thompson. *The English Landed Estate in the 19th century* (London, 1963), pp. 20, 306. See also G. E. Mingay *The Gentry: the Rise and Fall of a Ruling Class* (London, 1977).
4 V. A. E. Hardy, *As it Was, etc. An Autobiography* (London, 1958), p. 56.
5 Lionel Fielden, *The Natural Bent, Reminiscences* (London, 1960).

I lived here till 1926 when we got married. The house was then let. We lived in Ashley Gardens in London, Ovington Gardens and I was in the wine trade till 1931 when we joyfully came back again. Been here ever since. Brother Peter is two years younger and Michael seven. My father was born in 1868 I think. He was only forty-seven when he died in 1915. I think that's the right sum. I'm almost certain it was 1868 'cause I've got his twenty-first birthday gold watch from the tenants. My mother never would let on how old she was. Never, never. It wasn't till we met the coachman I showed you in the picture only a year or two before she died that he told her her age. He'd been here since 1895 and she was so angry that he knew, she had to admit it. But I can't remember.

I was called John because the eldest son's always been John for many generations. I got called Jock because I was confused with my father you see. He was John. Edward's after one grandfather and Evelyn after the second. Very simple. Peter was called after a picture in the billiard room and Michael, I don't know who. [Godparents?] We all had two of each. One was the uncle who was killed. The other commanded the Black Watch and was a very great friend of my father's and he died. He did very well in the war. He died about 1930–5 so I didn't see a great lot of them. One godmother was very old and died. She's a great-aunt almost. I stayed with her once in Scotland, once at Bewerley I think. Can hardly remember her. I don't even know. . . . Oh, yes the other one was Aunt May. I was very fond of her, looked after her in her old age. She died at ninety-one about seven or eight years ago. I don't know why they had such very elderly ones.

The big estate was Bewerley Hall near Pateley bridge which is fifteen thousand acres. My grandfather lived here originally and inherited Bewerley from his brother in 1883 and so he and the aunt, he was a widower then, all up-sticked and went to Bewerley and this was let to two or three people. When my father had finished at Oxford and done a bit in the army and been round the world he came here about 1895 and lived here till he was married in 1903. It was the eldest son's house, you see. And the old man, grandfather, married again, having got to Bewerley and got another wife and remained there till his death.

I remember the servants very well up to the First War, then of course things altered a bit, but they really altered when my father died. We had a cook, kitchen maid, scullery maid, a between maid, parlourmaid and a housemaid, God knows what they all did, inside. And outside we had the coachman, the gardener, an odd man and a garden boy. And we had three estate men, now we've only one and me. So it was quite an establishment costing very little. We never had to do anything or say anything beastly or rude to any servant, we'd have got absolute stick. My mother certainly went into the kitchen to see the cook. But not my grandmother. She never went. The housekeeper came to see her. Oh yes, my mother certainly did. I never remember the maids going in the garden. They would sit at the back on the lawn in the sun. I don't think they would be allowed in the garden. They would go down the stable yard to talk to the people in the cottages if they liked you know. They could go to the river for a picnic. I never remember them in the garden.

My father was a very keen composer of music, my mother was a very good pianist, they were both very good pianists, and he composed waltzes and quite a lot of hymn tunes and kyries and one or two music hall songs, and he would have maids who could sing and suddenly he'd have something in his head and there'd be a roar! The parlourmaid had a very good voice and our nursery-maid, oh I forgot the nurserymaids, I didn't mention them, she sang alto. Cook was a very good singer and one of the housemaids sang a bit and the gardener sang tenor. And they all sang this thing in parts which we adored of course. Most maids in those days came from Durham up north, Newcastle you know, miners' daughters. Yes, we went into the kitchen lots. I loved them all. They were all great friends to us boys and of course if they had a dinner party Peter and I used to creep down the stairs and snatch what we could from the dish coming out. Sweetheart them into giving us a bit of trifle. Nanny wasn't looking!

The coachman Jim Doyle was my great friend. He was very kind to me. He taught me to drive and he taught me to ride and I spent hours in the stables with him. He married the housemaid then, so they stayed on till the war. He stayed on till the Lord Derby scheme came up and then he went in the Veterinary Corps. He came back after the war and set up as a small farmer selling butter and eggs. The keeper taught me to shoot, aged thirteen, and trap a bit, and he was very stern, very stern, no messing about. If you did anything wrong you had your cartridge taken out and you just carried your gun. A good thing.

I spent hours with him, rabbiting or ferreting or trapping in the season you know. I learned a lot from Tom. My grandfather taught me to fish and the gardener was a very good fisherman. I think you know in those days the likes of us spent a tremendous lot of time with the nicer servants because they were so keen that we should learn what they'd acquired. They took enormous trouble with us, in the sporting world. And of course they were frightfully congenial. They wouldn't have 'taken a liberty' with you if you know that out of date expression. They were always polite. Curse us if we did wrong. Joked like mad. Pull our legs. But they never, like the nice hunt servants still today, they never exceed and they would no more have dreamed of getting tight in our company or using filthy language than you would. It was very easy, very friendly. We'd share a sandwich and steal a cigarette off them or something like that but all very friendly. Just a very happy relationship. They were very anxious to pass on their lore to us as young things in the same way that when I started hunting hounds with a very old delightful friend who'd been at it all his life, he was terribly keen that I should learn everything from him. He just happened to be kennel huntsman of these hounds when I took them on. He became a great friend. Been here since 1906 you see. And was exactly the same. He was desperately keen that you should learn what he could teach you and he'd pull you up sharp if you did the wrong thing. Very sharp. Not in public, not in front of people. You know, 'What did you want to do that for?' They were a marvellous race, really were. And I think all my cousins and similar age groups spent hours of time with the outside men either in the woods or by the river.

We'd just the two horses and my pony. My father didn't hunt you see, but I did from the age of seven. He was a great shooter and he liked driving that thoroughbred mare I showed you, but he had an awful railway smash before I was born, spending a penny in the train. And the train suddenly crashed to a halt and he put his hand through the window and got dreadful blood poisoning and he couldn't hold a horse. But he could shoot. He was almost dead before I was born, desperate blood poisoning. He used to lead my pony when I was little. And when I could go free he walked with me. He was a tremendous walker. He walked every day somewhere. And he took me. Oh miles and miles we went together. He was completely wedded to his estate and he didn't farm himself but like me he knew every field and fence and who it belonged to and the names of all the children, never mind the tenants, you know. We've always been a rather friendly entity. There was a home farm but it was let. My grandfather farmed it, then it was let.

I got this pony in 1911 and once I got going was allowed to go alone. I probably visited a farm every other day you know, if I was by a farm I'd always go and have a talk to them and so they'd give you tea or something to drink or something. We've always been great friends with our tenants. And I would call if I was going through a farm, get off and have a word. We had fifteen farms then. There were nine cottages and three in the yard, twelve, and the shop, the church and the institute. We owned the lot even the church. Still do. But we sold one farm. We've fourteen now. The shop was let as part of the farm. It's a little farm which is now expanded into an enormous sale of cattle food mixes. It used to be a general store. Bootlaces to bread, anything you wanted. Sometimes you hitched the pony up and went in and sometimes you just sat on it and had a bit of a gossip and then went on.

We only played with children who were within riding distance. We did play a lot of cricket and football with the gardener's children and the farm boys, at the top of the stable yard and on the lawn. We had a great deal of football and cricket with them you know. There'd be four of the gardener's children and perhaps a farm boy or so from the home farm and us, about six. Their father would play a bit. And we fished of course. As soon as we were old enough to learn we spent a lot of time fishing.

I had two nannies. I had Nanny Day to start with, I dimly remember, and then we had one called Wright who was with us till we went to school and remained my mother's maid. And they were very beloved and cosy and nice. They're both real old fashioned nannies. The three of us slept in the night nursery until I got bigger and then I went into my father's dressing room. We slept in the night nursery and we fed in the day nursery and the nurserymaid carted the trays up. When we were very young when there were two of us our nanny slept with us. Well then my cousin John Stansfeld whose parents were in India and Egypt, he came to live with us for the best part of five years, and if I remember he and I shared a room and Peter and Michael slept with the nurse till they were big enough to have their room.

When we got Anna our nurserymaid we had to talk to her all the time in French if we could, because she had no English when she came. And it's been very useful ever since. It was dinned into us that we must learn French because if we ever did anything in the world in a diplomatic corps or something which I had once had an idea I was going into, French was the language of Europe and if you couldn't talk French you were no good, and therefore it was always pushed at us. We had one governess who went as a nurse in the war, the First War. And we had another one. We were very fond of them both and they were very sporting. They used to run with a pony and climb trees. Gave us reading, writing, arithmetic and geography. And this one stayed I suppose till we went to school. I don't know who taught Michael when Peter and I went to school, you see I had bad eyes and I was late going to school. We more or less went together. And we almost went to Eton together. I think I went perhaps six months before him. But whether Maude remained with Michael I can't really remember. I should think she probably did.

The nannies never seemed to want to go out much. The nursery maids went out of course but I don't think the nannies ever wanted to go out. They sat and read a book if they ever had any time off, which was really only in the evenings when we were allowed to come down and see the parents after tea. We used to always come down, either here or to the billiard room. And she read to us always, my mother, she was a great reader, very good reader, or we'd play and sing songs or something. And I suppose poor old nanny then had a moment to start mending our clothes. When you were very little she brought you down and then we came ourselves after tea, provided they weren't going to something or had a shooting party, even then we used to come down when they had a shooting party, we always came down after tea to talk to them.

And they were very good about taking us out shooting, and hunting in the dog cart. I mean I always went with my father or mother when they were shooting here. I started at six I should think. There were no landrovers in those days. You had to walk. I didn't stay out all day but I went out quite a bit, and then came back with the ladies.

And in those days they didn't sit round the table having tea as they were. They all changed into tea gowns, marvellous, rather like a cocktail dress, and looked very elegant when the guns came in while they were eating. Then they all changed again for dinner. It's not a very good shoot but they'd probably have three a year. Well at a guess from memory, probably three guns and their wives if they had them would come, and then there'd be perhaps two locals came for the day and nearly always a singer or dancer, amateur for the evening concert. We always had music of some sort. The piano was in there you see, and they all sat round here and they sang. I remember that very well.

Father sang very mildly like we do. I mean not professionally. My mother had a nice voice but neither of them were at all professional singers. She was a brilliant pianist. She could accompany anybody, particularly the violin. She was quite good on the violin herself. Father started music at Harrow and did very well. Then he went to Christ Church and went on with it. He had two very brilliant teachers, both at Harrow and the House. He was frightfully keen on it, although not at all aesthetic. I mean he was a real sort of countryman shooter, but he did love his music. So many people like my father-in-law played the banjo beautifully and sang black and white minstrels with his brothers. They all did their own thing you see. Father published a waltz as he was dying in aid of war charities, *Valse Triste* it's called. And he sold a thing called *Animals German Band* as a music hall song, quite good. We still sing that occasionally.

I learned from my mother but I never learned to read music rather stupidly, and I can't read now but I can play nearly everything I've heard luckily. I've played in church for fifty years, psalms and hymns. She was professional standard; she'd studied it quite a lot in Dresden, the piano and the fiddle and she was more than competent to teach me what I know, and I amplified it a bit on the basic things that she gave me. My brother Peter hasn't a note of music in him, wasn't a bit interested. Never sang. Michael a little bit, but I don't know that he really followed up her teachings. She must have taught him a bit, by the time he was big enough to be learning we were at school you see. So I don't know what he did.

We looked forward to birthdays. They were quite an occasion. They never forgot them. We used to have a children's party from round about and we generally had a children's party in the Christmas time and we went to other children's parties in a brougham round about, which I enjoyed vastly. Peter hated them. They were the children of neighbouring houses up to six or eight miles away. You see there were quite a few big houses round there in those days, all with families. And one went to parties as far as the carriage horse could conveniently trot on a winter night with flickering lamps which blew out. There was a little dance – children's, Sir Roger and that sort of thing. Enormous feed. There were dancing classes up and down but I don't remember ever going to one. You see we're six miles from Settle, eleven from Skipton. Too far.

We could go to our parents any time of day or night if we wanted them. No fixed hours or anything. They were always ready to see us or tell us anything. We were up at six or seven yo· know in the summer. We were out with the ponies or shooting or bathing or doing something. We'd go and rouse them up and tell them what we were going to do or where we'd been, probably been out by then. We used to often ride up and enquire if people were sick. We went to all sorts of places. I remember being sent out every other night in pitch dark to Hellifield station to get the evening paper to read the casualty lists and tie the pony to the railings and go up to the station and get the paper, and trot home in the dark. Nobody seemed to worry about that.

We had breakfast in the nursery certainly till we went to school but the trouble was my mother being Edwardian never would have breakfast till half past nine. That was the time you see. And so we got frightfully bored and we were always out by seven or eight. And we much preferred having it in the nursery at half past eight or nine than waiting till half past. I suppose eventually we came down and then we always had lunch with her in the war at quarter past one. I think we had tea in the nursery until we'd just this old maid left and the cook and then of course we started feeding with her all the time. I don't think we had dinner downstairs till we were at Eton. We just had a snack. Being in the war you see it wasn't much of a dinner. It was a herring and a bit of rice pudding or egg pie or whatever we could have then. It wasn't a smart affair at all. We didn't even change. Well I mean we put on a tidy suit but we didn't dress any more. Hadn't got the clothes then.

If we did wrong we were sternly ticked off. I can't remember ever being smacked or beaten, possibly one on the hand. But a ticking off from either parent was quite something. You didn't like it. We didn't do it again. My father particularly. I never remember having to be hit, but they were both pretty stern if you did wrong. But it was finished with then. I was a bit frightened of my father. He'd quite a temper and when he roared people jumped. You didn't know what was going to happen. It might not have been much you know. Somebody had left the door open and a draught came, a tremendous roar, and you thought is it me or her that's left the door open. We were respectfully frightened shall I say. All I remember being nervous about was going up the stairs with one guttering candle. That loo at the top of the stairs had a big thick curtain, nobody was allowed to know about loos in my mother's day. And it used to have a draught and it used to move and I used to tear past that door. I never remember having nightmares. The place was full of rats and noises off and owls and things. They never bothered me.

[Sex education?] Never mentioned, no. I can remember sitting in a carriage or a cart or something outside and my cousin beside it. But before getting in the cart he must rush into that loo. He did, very quickly, and pulled the plug and we could hear it outside you see. And he got the most terrible ticking off from my aunt, his mother, for daring to make a noise like that when ladies were present. It's almost unbelievable now, isn't it!

Religion for one they were strong on. We never thought otherwise than of going to church. I suppose the usual hopeful things of truth and honesty and not telling lies. Respect for elderly people. Respect and – consideration isn't quite the word – for children of the tenants, of the tenants themselves, and their interests and little things like that. I mean you were very soon taught if you saw a nice meadow of hay not to go and gallop through it on your pony. Hell of a row then. That sort of thing. We were brought up very Empire minded, read lots of *Our Empire Story* and Walter Scott and all that. They were great Empire fans, both of my parents. I was a Boy Scout at school.

At Bewerley prayers were said every morning. The whole household were expected, didn't get off unless they were actually cooking breakfast. But we never had 'em here. They were great Christians Father and Mother but they were extremely cheerful Edwardians, enjoying everything. Don't think they were solemn religious people, they weren't. They were good Christians but I don't think that either of them ever thought of having family prayers. Not their line. Well they wouldn't be up in time probably! We did have one church warden in our little church in top hat and black coat. It's only a chapel of ease you see, part of the parish, but it's not the parish church. It's our own little church. Dad always attended. Slept in the family pew. She played. There was a Sunday school. My mother taught in it too and one of the farm daughters. Mother gave us a great grounding. I managed to get a certificate in scripture; I'm sure I'd never have got that without Mamma. She used to come and hear our prayers and talk a bit about that and on Sunday she'd talk a bit about it or read bits of the Bible. I think Mamma always said grace. Towards the end of her life she may not have, I don't think she did, but I think we were brought up to say it and in the nursery too. I can't remember whether my father did or not. And every Sunday evening always we sang hymns for an hour. I remember the first nanny crooning little go-to-sleep ditties, but my mother was the best at that. She used to come and sing us to sleep occasionally. She was the organist in church you see, and so we were all encouraged to sing. In the palmier days when everyone came to our tiny church all the farmers came, all their children and she had the aforementioned maids and the gardeners and schoolteacher who sang alto, and she did drill them into quite a good little choir. Now there's about six or ten, it's rather sad. Oh and one or two farmers sang extremely well. I sang in it like mad. No, not Peter or Michael, he was too young.

I went to school just outside Winchester, Winton House. It was in 1917. It was the coldest winter of the war. It was very very bitter. And I only got in by the skin of my teeth. I was supposed to have bad eyes then and a bit of a heart. I don't know why. Never bothered me since. So I was given a four-wheeled dog-cart and an old pony, boy scout hat and I used to drive to the hospital which I adored of course, free for all you see. Clattering round. It was very trusting of them. We got bowled over by a three tonner one day, but no harm done. I used to go to the different camps with my boxes of bottles from the hospital. I can't think why they let me go. And I was out two and three and four hours. I was terribly homesick. Loathed it at first. I knew one or two boys and this cousin was there, he looked after us. I was very happy later. I hated going. I went to Eton in 1918 just before the end of the war. I enjoyed it all once I got settled in. I hated it at the beginning of every term. My mother didn't visit me at Winton House, she came to Eton occasionally or we went up to London to see her. She never left here. She wrote to us twice a week sometimes, certainly once, always. She was a very good letter writer. I was in the house of a man called Byrne. Dear old boy. I was very fond of him. I was very happy there, beagling, football and rowing in the House Four.

Fagging didn't bother me. I could run very fast. The last boy has to do the job you know. Always a bore if you were reading something. I got beaten twice and that's the end. I'm still all in favour of it. We were beaten by the Library which is really the prefects. You knew you'd done wrong and you got it and you just had to bend over and you got four or six. And that was it. No afterthought or animosity. You were just forgotten. I enjoyed life and I tried, I was always in training for something. And justifiably you got smacked. I never felt ill used. I was very bad at science. We had to do a bit. I just went on the ordinary Latin and French and maths and history. [Army class?] Never went in for that. It was just starting after the war and a lot of chaps did go in for it but I'd no intention of going in the army. I never bothered. I just did the ordinary curriculum till my time was up.

I can't remember wondering why there were rich and poor. Probably in those days there were certain stations in life, sounds rather an old-fashioned word, and money and belongings. People seemed more used to belonging to one or the other and it wasn't such a surprise. I think we accepted it and I think most people did. Mind you, the roofs were kept dry and the buildings were kept up. We had these great black-leaded ranges which they thought were marvellous. Some of the pensioners were certainly very poor, but if they belonged to the place and retired, they nearly always got a pension. They were never just dropped. They were nurtured even if they had to go to the workhouse as being crippled or very hard up. There were certain people, not so much down here in this vale but on the hill farms, perhaps a husband and wife with seven children, in a bad winter who were very near the breadline, in fact pretty hungry at times, but not down here. They didn't swim into our ken. But you see it's all a matter of comparison.

There were distinctions certainly, even in those days. There were distinctions, in that way between old landed proprietors, and people who'd made a fortune and bought land and moved in, and were going on – slight you know; then also severe distinctions between the upper servants and the lower ones, the butler and cook, that you may have read about and heard. But it was true at Bewerley when they had these enormous parties and they brought a valet with them, Lord So-and-So's valet took the cook into dinner, and the butler took Lady Whatnot's maid, that was very strict protocol, into the Servants' Hall. Then they went out and had pudding in the Housekeeper's Room, leaving the rest of the staff in the Servants' Hall – and they fed very well indeed.

There was a distinction between the farmers and the farm men, servant men they're called round there. Farmers were well paid on the whole and servant men badly paid of course, terribly badly paid, but again in many cases had a cottage and a pig and garden but there was a distinct line there, although many of the farmers sent their daughters and sons to be trained as somebody's servant lass or servant man, until they were able to save up enough money to start a farm, a little farm. So there was a definite social division there. But at a dance or whist drive, they would dance with each other happily. There was a distinction between ourselves and the farmers because of the money probably. They wouldn't expect to come to dinner naturally. But they always asked you in and when we had a party, we used to have a party occasionally and open the garden, and perhaps have a tea-party or something. They'd come to that. They never shot. They do in other places now. But I think that's more modern. Doctors and lawyers, they came to lunch but they didn't come to dinner, and their children came to tea and all our parties, children's parties. They'd come and play tennis and their wives. They wouldn't dine. At shooting parties – friends and relations – they wouldn't be asked to dine to meet them.

[People in manufacturing?] They'd be in a different social outfit. They would come to garden parties. When they'd been long enough and got a shoot going they might come and shoot, but in those days wives didn't shoot a great lot unless they were bred and brought up to it, like our sort of aunts and things. The ordinary manufacturer's wife did not shoot and so she didn't have to be asked. It still appertains up to a point. And they're not used to it and they don't like it. Wine merchants were quite a different type of chap a lot of them. Some of them had been in it for two or three hundred years and in the wine trade they were sort of handed on from father to son rather like the land. And they'd travelled and they'd shot and they'd raced. They weren't tied to the mill or tied to the office or the ironworks you see. The local tradesmen would come to ferret hunts.

My parents did quite a lot of local things. For instance they organized the building of Hellifield parish church and they were both on various committees. Nothing like the extent that we have been. He was on the Bench for years but they weren't politically minded. They helped a bit at elections. I can remember going in the Victoria with flags flying and true blue for this you know and being hooted at. They were not very active but they were very great Conservative supporters. I suppose he'd be on the local committee in Hellifield probably but that's all.

They liked the servants to be Conservative. In those days, well they were divided between Conservatives and Radicals round here and the Methodists who are very strong. There were a lot of Methodists round there. They were mostly what they used to call Radicals in those days. Liberals. I can only remember one Roman servant and that was a French nurserymaid we had. I don't remember any other RC servants except Jim Doyle. He used to go to Settle Roman Church every Sunday and Anna occasionally. But all the rest used to come to our church so they can't have been. We picked up swearing from the locals here. I expect we did. I think we must have done 'cause all the locals swear a bit in Yorkshire and don't think anything of it. I do remember swearing now you mention it. I remember my brother swearing and my mother sending for the doctor to ask him what it meant!

My father really was in a sense a war casualty. He was longing to go to the war himself you see, having been a gunner. But he was put back by this broken arm, this broken wrist. They wouldn't pass him. All he could do was to go and buy horses for the government. And he stood about for hours, saturated, waiting for the train. He was buying remounts. Coming home in an open dog cart, he got pneumonia. He was dead in three days. It just wrecked her, poor darling. But of course she still had to cope with the day-to-day staff on the estate, farmers coming to see her. Then she got an agent to help her. And she was desperately hard up you see with my father's death duties and my grandfather's death duties coming on and all. She was very pushed indeed. She wasn't very keen on taking advice I'm sorry to say. She hated figures. She wasn't very good at them. She worried desperately poor dear but she kept going. She kept us educated and somehow she got by.

Her father was a parson in the Cottesmore country at Manton, they also lived a long time at Billericay. And he used to hunt a bit. He never had much money. And then he suddenly became a Roman Catholic, baled out of the church which shocked her very much. But they remained great friends. He used to come and stay. I can remember him. He died in 1910 I can just remember. She had this very smart brother who commanded the Gordon Highlanders and was killed at Loos shortly after my father you see. And she had a sister in Warwickshire who died a couple of years ago. She came to stay very rarely but I loved her 'cause she was a great hunting woman and she used to tear about with me on my pony, 'cause I used to get up on the back of it at a pinch behind her.

At the salient time between 1914 and 1919 hardly anyone went anywhere except on leave or came for a weekend, some old friend who happened to be travelling. It was pretty grim. Not many cars you see, she wouldn't have a car till 1926. If she wanted to go to the station she ordered a brougham from Hellifield or a wagonette took her down. And our old coachman would run her about occasionally. But there was always horse transport. She would not have a car, although she eventually learned to drive quite well. We only had a telephone in 1931, we only had petrol gas and candles. We had a candle in the hall and it was cheaper for us. And she would only have petrol gas because it was better for the complexion than electricity! We had to wind it up every day. Well a lot of that was cut down in the war, you couldn't get the petrol. So we had guttering candles all over the shop. She never held a party. We got her playing tennis again. She played a tremendous lot of tennis with us. She was very good. She'd adored a party, adored dressing up, adored travelling. Just wrecked her, poor dear.

We had very little pocket money, tuppence a week or something like that to buy some sweets at the village shop you know. We played cowboys and Indians, preferably on ponies of course, which was great fun. And charades. Dumb Crambo my mother was keen on. Dressing up we were very keen on. She was awfully good at sketching; my father wrote a few poems, comic poems, but I could never sketch. We went on average for a month to Bewerley every July–August. Ponies, dogs, everything and the governess.

I was very fond of my grandfather. Of course, he was ninety-three when he died, so he was pretty old, when I was staying. In the war he was in his late eighties you see, so I used to go for walks with him and if we'd been shooting he wanted to know everything about the day and which was the best drive and what the dogs had done. I was very fond of him but he was in a rather hard generation. My grandmother was his second wife and she was very sweet to us. We loved her. And my mother's mother we were very fond of too. They were very kind to us all. She used to come and stay, yes. She was a cheerful old soul. She really enjoyed life. And my mother and father of course went for the three shoots, sometimes we were there, as we got bigger we were there for a shoot, grouse shooting. And other times they'd have us when they hadn't a party, but we went about a month a year. No week-ending then. Had to go by train you see. Change at Leeds, go to Harrogate, change at Harrogate and go to Pateley, quite a trip.

They had tons of servants. Grandfather had a butler and two footmen, always, in the dining room. Everyone went to bed at ten and there were sixteen candlesticks, silver ones, with beautiful little candles, and there were little oil lamps in the rooms, and the second footman spent quite an appreciable part of each day trimming all those candle wicks and polishing the candles and seeing that the burners in these little oil things worked. Well you couldn't expect a parlour maid to do that. A butler here wouldn't have had much to do really. A parlour maid could do her parlour-maiding and her silver and look after them and she could clean her pantry and do other jobs which a butler probably wouldn't do.

Occasionally we went to Scotland to an old great-uncle of my mother's. We used to go to Morecambe with a gorgeous fortnight to bathe and dig in the sands or Grange or Scarborough. Be about June I should think. That was our annual trip. We stayed in the old Midland Hotel at Morecambe which is right on the sands. Had a sitting room, nanny and nurserymaid. Straight out into the sea. Mother came for a bit, you know, a few days perhaps. No, I don't remember my father ever coming. I think they used to, if I remember, they probably went on a little visit themselves some-where. They occasionally went away for their little holiday as I say, abroad occasionally, or to Ascot perhaps, or London for a fortnight or they went away to shoot quite a lot. They went and stayed in different parts of Yorkshire to shoot. And in the grouse season he was away quite a lot, shooting. In London they stayed in Brown's Hotel or somewhere like that where my grandfather had stayed from the 1860s. They always stayed at Brown's Hotel. I can only remember going once to see Hamley's toyshop and the circus. At Eton we used to go to London for the Lord's weekend. Mother used to come down to see us. We went up for the weekend, stayed in a hotel somewhere. We only went to the three seaside towns. We led really a very peaceful sort of life I think. With our ponies and guns and dogs we were really as happy here as anywhere.

9

Joan Poynder

Joan Poynder's father was Sir John Poynder Dickson-Poynder, 6th Baronet. He was born in 1866 and was active both in county and national government, serving as High Sheriff of Wiltshire in 1890 and as Member of Parliament for Chippenham from 1892–1910. In the Boer War he was ADC to Lord Methuen. He was created Baron Islington of Islington in 1910 and went to New Zealand as Governor General in the June of that year. He was Under Secretary of State for the Colonies from 1914 to 1915 and for India from 1915 to 1918. In 1896 he married Anne Beauclerk, daughter of Henry Robert Duncan Dundas of Glenesk.[1] Joan was their only child. During the First World War she joined the Red Cross and after nursing in six English hospitals managed to get to a French hospital although at nineteen she was considerably under the required age of twenty-three. She married Edward Grigg in 1923 and had three children. Her husband served as member of Parliament for Oldham and Altrincham, was Governor of Kenya and later Joint Under Secretary of State for War (1940–2). He was created 1st Baron Altrincham in 1945.[2]

Joan Poynder's[3] great interest was always hospitals and when she was in Kenya in 1928 with her husband as Governor she founded three hospitals, two for Africans and one for Asians, all with training schools for nurses. She also started a nursing association of trained nurses from England for the English settlers and officials. During the Second World War she served on the District Council. She was Governor of the local grammar school which later became comprehensive. 'I don't think I'm naturally passionate about politics but I'm interested in the end product. I want certain things to happen. A lot of people are just interested to have a game, aren't they? But the end product has always interested me. I was interested in the betterment of people and that way I'm interested in politics.'

As a child Joan spent very little time with her mother. Edwardian upper class parents followed their Victorian parents in their attitude to babies and children. Breastfeeding was not in vogue, a special cow being often kept on the estate for the baby, and parents did not concern themselves with the baby's routine and habits. A nurse of many years' experience recalled in the 1930s that twenty years earlier she would not have dreamed of asking a father if he wished to see an infant have a bath as it would have been thought very bourgeois and too familiar. Nor would Edwardian parents look after their children on their nanny's day off, for Edwardian nannies had no days off; they would not expect to go out and leave their charges to anyone else, except perhaps the nursery maid or under nurse and then only for a short while.[4]

The family nurse was therefore a most important influence on the child, and had almost complete authority over it. Children ill-treated by their nurses rarely complained and the parents were usually too distant from the nursery to know how their offspring were treated. Good nurses are often spoken of with greater affection and warmth than parents by their charges, and Joan's nurse, Nanny Wiltshire was an unusually good one. She was not unfortunately to stay as long as Joan needed her because she wanted a baby 'to take from the month' and Lady Poynder was not able to have any more children. Old nannies sometimes stayed with their families as maids or housekeepers when their youngest 'baby' grew beyond the nursery stage and the children could then keep contact, but Nanny Wiltshire was a young woman. With a good, intelligent nanny this independent-minded child flourished, but the govern-esses who replaced her in no way made up for the absence of a mother's day-to-day care, and lacking also a brother or sister, Joan was very lonely. Governesses were invariably unpopular, and with one exception Joan's were not a success.

Governesses were a fairly recent innovation dating from the end of the eighteenth century.[5] They belonged neither to family nor to servants and thus lived in a status and sexual limbo. They lunched with the family but did not dine with them except if needed to make up numbers at dinner. They were very often French or German and suffered on this account from English boys and girls, confident in the superiority of the British nation. They were not usually fit to take over the upbringing and education of a girl till the age of seventeen and many girls attended classes in the Parliamentary season at Miss Wolff's, or went away to school for the end of their education, but though Joan longed to go to school she was not allowed to.

Would the Poynder parents have taken more interest in their child if she had been a boy and able to succeed to the baronetcy and Hartham Park? Sons were of tremendous importance in landed families and as daughters could not usually inherit, failure to have a son could be the cause of great distress. An heir to Hartham would have probably been freer to explore it and mix with the tenantry and learn to shoot and fish, while Joan felt herself restricted and watched over. He would have gone to a public school and been less isolated, but whether he would have had any more parental attention is hard to say for Lady Poynder's interests lay beyond family life. In this, she was a typical Edwardian aristocrat. A contemporary social commentator deplored the restlessness of society people blaming it on French influence, continental travel and liberal views that regarded the old virtues as obsolete. Upper class Edwardians lived much less at home than their parents had, being always on the move between London, Biarritz, Bordighera, Cowes, Goodwood, Ascot, Newmarket and each other's country houses. Nor were the women the settled matrons he believed their mothers to have been. 'The identity of interest of husband and wife' was undermined and 'the flirtations of girlhood are perpetuated or reproduced in what was once the staid and decorous epoch of matronhood.' They entertained their admirers at five o'clock tea while their husbands were out and lived for their acquaintances rather than their children.[6]

But Lady Poynder was not content simply with fashionable London society. Her interests were less conventional: she liked intellectuals, writers and musicians and was almost a Soul being friends with people in that orbit, for example Margot Tennant, Maurice Baring, Lady Desborough and her son Julian Grenfell. The Souls, who formed their coterie in the 1880s, were a group of aristocrats who included Arthur Balfour, George Curzon and George Wyndham. They had literary and intellectual interests rather than being centred on the turf, and preferred acrostics, literary allusion, parody and satire to bridge and baccarat.[7] Female Souls, all but one of whom were married, were 'illustrious in their homes around which men fluttered like moths'.[8] It was a world in which a teenage girl would have been an embarrassment as girls were supposed to be quite innocent and untouched until marriage, and fashionable society's conversation was not decorous. So Joan was kept in the schoolroom much longer than the daughters of country gentry and it was not until the First World War that she got free.

NOTES

1 L. G. Pine *The New Extinct Peerage 1884–1971* (London, 1972), p. 157.
2 *Debrett's Peerage and Baronetage* ed. P. Montague Smith (London, 1980), p. 48.
3 The interview with Joan Poynder was begun by Ann Jungmann in 1974 and completed by me in 1976.
4 Lady Muriel Beckwith, *When I Remember* (London, 1936), pp. 257–9.
5 Lawrence Stone, *The Family, Sex and Marriage in England 1500–1800* (London, 1977), p. 384.
6 T. H. S. Escott, *London: Its People, Polity and Pursuits*, vol. II (London, 1879?), pp. 7–17.
7 Margot Asquith, *The Autobiography of Margot Asquith* (London, 1920), pp. 173–201.
8 Nicholas Mosley, *Julian Grenfell: his life and the times of his death* (London, 1975), p. 15.

I was born in Wiltshire in 1897, at the home of my father called Hartham Park. I am an only child. My parents had a house in the country that was my father's heritage and a house in London, 8 Chesterfield Gardens out of Curzon Street. It was one of the first houses built there. That's when I was about nine or ten I suppose. I lived at Hartham Park till I was twelve and then my father went to New Zealand as governor for three years and we came back and I was there on and off till the First World War.

The house was started by Wyatt and added on to. A most charming country house in a park, large park, with every kind of tree and then a very good garden which my father improved, and an old stable yard which was rather older than the house with lots of rooms for horses. And we had quite a lot of land and a good many farms in Wiltshire, and there were especially lovely woods round the house and a great many rooms. Well I'd have to add up but I suppose one could put up a lot of guests. There must have been about fifteen spare rooms for guests and a lot of rooms for the staff because there were a great many. There was a billiard room and my mother had what's called a boudoir, a drawing room and a library, dining room, two drawing rooms I think. I had lovely nurseries. There were not as many bathrooms as one has now and a lot of them the old kind surrounded by wood.

The house in London is still there. It was built I suppose might have been the 1880s, rather an ornate house, and it had a lovely ballroom and a great many rooms. It's a cul-de-sac opposite what was Chesterfield House. I had lovely nurseries in Chesterfield Gardens with a lift. It was always a great amusement for children when they came to tea. My parents and I came up to London in the summer and sometimes in the winter, but went back for the sort of things people did in the country, a certain amount of hunting and a certain amount of shooting I suppose, that sort of thing. And some weekends, not so much when I was a child I don't think. I didn't do weekends there.

There was always a butler and about two or three footmen and what's called a groom of the chambers, an odd boy and an odd man and three laundry maids; three or four in the kitchen; three or four housemaids; a lady's maid. My father always had a valet. Those were inside. Outside there were many more. There were all the people in the stables, a lot of gardeners. People had a great many. The servants had a whole sort of wing, lots of bedrooms, and the upper servants had a steward's room and the others had the servants' hall. It's very spacious in the country. And the housekeeper always had a sitting room and a store cupboard where she kept things.

The upper servants were the butler, the housekeeper, the lady's maid, the nanny, the cook, possibly the head housemaid. But the head housemaid always had her own sitting room too. This is before the First War you know. We always called the cook Mrs and the lady's maid was Miss. The butler was Mr. And I always called them like that. The lower servants had their Christian names. My nanny would call me by my Christian name, but when she would be writing to my mother I noticed in old letters she called me Miss Joan. They were formal in those days.

There was always a servants' ball. The master of the house used to open it with the housekeeper and the wife with the butler in some form of dance. Whether it was a waltz or whether it was a quadrille or what I couldn't really tell you because I don't really remember attending that because you see it all happened before I was seven. After that there was a war and there was nothing of that kind. They had a reading room and a billiard table at Hartham outside and they had cricket matches and they had a lot done for them. It was a sort of community; and I remember meeting one of the sort of housemaids long afterwards somewhere and she said, 'It was the happiest time'.

A lot of them intermarried. They didn't have very high pay, but of course it was very much higher because things were much cheaper. You see it was really relative. They weren't given very good presents I don't think (I'm saying before the war) after that they did. They would be given a roll of stuff to make a dress, that kind of thing you know, the under servants, of which there were a great many. And starting at fourteen always. Certainly the house-maids had to get up early and all that. They lived comfortably otherwise; rather spartan rooms but they certainly had very good food. And the surroundings were pleasant. I was always friendly with them all. I liked them. They were there many years most of them. Till we went to New Zealand they'd all been there since I was born.

The women servants, maidservants, had these print dresses, never very much colour, and they were given those at Christmas as I tell you. And they always changed into black. And the men, footmen, you see we didn't have women parlourmaids really, we had men, they had a uniform of blue with a crested button. They crested everything in those days. They crested their carriages and everything they used practically, even children's prams, quite ridiculous, and plates. We've got some plates with the crest on here you can see.

They had a habit of the footman having the same name William or Frederick. One of the footmen always had to sleep on a bed that went up into the wall in the pantry. He was supposed to look after the silver. He didn't have a bedroom.

I had two French governesses. I was never taught by anybody English. And I had a very wonderful nanny. My meals were brought up on trays, a long way to the nursery. A hall boy brought it up on a wooden tray and nurserymaid put it on the table but nobody waited on us. The nurserymaid and nanny ate with me and any child who came to tea, or staying children. Just sort of nursery meals, I can remember being so small that my food was all made into a sort of mush on a hot water plate. For breakfast one day I had bread and milk and the other day porridge. Not often eggs. No orange juice or as much fruit as children have now. A lot of bread and butter. You had to finish up your food. And very plain food. Nothing rich. Tea was just bread and butter and you had to eat about three bits of bread and butter before you had jam or before you had cake. And the cake was plain. You weren't allowed a lot of cream. You couldn't go and eat (I used to try) as much fruit as children would like and a lot of strawberries. We were given an allowance of anything like that although there was plenty. And you didn't have many sweets.

My mother probably had breakfast in bed, my father had it downstairs. When the governess came I had breakfast with her in the schoolroom. The nursery was then turned into a schoolroom and I had meals in the schoolroom. Afternoon tea was always in the schoolroom. I never had dinner. I only had a glass of milk and a biscuit. I was kept back a long time. I did not dine with them till I was really grown up, even in New Zealand. When I got to the sort of schoolroom age I came down to lunch. I think about nine, eight or nine, and sat with my parents. But they wanted me to wear a napkin round my neck. And I thought this was tremendously sort of undignified. And so a footman used to bring this round with a safety pin. And I used to hold on to it and you have a lot of purchase if you do that and he used to get purple in the face and so did I and after a bit we were made to stop it. But I minded that desperately and of course that was awfully wrong because I certainly knew how to eat by that time and anyhow it's not the way to do it. I remember that very well. I was about eight I suppose. But I didn't before that ever have meals downstairs. It was when I had a governess you see. And the governess came down too and nobody ever spoke to her and she was furious. They had a very lonely life, governesses. And they were therefore rather difficult to their pupil. It wasn't at all the ideal way of being educated.

I called my mother Mummy. She was very amusing. I don't know that she was a sort of ideal mother for a child but she was quite easy to talk to. In a way you see you didn't have quite the intimacy that people have with their mothers now when they're looked after entirely by their mothers, and it's a different relationship, I think. They were a bit more aloof. And you didn't know them quite so well as people know their mothers now. I remember being punished, I think rather unfairly too, for quite small things really. I mean grown ups were irritated. [Why?] I don't know, not being obedient or something. But they were not reasonable always. That's why I remembered it; children always remember I think things that were done unfairly. You might be sent to bed or you were scolded. I don't think my nanny would have decided on punishment. My mother and the governess would have.

Many children now have a much easier time. One was made to grow up and face things in life much younger than people are now really. More adult I think. I was awfully lonely. I don't remember it so much when I was with nanny or when I was a little child. It was after that. There are things children don't discuss with grown ups. And I think as an only child I discussed worries with nobody really. An only child's rather different to a family of children. I might have talked to my nanny because I know when she went for her holiday my mother always told me that she tried to find out if I was missing nanny. And I was about three or four. And I said, 'No – I . . .'

'Why don't you say?'

I said, 'Well I don't tell people my thinks.' And I think that was always the same with me. Just some people are more reserved than others.

Nanny was with me till I was eight. Then she was ill and she went to the Crown Princess of Sweden, brought up all those children. You see my mother had no other children. Nanny always wanted babies. I think that was it. But it's a great break for me, especially when she left. Grown up people never realized how much it meant I don't think. But she left and I had an old French governess who came for a year with her who I loved very much. And they thought she was too old for me. They got a younger one which is no good to a child. They got a rather disagreeable younger one. So I had two new people at once which had a great effect. She only stayed for a shortish time. Then they got this Alsatian who stayed with me until I was sixteen who was a good teacher but I disliked her so much.

I think nanny taught me reading and writing. In fact, there never seemed to be the great difficulty about reading that people seem to have now. For one thing I was read out to a tremendous amount. And books were read over and over again like *Alice in Wonderland* which I liked from a very young age. But you had it read several times and you asked for it and Mrs Molesworth's books, and I knew them all, I've still got them all.

My nanny was one of those extraordinary people who was, I don't know, she was just without any kind of snobbishness. But not in any aggressive way. She had a baby when she was young. And nobody knew that – anyhow it was all suppressed. You see most people were brought up by sort of old maids who were nannies and who were narrow and she was none of those things. And she did somehow make me realize that people were the same and you must not be a snob and you must not sort of think yourself better than anybody else. And that I never lost. And you see the Jesuits always say, 'Give me a child for seven years and then anybody can have it', and that's what happened to me. She was the great influence and nothing else moved me. I loved her very much. I had a marvellous time. I can look back with absolutely not an unhappy moment. She was a very remarkable person. When she left I stopped being in the nursery. She liked this French governess, got on very well with her, who was elderly, had been with various families, the Salisbury's I think before, and was an outstanding teacher, my parents never realized, so that I learned French for a year with her. But with the other governess, the Alsatian, I had to learn German and French and nothing else really. She didn't teach anything.

I went to the south of France to a villa at Bordighera when I was three for a few months. When I was seven I went to Paris. I remember particularly the train and drinking chocolate and spilling the chocolate down a moleskin coat and being very scolded. I remember driving round the Champs Elysées in a fiacre and they took me to a toy shop called the Nain Bleu and bought me a trunk containing a doll with a trousseau. And then I went to Fiesole and the house had been a monastery. I managed to persuade the governess not to give me lessons but to spend two days going round the picture galleries in Florence which made a great impression on me. I went for a short time to a day school in Paris when I was about eleven and I caught whooping cough.

In the country I always did a lot of riding. I was tremendously keen on riding. I covered a lot of country and I knew all the country very well round. And when I was very young I even hunted with the Beaufortshire when I was about seven, eight, nine. And we had this stud groom called Mr Faircloth whom I liked so much, I loved him, who taught me to ride and went to New Zealand with my parents. So I rode and I rode about the garden and the woods and everything. I suppose I was taken for walks with nanny. I played a lot with toys, especially with a doll's house. Toys meant a lot to me. They were very good toys in those days. You kept them carefully, I think much more than they do now where children have a great many rotten toys and throw them away. But one had big solid toys you didn't forget. I could play anywhere at all in the garden. I think I was rather supervised. I always wanted to get off by myself.

I came down after tea dressed up, and I don't think people played with children as they do now but I was very observant. I noticed the grown-ups very much. They were very pleasant to me.

I enjoyed that. At lunch I wouldn't have talked a great deal when grown-ups were there. I liked listening, but I was not stopped from talking. Nobody suppressed me at all. They had a lot of guests, interesting people, political people, you know. People of that time. I watched the grown-ups a lot but they never spoke to me. Hardly ever.

I went to bed at half-past six or seven until I was fifteen. Nanny and afterwards a maid looked after me and my clothes. My mother did nothing for me really, except that I always went down to see her and she talked to me a lot, and she did read out sometimes. She visited cottages. She went and talked to the people. She liked doing that and I used to like going with her. She was a very approachable person and enjoyed different kinds of people. My father liked the garden very much and he told me about trees and things in the country and I rode with him you see. I rode every day in London in the Row for instance.

I went with my mother if we stayed away but nanny probably came too. And I went to the sea you see, that was a thing children did, sent to the sea in lodgings. And we had a sitting room, rather gloomy bedrooms and rather frightful bathrooms, I should think. We enjoyed it very much, and I was sometimes very excited by it. We dug in the sand. I don't remember doing anything else very much, but going down to the beach and paddling. You were never allowed to paddle or bathe till you'd been there about a couple of days. They had all those funny ideas. We dug with a wooden spade or something, one always wanted to buy the iron ones, but they were very difficult and one always got a new bucket, a shrimping net and a boat, and you paddled and you bathed. Rather uncomfortable bathing dresses. But I swam you see. I learned to swim young in the Bath Club. That was one of the things I did do in the way of sport. And I won a medal. I've always swum. I was taught very well there.

I went to Ramsgate and Westgate and Filey. That was when I was much younger, and we sometimes went with other children. The Somersets were great friends of my parents, the Cavendishes I went with. Their nannies were there. The nurserymaid went, yes. It was always in the summer for I should think about a fortnight, that's all. I should think we enjoyed it very much. My parents didn't have holidays in that sort of way. They went on shooting parties or stayed with friends or something. I don't know what they did. But it was just that it was thought good for you to go to the sea. And then of course I went to New Zealand you see, and there was no question of going to the sea when I was twelve. But I did go with my mother once to Cornwall when I was eight. I do remember that. But she took a house that time. We didn't go into lodgings. I think my father came. I can't remember quite. He was busy. He might have been down, but he wasn't there all the time.

On Saturdays I didn't do lessons the same as other days. I didn't do lessons in the afternoon but I had them in the morning. On Sunday I went to church. I remember being made to wear rather different clothes which irritated me. I remember the Zoo on Sundays, always on Sundays. And I only once went on Saturday with Elizabeth Asquith who was a friend of mine. Mr Asquith was a friend of my father's, and we went on an elephant. You couldn't go on elephants on the Sunday. They didn't have the elephants. And we both got measles. The reason was there was a danger you know, with the sort of children who came to probably the central part of London. There was an awful lot of contagious illness, and they were very dirty too. There was great dirt. All that has gone. And I also went to concerts which I enjoyed very much at the Queen's Hall with Sir Henry Wood, and there were short concerts on Sunday afternoon which even when I was quite young I enjoyed very much.

I went to a Sunday School for a short time. It was given in London by the Duchess of Bedford for the little neglected children of the rich. But she got very high church and in the end a nun appeared I remember. The thing was that we had to paint a picture and I brought mine home, this picture, to show. And I loved this place, this school, because I was always alone and I knew the other children, we were quite small and had quite fun, and this painting was quite amusing to do. And then there was one painting (my parents took me away, they got worried about it) which was the gates of heaven which I'd got in yellow paint, and then there were the gates of hell, and I hadn't got a nice black paint. And I went to them and I said, 'I don't think this is black enough for the gates of hell, do you think you could get me some black paint,' and then they were very worried and they took me away because they thought this was odd stuff. And I said, 'Well the only thing I really like about it is the end. We're given a very good sponge cake and a glass of milk', and that was the only impression.

I was very small. I was only about five or six you see. And anyway I was brought up with a lot of teaching of Old Testament things which children aren't now, which is a great pity, because they're fascinating stories. They're as good as any fairy stories. And I learned those very young with my nanny when I was five, four or five.

My governess was Lutheran. She was very very much sort of anti-Catholic. But she had the effect of making me rather tolerant I think. I disliked her so much. There were two kinds of grace when you were very small. It was 'Thank God for my good dinner.' And then there was 'For what we are going to receive make us truly thankful.' But no grown-ups said grace. There again it was a funny thing you see. In time it occurred to you, 'Why should I say grace when they don't?' And I was the sort of child to whom those sort of things always came. Religion meant to me what I think it does to every child. They've got an idea when they say their prayers it's a good thing that they must remember all the people they're fond of. I think when I was about thirteen or fourteen I thought a bit more about it. I've always been a person who likes looking at the words. I don't accept anything very much. And most people of that period always went to church you know. It was a thing people did. What they took in from it I don't know but they felt they had to go to church. We had a chaplain called Mr Andrews who gave me arithmetic lessons which weren't very successful, and church history which I found very dull with him. I remember him very well. And his wife used to come at Christmas time and she couldn't bear crackers, they made her feel ill so my mother thought her an awful muff. I can remember that too.

Christmas Day was marvellous. And everybody took part. There was a huge Christmas tree and choirboys because we had a chapel. The choirboys came and sang carols. The chapel was a little way off. It was built by my great-uncle. And we had our own curate specially from a little place called Pickwick, near Hartham, and had these services. One always went to church. And all the staff were given presents and came and got them off the Christmas tree. We had villages you see and my father gave a Christmas tree to the village children. There was generally a house-party and there might be my cousin who was my age who was killed in the war, and just the staff. These other parties were given at different times for the boys and girls in the village school. There was always a tree in every village and the children were given an orange and some sweets and a toy. A lot was given.

I had a Christmas stocking. I generally opened it about four o'clock in the morning because I never went to sleep. I never slept all night. I used to make my presents and gave them from my pocket money. That's a very good plan I think. I had a real sense of giving. I'd spend ages making sort of book markers. I gave them to everybody in the house. I gave my parents something I'd made, a picture or something. Always something I'd made.

On Christmas Day I was made to do a play myself. I was made to recite in French and German. I had to play alone which is torture. It rather spoilt Christmas day. My governess made me do the plays. She found solo parts which were partly singing and partly funny French things which you know you get in France. And then very very long German poems like a long thing about Wilhelm Tell by Goethe, Schiller rather. I was dressed up as Wilhelm Tell and that you see. And it was a great strain that. And then there was a thing 'The telephone' I remember doing which was a farce and I was dressed up in my cousin's clothes, as a man. I was then only about ten. But it was a great strain. And all the guests watched this and it was quite funny. But I never had a chance to act again. But I had to do all this and carry the whole thing. It was such a strain. To act with other people is great fun, but alone it's no fun at all. You've got to be a sort of Sarah Bernhardt to like to recite and I didn't like reciting at all.

In Hartham we had a proper estate agent because my father had a lot of land and a lot of cottages and villages and things. There was a young man called Mr Dunn who was kind of under him I suppose, and I remember him because the second governess I had before I had this monster, she had a thing about this Mr Dunn. I think she ultimately married him. But anyhow he had a little office in the yard, stable yard, and this suited me very well because I hated going for walks, and I used to play about and they used to sit in this little office in the yard, stable yard, and I said, 'I'll let you know if anybody comes around.' So I did this which was great fun for me. And then I said, 'And why not (in lessons constantly I learned nothing) give me copies to do and addition sums, because then you can leave me and go,' which she did. That didn't last long as the housekeeper gave them away. And then she was sent away. And she was awful because she told me that the next governess who was the German governess was going to ill-treat me and I was very disloyal if I was nice to her, so I wouldn't speak to the new governess. And then she held that against me always. And the sort of things now you see one's Edwardian parents didn't think of, which was terribly cruel, that when these governesses arrived they came in and the schoolroom was high up in the houe with a very dark passage to get to it, and the one who was going, left as the other one came and they met in this passage and there was me cowering, a little girl, these two women looking at each other. Because one's mother should have been there to help you with the new governess but she wasn't. And the governess who came she had a sort of flat cap they wore, and I remember a rug with a strap round and a very ugly fierce face, the German one, the Alsatian.

And I remember when the other French governess came, the one they sent away, Madame Levido, was very lively and used to box my ears, but she was much less unpleasant than the half-German one. But when she first came for some reason she wasn't in the schoolroom, she was in the billiard room. This was in Hartham, in the country, and I was sent down to see the new governess. And I remember opening a door, it was a rather large room, and I could only see black hair coming above this chair, and I was so terrified because I hated governesses you see and was frightened of them. And it took me a long time to have the courage to go and see her. You see, that was a terrible thing that they would have done. They didn't realize what it meant to a child, a new person coming. And not to introduce you to them.

I began German with the Alsatian, which I always disliked very much. But nearly all lessons were in either German or French, and very few English lessons. My parents didn't talk much to her at all. My mother spoke a little German, my father didn't at all. And they wouldn't have talked any foreign language. She was Scottish, my mother, she'd been brought up in Edinburgh, I think with governesses, German governesses. That's why she knew German. She hated her governesses. And she'd let me have these awful governesses. And she was very funny my mother and she said, 'I never see machinery that I don't wish they were full of governesses.' And yet she gave me these horrors. But that's one of those things you can't understand. Simply because those people at that time felt they couldn't send away their only child to school, and I longed to go to school, because I loved my contemporaries. I would have loved school. Girls were not so much sent to school. It was beginning and some people did, and when they were older they did, but you see I went to New Zealand when I was about twelve or thirteen and before that they wouldn't have thought perhaps of doing it. And there were classes for certain things, but I always had the governess and it was not very much good really.

Yes I did go to Miss Wolff's, indeed I went to Miss Wolff. And I particularly minded it because it was in a house in Mount Street and there was a long table and I didn't like Miss Wolff at all. She had been a private governess. She had what the French call a *face à main*, which is a thing you know on a little stick, a lorgnette. And she used to look at books that way, and there was a long table. And round in this room the governesses and nannies and people who brought the children sat. They stayed. Including mine. And she didn't like me going to these classes and the idea was that I should mix with other children, and of course it was the worst way to do it because I was asked questions about things I'd never been taught, and very few didn't answer well, things like dates of the English kings, I had never been taught at all. I made wild answers and then they all laughed, including all these governesses and nurses. I've never felt such torture! And my governess was so furious about this that she made me lie on a backboard which was a thing you had in those days made of baize and a hole for your head, and she made me learn the kings of England and their dates from William the Conqueror right up to the King, which I must say has been marvellous to me. I can't be put wrong.

Then my other thing was Monsieur Roche who some people found a very good teacher, but I was very young again and that was someone miles off. Again the same system of a table and you had jettons, little things you know, counters, if you answered properly. And he hadn't taught you, he just asked you things out of the blue, and I never got any jettons, and there were always brilliant pupils who did and you had to count them in the end which was very humiliating. And then he made one learn a verse of poetry and that tortured me the whole week because I didn't know whether he was going to ask me. I was just so nervous. It was the wrong sort of way to go to school you see. It was only once a week and I dreaded the whole week, the most awful thing of going to Monsieur Roche. I learned nothing of course, there was no way of learning, just the questions and these rather bright children who learned other things. It was real torture, and that wasn't the sort of school I wanted to go to. Monsieur Roche had classes and a lot of the people even rather older than me went to Monsieur Roche and liked him and he I believe was a good teacher, but I can't see that you can remember going once a week like that. But Miss Wolff had proper literature classes and English classes but I didn't go very much you see because the governess didn't want it really, she said I would never go; twice a week for a history lesson, something like that, which wasn't really going to school at all. You never mixed with the children, you just came in, sat at this table and went away. It was only for one term. I went only when I was in London, and only for one term.

And then I remember when I was much younger going to extraordinary classes which I think the Duchess of Sutherland ran, for literature. Well I was much too young for it. I was then only about seven. But there were a lot of older girls at it who were quite good and they knew all the answers and had read the books, Dickens and that, whom I had never even heard of. But luckily this class was done in a drawing room, there were various children of my own age, including Bimbo Tennant whom I was very fond of who was afterwards killed, and we all sat on the floor. But she was very nice, the teacher, but obviously thought we were much too young to bother with. And we all had to write essays and she used to give us a subject, and my governess used to write the essay and I copied it out and she was always very praising naturally, because it was quite well done. But I remember some of the questions that were asked and what Dickens and Scott and these older girls knew, and I stored things up you see, and made up my mind to read them. And I did read a lot you see. I taught myself tremendously by reading. I was a great reader, especially as I had this foreign governess. So I never stopped reading. I read the whole of Scott, the whole of Dickens and most of the classics myself.

My parents left it much too much to the governess because they hated her I think. I spoke French you see, and German – one language one week and one the other. They knew I spoke French and they knew I was doing a lot of French. I don't think they bothered much about girls' education beyond that you know. No Latin or anything like that, not that I think that's necessary. Very little arithmetic. I did some. Well you see it was in French and she was a bad teacher because she got very cross, so we got so angry over it that in the end we gave up doing that and consequently I can just manage my bridge scores. I didn't really do any.

I played the piano. I was taught the piano. Everybody was whether they were musical or not from an early age. My mother played the piano a little, not particularly well. She'd been taught. I was going to dancing classes very young in London, to somebody called Mrs Wordsworth, a lot of dancing I did and gymnastics. My parents read everything I think. My mother being Scottish liked Scott and she read all the novels of that time, and I heard her always discussing books, so I read a great deal myself when I was young. Both of them were readers. Both of them.

On my birthday I had all the usual things, a party and a cake. Mother and Fathers' friends' children came. My mother did play games. She played, I remember, blind man's buff and those sort of games with me at parties. But I don't remember her playing the other games, Old Maid and things like that, much fewer games you know for children, and grown ups did not play with them as much as they do now. I think there was croquet but I can't remember playing it very much. I did play yes but not very prominently. I went to lots of parties, children's parties. There were wonderful children's parties and she took me there. And I was bridesmaid very often. There were fancy dress parties, I've still got some of the fancy dresses, and dancing and cottillions and mostly dancing with music, and things called the Barn Dance and the Lancers and those kind of dances, Sir Roger de Coverley. Children did that. And otherwise there were sort of games like blind man's buff.

There was an idea that you played only with the children of people that your parents knew but I didn't actually come up against that. I knew it was a rule. I knew the village children. They used to come to tea with me. We visited them a lot. My mother visited them a lot. I think I had no feeling about people being superior or inferior at all, very little of that. It never occurred to me that there was any difference between the children really except that they had less things than I had. I would have given them some of my things. I remember going along to farms to tea, and playing in the farmyard a lot. I loved animals. Animals played a large part. One was always given pets but you had to look after them, rabbits and guinea pigs and dogs and birds.

My father was Member for Chippenham. He belonged to the Conservative Party, he was in the khaki election. He was also in the

Boer War. He went out in the Yeomanry. Then he became a Liberal at the time of Free Trade, came under Mr Asquith. I didn't know why he changed because I was too young then. I felt that everybody was passionate about it even when I was small because I felt they were his enemies. First of all there was a toy shop in Corsham where the man was a Liberal and I loved buying. You know one could buy cheap toys like those wonderful wooden painted dolls which cost about sixpence. Now they cost about ten pounds. And he was a Liberal and I thought it was wrong. He had a long beard and I was rather frightened of him, because he was an enemy of my father. Then overnight he suddenly became his friend. That was as far as I understood politics. I did take part. I went round on a pony which was quite wrong and said, 'Are you going to vote for him?' And at one place, Sherston, I remember he had rotten eggs thrown at him while he was speaking. And I remember riding back to Hartham, gates of Hartham, and this is quite true and the horses (we were in a carriage, a horse and carriage that time from having come from the poll at Chippenham) the horses being taken out of the shafts and we were pulled all the way, which is about a mile and a half to the house with torches, people, and it was wonderful. That often happened I think. The Boer War I can't remember but I only remember sitting at a table and doing invisible painting and Lord Roberts and Kitchener coming up and being visible. I do remember that. And I can remember wearing blue ribbons at that election. And I do remember very far back you see.

My mother was a great influence. She knew a lot of these politicians very well. She knew Winston Churchill very well in that way. The people who came to stay were politicians and they talked about it, but I wouldn't say she was the sort of person who might have become an MP or was dedicated. She wasn't that type. She was a great social person and knew a lot of people. She had a lot of friends. She was a very well-known person, my mother. She was a great mimic. She was very funny. She made friends with a lot of sort of prominent people of that time you know. Politics was very social anyway. An awful lot took place at luncheon parties and dinner parties. My mother I think was a very unconventional person. She'd make friends with people outside her coterie. She wasn't a Soul, if you've heard of Souls, but she was verging on that. Maurice Baring was her great friend. She wasn't narrow at all.

And she was a great one to laugh at people. But on the other hand of course they had their conventions which they couldn't really escape from. But she would have if she could I think. My father was a very good mixer with anybody. He hadn't got any of those sort of inhibitions. And I think although I didn't see all that and one was brought up conventionally, I absorbed from them a wide outlook and no prejudices.

[Sex education?] Not really no, because I read a great deal and you stored things up. My mother never did and my governess said, 'I will tell you things, they're the things you should know, *très gentiment avec les plantes.*' Well I didn't care for the governess. I said, 'I don't want to know it *très gentiment avec les plantes*, I will find out.' So from then on I said, 'Well I know a few sort of things, I'll go down to the *Encyclopaedia Britannica* and I will find out all I need to know about my body, or body generally and that'll help me,' which I did, about fourteen. And I never asked anybody. And directly you went to hospital you learned everything there was to know.

Before the First War I grew up into a very different world. Completely different. I suppose they thought I was going to be conventional, make a sort of marriage they approved of exactly and go the ordinary way. I mean people did. But I wasn't after that war. The war changed everybody. I mean one was brought up without much education really. I mean the education of a foreign governess. There wasn't much scope as there is now. You weren't brought up to have a profession. I was brought up with a principle. Very much so. And one was taught all the old Bible stories when you're young which you may or may not care for when you're older. But it brings you up with a standard, which I think is lacking now. Everybody was brought up to do public service. They did, my parents, mostly my father. And it's all through my life been a thing I've thought important. When I was sixteen I had this year in Paris as I think I mentioned. I was going to have a year, it was the usual thing for girls then, to have a year in France or somewhere and a year in Germany. And I for some extraordinary reason which is lucky for me, made a great fuss and I said I must do the French first. I must go to Paris. So I had the year. And of course I wouldn't have had that if I'd had the year in Germany. It would have been an uncomfortable year I think and I'd never have had the French. So I never had the German for which I was very glad really. But then after that you would come out but I would have tried to go to university I think. Very few went. And it meant giving up the sort of balls and the fun that would have been provided. I had this passion for independence you see and I knew that I wasn't going to get much in the pre-war days except through marriage. But it wasn't necessarily a thing that one wanted to do at once. But luckily I got it immediately by pretending I was much older and going in for nursing. Which nobody could stop me doing.

My generation was pretty well wiped out. So I always said to my parents, because really there was great difficulty about inheriting because it was supposed to only go to a son, and they were very upset about having no more children, having only me, 'But of course I'd have been killed. I was just the age.'

Appendix

The first project 'Family Life and Work Experience before 1918' was financially supported by the Social Science Research Council. Five hundred men and women were recorded, and a lengthy questionnaire was used. All were born by 1906 and the earliest in 1872. We wanted the interviews to represent the Edwardian population as a whole and so designed a 'quota sample'. This is a list of categories of various proportions into which people had to fit in order to be included. The sample was based on the 1911 census and consisted of 444 people. The proportion of men and women was the same as in 1911. We managed too to keep the proportions of people living in the countryside, towns and conurbations correct and also the balance between the main regions of England, Wales and Scotland. We tried to approximate to the distribution of social classes in Britain in 1911 by dividing the sample into six major occupational groups taken from the adjusted census categories of Guy Routh's *Occupation and Pay, 1906–65* (1965). Those people who were not working in 1911 were classified according to their breadwinner in 1911, normally the father or husband, but in a few cases the mother. We had to do five hundred interviews because some interviews were incomplete or turned out to belong to a different category than anticipated. Interviewers were employed for areas where Paul Thompson and I and our colleague Trevor Lummis could not work because of distance. Like ourselves, they found their subjects through personal contacts, appeals in the local press, welfare agencies for old people, old people's essay competitions. Of the interviews in this book, Geoffrey Brady, Clifford Hills, Florence Atherton, Annie Wilson and Tommy Morgan belong to this project.

Two projects, also supported by the Social Science Research Council, followed. One was on Trevor Lummis's 'The Family and Community Life of East Anglian Fishermen' the other mine on 'Middle and Upper Class families 1890–1920'. With the help of Ann Jungmann I interviewed sixty men and women who were born into the families of landed gentry, professional men and wealthy manufacturers before 1908. A questionnaire was used similar to the one used for the first project but adapted to suit the different domestic circumstances of better off people. In addition more attention was given in this survey to sex roles and the responsibilities of husband and wife for decision-making in the home. Joan Poynder, Esther Stokes, Henry Vigne and Jock Yorke were interviewed for this survey.

Appendix

The names of the subjects of this book are all the real family names (maiden names of course in the case of the women), with three exceptions. A member of Geoffrey Brady's family wished his surname to be concealed and his widow decided to respect her wishes. Brady is his second Baptismal name. No relative of Tommy Morgan or Annie Wilson could be traced so surnames were invented for them in accordance with the guarantee of confidentiality given to everyone when originally interviewed.